Pakistan

THE CONSOLIDATION OF A NATION

PAKISTAN

The Consolidation of a Nation

WAYNE AYRES WILCOX

Columbia University Press, New York and London

First printing 1963
Fourth printing 1969

SBN 231-02589-0
Library of Congress Catalog Card Number: 63-9873
Printed in the United States of America

FOR MY PARENTS
John and Magdalen Wilcox

Preface

Pakistan, the largest Muslim country in the world, made its international debut at an independence ball held primarily for its Hindu sister, India. And despite its size and importance, Pakistan has remained in the shadow of India since 1947, attracting attention only occasionally by its unstable cabinets, unique communal ideology, curiously split territories, or many quarrels with India. The world has therefore come to know Pakistan only through the headlines of recurrent crisis and little attention has been paid to its more basic dimensions. In particular, scant notice has been taken of the central role of its government as the coordinator of a bereft and divided society, a mission which for Pakistan was of herculean proportions. The problems attendant to the shaping of such a nation demand attention and sympathetic concern.

This narrative attempts to explore the molding of Pakistan and focuses on the sometimes tortuous efforts of its leaders to introduce effective, uniform, and democratic government to a people who, until 1947, lived under petty princes and tribal chiefs. The society of the Indian princely states was the most tradition-bound in the subcontinent, and in the efforts of the government to stimulate change are seen the difficulties, and also the promise, of the remaking of a nation. The subject is more important because the government failed in Pakistan, and with the collapse of constitutional government in 1958 democracy as a way of life for the new state was questioned. Indeed, the questioning is assuming increased importance throughout the Afro-Asian world.

Unfortunately, the lessons of the failure in modernization and democracy in Pakistan are largely unknown, even at home. There is no lack of hasty judgments and hazy prescriptions, but empirical studies of political and social behavior are practically unknown. One cannot but contrast India and Pakistan in this regard, and note the debt that India owes to those who laid bare some of its problems, regardless of their momentary unpopularity.

This book first introduces the nature of political society in the princely states with the coming of nationalism and independence and then traces the response of the princes and their people to the needs of a new era. The states were a much heavier liability to the newly independent dominions than has generally been known, and in the undeclared war for the states was born a set of new and crucial problems for both countries. As we see the states brought into closer contact with the central government, the focus shifts to the dialogue between traditional society and the modern state, and some of the problems of nascent democracy are explored. Finally, the role of the states in the federal controversies of constitution-making is considered. Some important and generally unavailable documents are given in the appendix. In the intensive analysis of a segment of Pakistan's political life may be seen the elements which lay at the heart of the nation's dilemma, and which frustrated successive governments in their sworn task of reshaping an old nation.

Much of the information found in the text was recorded in interviews with officials and politicians of the state and central governments in Pakistan. Frequently, and understandably, some of these men wished to remain anonymous. Their colleagues who spoke openly and for the record are no less praiseworthy for their candor, and to all the author is most grateful. While much that follows is critical of the policies pursued by these same leaders, it is necessary to remember that their problems were of a magnitude hardly imaginable in the West. In any case, they deserve praise for their service in the face of so much criticism that has been unfair and irresponsible.

The field research for this study was made possible by timely grants from the Council for Research in the Social Sciences, and the Near and Middle East Institute of the School of International Affairs, both of Columbia University, to which I am deeply indebted. I am grateful to the government of Pakistan, to George Philip and Son, Ltd., London, and to *Dawn,* for permission to base the maps in this book upon maps published by them.

Thanks are due to Latif Sherwani of the Pakistan Institute of International Affairs, who smoothed the way for numerous interviews in Pakistan and to Professor J. C. Hurewitz of the Near and Middle East Institute of Columbia University, who read the manuscript in its various stages of imperfection, made valuable observations, and in many ways facilitated its publication. It is a pleasure to acknowledge my deep debt to I. H. Qureshi, formerly visiting professor at the Center for Pakistan Studies at Columbia, and now vice-chancellor of Karachi University. He read an early draft and patiently counseled its improvement both in New York and at Zeba Manzar, Karachi. My wife was both a sensitive editor and constructive critic and let neither thankless task ruin her good humor. For the shortcomings of the book the author alone is responsible.

W.A.W.

Delhi
December, 1962

Preface to the Second Printing

The new printing contains changes in the section on Kalat, pages 75 through 81. I am indebted to Douglas Y. Fell, I.C.S. (ret.), a key official in the Kalat government in 1947–48, who made available to me hitherto unpublished private papers which justify a slightly revised treatment of Kalat's tardy accession to Pakistan. He does not, of course, bear any responsibility for the interpretation I have placed on these materials. No other revisions have been made in this printing.

W.A.W.

New York
January, 1964

Contents

PART ONE

The States in Contest

It has been by a policy of Protectorates that the Indian Empire has for more than a century pursued, and is still pursuing, its as yet un-exhausted advance . . . . some were annexed, others engulfed in advancing tide, remaining embedded like stumps in an avalanche, or left with their heads above water like islands in the flood.

George Nathaniel Curzon, The Romanes Lecture, 1907

I

Islands in the Flood

The most serious single problem facing the leaders of India and Pakistan immediately prior to their independence in 1947 was the disposition of the Indian princely states, quasi-autonomous protectorates scattered throughout India. The nationalist movements of the Indian National Congress and the Muslim League were legally prohibited from organizing branches in princely territory with the result that when freedom for British India was granted, the princes remained outside the political settlement. The efforts of several rulers to assert their independence and the conflicting efforts of the nationalists to draw the states into either India or Pakistan preoccupied statesmen throughout 1947. A month after independence the unsolved problem plunged the new nations into a war to which a genuine peace has yet to be concluded.

Nor were the disputes concerning the principalities solely an international problem. Both India and Pakistan inherited vast regions which had been denied the educational and economic development brought to the rest of India by the British.

Many states were kept as antique showcases of medieval India and their rulers laid more stress on pageantry and pomp than on hospitals and schools. The political society of the states was almost static, and it fell to the struggling democrats of the twentieth century to bring it parallel to provincial standards in response to the needs of the new era.

The obvious question, in reflecting upon the bloodshed and torment of the problem, is why the British allowed states to exist within the Indian Empire. Had the state people been joined with the majority of their fellows, there would have been no war over Kashmir, no strong feudal-Rightist parties in Rajasthan and Orissa, no vast expenditures on privy purses or the special rights of the six hundred Maharajas. The answer to the question lies in the pattern of imperial strategy in India and in the queer alliance against change which marked the early decades of the century.

The creation of the states

Early in the eighteenth century the last great Mughul emperor died, and in the wake of his death disorders shook the administration which had given India good government for a century and a half. The imperial disruption coincided with European expansion, and the British East India Company was caught up in the struggle for the remnants of the Mughul empire. Company leaders faced not only French, Portuguese, and Dutch soldier-statesmen but local Indian rulers of solid, if uneven, ability. The Company was sorely taxed to claim even the eastern fringes of the vast land, while in the west, Afghans, Sikhs, and Marathas in their turn won control of impressive realms and prepared to meet the westward advance of the Europeans.

Most of India lay divided, ruled by local lords and petty

kings who reflected diversities of language, religion, caste, and tribe. Stable societies in many of the regions of India developed unique cultures, their languages produced literature, sects and major faiths cultivated separate world views, and castes and tribes lived in a closed but all-embracing universe. As the veneer of Mughul control ruptured, regional leaders representing these interests and nations sprang up, only to be smothered, one by one, by the East India Company.

Another class of local rulers destined to outlast their stronger Indian rivals were the freebooters who seized power in the chaos of decaying imperial rule. Having no following but bands of soldiers, these *condottieri* often laid claim to vast tracts of land. They were, at best, a temporary phenomenon which would pass as regional kingdoms expanded, but nothing was known of the future policy of the British which would preserve these petty fiefs until the mid-twentieth century.

Regardless of their local power, the Indian rulers were seldom a match for a well-organized aggressor. They were parts of a house divided whose scattered legions and assorted battle plans were inadequate to meet the concentrated strength of the invader. The Aryans, Asoka and Akbar, had conquered India piecemeal just as their successors, the British, would someday conquer it. But after conquest came the great challenge of Indian rule for the diversity which made conquest simple made rule difficult. Local insurrections and rebellions plagued every ancient Indian kingdom. Imperial governments took great pains to induce loyalty including the conversion of the local population to an alien faith, intimidation by locating garrisons in troublesome provinces, and intermarriage with strong tribes or groups. While some empires lasted longer than others, no Indian conqueror held political control over all of the subcontinent at the same time.

The British trader-soldiers of "John Company" evolved a

new system of rule which hobbled India by harnessing its
internal divisions. The invaders were initially deprived, by intent and distance, of the power of the Home Fleet. They had
to move cautiously and utilize local alliances, and made little
attempt to destroy every native government or conquer every
square mile of territory. Even Christian missionaries were
forbidden to enter company lands to disturb the traditions
which were their prime ally. Because local princes of the first
rank were often strong enough to pose a threat to the Company, many of its allies were insignificant rulers.

The strategy underlying the diplomacy was simple. It aimed
at creating an Anglo-Indian alliance in a particular region to
intimidate or defeat threatening local adversaries. A broader
system proved unnecessary because no single foe or coalition
was sufficiently strong to overcome the British. India was already divided, it only waited to be conquered. By 1800 the
Company had eliminated European competition, subjugated
Bengal, and moved into central India, all the while contract-
ing new alliances, overpowering divided foes, and consolidating
gains without upsetting traditional life in its dominions.

As the frontier was pushed west, former allies remained behind the lines, oftentimes in control of important terrain.
Should they be disarmed and humbled or left alone? The
danger of an empire riddled with independent chiefs was apparent—the chiefs might tire of the alliance and strike the back
of their former friend. Nonetheless, British officials believed that
further expansion could be accomplished only if resources were
massed in the west instead of being spread in garrison duty
and would be facilitated if the yet-independent western princes
had confidence in British promises. There were also venerable
pledges of support and friendship between the Company and
the rulers, although they were not sacrosanct. The ultimate

decision, after several experiments with alternatives, was to respect the alliances. With few exceptions the remaining princes were too weak, too divided, and too cautious to pose a serious threat to their suzerain. In the course of time, the rulers were made to understand how completely their thrones depended upon the continued tolerance of their "ally."

The dual character of British and princely rule did much to prevent general hostility to the Europeans. Members of a religious, caste, or linguistic group displaced in directly administered areas might find a place in the service of a ruler of their persuasion. Thus the princely states, without posing a serious threat to British rule, provided a safety valve through which frustrations and antagonisms could be vented without endangering a wider community. Their role as sanctuaries of traditional India would become increasingly important as westernization began to convulse the subcontinent.

The transformation of the states

By 1850 the Company was supreme, and in the full flush of victory it questioned the value of the princely alliances. The role of the states in any case needed redefinition in the context of the new all-India administration. Imperial planners decided to restrict the autonomy of the rulers by isolating them from potential friends, limiting their external intercourse, and disarming their military forces. The maze of princely and British administrations was interwoven with new facilities of communication and transportation. Troops, concentrated in centers throughout the subcontinent, were capable of high speed transfer. For the first time in history, the effective governance of all of India was possible.

Within the states, British resident officers seized more and

more initiative. Maladministered states might be transferred
to British control and erring rulers might be deposed. At the
zenith of their new power, the once tactful traders had become
harsh masters, dictating the detail as well as the spirit of their
new India.

In the directly administered areas, the Company's men systematically destroyed the ruling elite and substituted their own
agents. Because the Muslim community was largely dependent
on employment by the Mughul administration, it was crippled
by the changes. Opportunities to join a state army or administration were restricted because the rulers were paring their
services in obedience to British dictates. Steeped in the traditions of soldiery and administration, the Muslims were crowded
from public life and deprived of employment and status.

In 1857 the long-pent-up hostility between East and West
erupted in the Mutiny. While the Muslims were not alone in
the rebellion, they had every reason to applaud it, support it,
and join it. Throughout all of northern India the fires of war
burned; that is, except in the princely states. After the Red
Fort fell to the British and their revenge was taken, they lavishly
acknowledged their debt to the princes. A policy of support
for the division of India was enshrined in imperial dogma for
ninety years, the full span of British rule, and notions of indirect administration spread throughout the colonies. Another
policy which was equally important in the future was the
crushing of the Muslims of India.

Dual administration in India

Ranking in importance with the creation and later transfor-
mation of the states was the decision of the British government
to administer India in halves. The directly controlled territory,

British India, was the more populous and important part while Princely India, some six hundred islands in the British sea, was answerable to the Crown imperfectly through a political department. The legal connecting link between the two halves was a body of political usage and mythology called paramountcy.

Paramountcy covered a multitude of arrangements but generally provided that the control of foreign relations, defense, and communications were British prerogatives while internal administration, so long as it was solvent and not completely debauched, was the ruler's domain. Underlying the whole concept was British sufferance. When currency, taxation, justice, and later economic development became important to the paramount power, the implications of the term multiplied and the exact degree of British involvement in the internal affairs of each state was adjusted to individual situations.

The implications of duality in India were far-reaching because the rulers, no less than the British, were often unrepresentative of their people. Recruited in large part from states with flimsy administrations, the allies of the Company and Crown were primarily creatures of the frozen politics of British conquest and not of the popular will. The religion of the prince, for example, was not always that of his subjects. Religion is important in any traditional society and is particularly so in India where it regulates minute details of daily life, conduct, and even diet. It was more important because of the epic clash of Hinduism and Islam, the major faiths, which are sometimes antithetical in their practices. For example, an orthodox Hindu prince might ban cow slaughter in his state and thereby deprive his Muslim subjects of their primary food and occupations.

Similarly language was frequently linked with religion or place of birth, thereby closing off the state peoples from their

government which was conducted in a foreign tongue. Affairs
of state and recruitment in the bureaucracies were limited to
members of the ruler's community while a majority, perhaps,
of the state peoples were condemned to second-class citizenship.
This was not a novel relationship to the long-suffering Indian
peasantry, but with the rise of religious nationalism and democratic ideals in the twentieth century it spelled disaster.

A second implication of the division of India was that the
states were small economic entities sure to lag behind British
India in material advancement. The Company had sequestered
the fertile Indo-Gangetic valley, the great ports, the key rivers,
and the important towns. With a few notable exceptions, the
princes governed rural India, the marginal lands of hill and
desert. They could not generate the capital for economic expansion, and a heavy burden of ceremony, tradition, and inefficiency swallowed up the modest available budget surplus.

Predictably, the position of the states in relation to the provinces deteriorated rapidly. Machine competition impoverished
local handicrafts and rural indebtedness spiraled. While the
effects were general, the provinces received factories, railways,
and roads while the states reaped only the undesirable fruits of
foreign conquest. Denied as well the new techniques of organization, state societies atrophied, their cultures increasingly shot
through with smallness and superstition. Where once the
princely courts had glittered with the displaced artists and
thinkers of the crumbling empires of India, they now lost even
their promising young.

The sole hope of the state peoples was their ruler. With his
purse and patronage, learning and contacts, he might be able
to lead his subjects into their new responsibilities while allowing them to maintain their self-respect. As a member of state
society privy to British life, the prince might be able to blend
the soft of the old and the vital of the new to regenerate his

state. The rulers failed in this difficult task. Frequently more concerned with Mayfair than their villages, involved in paternity suits as often as economic reform, the rulers fell victims of their political irresponsibility.

As well, traditionalists in the provinces failed to equip their young with insights and strengths to meet Western civilization and emerge culturally intact. The flood of the scientific revolution devastated Indian society and its thoughtful members found they could meet it only on its own terms. The Muslims were too proud to believe that Christian Europe was superior, or that they could no longer rule. As they tumbled ever lower to the bottom of the caste heap, the disenfranchised Hindu was learning British ways in banking, commerce, clerking, and the professions. He probably enjoyed seeing the communal tables turned on his former masters and yet, in Western dominance would come the revitalization of all India, including Indian Islam.

By the beginning of the twentieth century, the new India stretched from the very gates of Kabul to Rangoon and south from Tibet to Ceylon. South Asia was answerable to one master. The Indian people were, like Gulliver, tied to the land by a few adventurers from a small island in Europe. With Indian society weak and self-contradictory, the former ruling class utterly destroyed, and the conquerors every day stronger through the gifts of technology, the British prize was a universal empire unprecedented in the history of the subcontinent. Her Majesty's Viceroy could rest well, musing over the glories of the Victorian Age.

Princely state organization

In their fitful advance across the peninsula, the British had gathered a bewildering variety of states, some of which were

vast and others miniscule, some rich and fertile and others
barren. Since they belonged to no one mother, they bore faint
resemblances to one another but were, however, quite similar
to the adjoining lands whose language they generally shared.
Where there were no special problems the states came to have
common features.

Nominally, the fountainhead of state policies was the ruler
acting through his court, but behind all actions and scarcely
in the shadows stood the British Resident.[1] Acts of the state
government were issued as royal decrees even though they
were drafted, discussed, and approved by advisors and the
Resident before promulgation. In many states the ruler did not
trouble himself with administrative affairs and vested his authority in the new prince, who might be either an officer of
the Indian Civil Service or a promising provincial politician.

The gentry of the states, not without power in the semifeudal
societies, were occasionally called together in a durbar[2] (meeting in a royal court) to legitimize a departure from state tradition or to witness the birth, marriage, death, or deposal of a
prince. Their primary influence, however, was exercised through
the social life of the states.

Princely governments were not modeled on the famous Indian Civil Service, renowned as one of the most efficient in the
world. The whole notion of a merit examination is alien in a
traditional society in which loyalty and position are more important than impersonal attributes. Inefficiency was not a major
problem because few services were provided and the average
sinecure post was part of a well-understood and approved system of patronage. As one candid state bureaucrat put it: "This
isn't the President's staff of the United States. Sometimes we
are as lazy as hell, other times we work all night but there
is no office procedure."[3]

Military forces in the states were either strictly controlled or entirely disbanded. Except for the often tattered guard of the household china which had little need for modern equipment but was physically respectable, troop recruitment for ceremonial duties was based on state patronage rather than fitness for combat. There must have been a considerable demand for uniforms for portly figures.

In some of the more progressive states, an independent judiciary was organized. This was a deviation from the British Indian pattern which unified lower administrative and judicial functions but was part of the transfer of real power from the hands of state politicians to specialists on loan either from the Indian Civil Service or the provincial governments.

The pace of state life was slow. The ruler often spent his summers in the United Kingdom entertaining his noble peers while in winter residence in the state he presided over a continuing succession of balls, receptions, visits, shikars (hunts), and festivals. He planted trees, opened new canals, donated gifts to the state's needy, and presided at meetings, but the soul of administration was not his concern. Having neither power or responsibility, he was a free spirit, at least until 1937.

Least like the stereotyped petty kingdoms of the romantic novel were the principalities of western India, dotted along the arid Persian and Afghan frontiers. They were, of course, part of the problem of a live and contested frontier behind which lay Imperial Russia. Their tribal populations added interest because of their well-deserved reputation for belligerence and independence. The tribesmen scarcely recognized any interior authority, let alone that of a foreign invader, and the British were faced with the "Yagistan" of old. They first attempted to conquer the area but were made to pay too dear a price. They then sought to buy tribal loyalties but succeeded only in

whetting the appetite of the Pathans and somewhat calming
the Baluchis. Finally they resorted to the defenses bequeathed
to them by history and geography and attempted to contain
the warriors in their own country.

The prince, more accurately the paramount chief of a certain region, was constantly challenged to prove himself both
within the tribe and in diplomacy, war, and maneuver with
the British. The Indian army, rather than protecting the rulers,
was often sent against them, sometimes in practice and other
times in anger. The tribesmen continued to do as they pleased
and they were pleased to fight and plunder.

The governments of the tribal princely states were as unique
as their populations. The ruler drew his court from his tribe
and used the subsidies paid to him by the British for retainers,
comforts, and the implements of war. The payments, justified
in the name of law and order by the British, were dispensed
by a political officer charged with tribal affairs. The officer had
tribal troops under his command but so long as the affairs of
the states were reasonably placid, payments were made and no
questions were asked. In the event that the British withheld
payment of the subsidies or attempted to dictate terms, the
ruler ordered guerrilla war.

The actual business of government was transacted in the
ruler's court or in local jirgas. The jirga, or local assembly, has
historically met to decide disputes on the basis of customary
tribal law. Since real power in the society is local, the jirgas
were capable of both adjudicating and enforcing their will. So
long as the tribal system lasted, the primary influence of the
ruler was exerted in his control of the funds and arms given
him by the British with which he maintained his authority.

Until statutory law was needed to establish guides for a rapidly
changing life, the monarch met individual needs for equity in
his court. More characteristic was a pattern in which the ruler

saw his task as the suppression of rival tribes and leaders. In all of the polities, the control of the prince over local law and order was tenuous and political life was "mean and brutish."

Reorganization, 1919

The variety of political and legal institutions and the imprecision of the treaty relationship between the British and the rulers troubled both parties and were intensively studied prior to the Government of India Act, 1919. The princes were interested in codifying state practice so that expanding British interference would be checked by legal restrictions. The Indian government sought to group those rulers having substantial internal sovereignty and differentiate them from the quasi-autonomous jurisdictional units with which the subcontinent was filled.

Bahawalpur, the premier Muslim state in western India, may be considered representative of the new governmental organization. A cabinet was formed under the leadership of a *mushir-i-'ala* (chief advisor), numbering among its eleven members a foreign minister (who could deal only with the British), a minister for revenue, the chief judge of the state court, a minister for the royal household and the ruler's private secretary, a minister for irrigation, and three members with various portfolios. Bills might be drafted by the responsible minister, passed by the cabinet, and submitted to the ruler, but the prince was free to act at his own discretion. In fact, the ruler could issue decrees without benefit of cabinet advice. While it would be misleading to suggest that the sovereign held unlimited internal authority, his wishes as the ruler and, generally, as the largest landlord of the state could hardly be questioned except by the Resident.

Revenue and irrigation ministers were frequently chosen

from the technical services of British India, and in any case
the web of obligations and interdependence woven by the
British snared the ruler. The increasingly important cabinet
and the heavy burden of British advice squeezed the ruler out
of politics. Importantly, the real control of the prince came
from his suzerain and not from the people of the state, a fact
of crucial importance in the decades to come.

As the economic life of British India impinged on Bahawalpur, its society could no longer be autonomous. Tied by
communication lines, economic markets, and even irrigation
canals to a broader India, the isolation of the state peoples
was ending. The fictitious barriers of the different colors on
the map ceased to restrict the flow of ideas into the backwaters
of rural India.

The 1919 reorganization of the Indian states did not signifi-
cantly change the tribal states which were considered part of
the general frontier situation. In Kalat, however, lawlessness
and anarchy were such problems that the British assumed indirect management of almost all the state. The Khan actually
controlled only five of his state's eleven districts and lost all
liaison with the autonomous southern tribes. His army num-
bered 461 men armed with twenty-nine cannons of which
twenty were unserviceable, and the other Baluch states possessed an even less impressive establishment. The northern
states were deeply involved in the Third Afghan War, which
also affected Kalat, but the government had little desire to
"reform" the rulers who were, with some exceptions, struggling
against the Afghans.

At the dawn of an era of revolutionary nationalism, the
states were a century behind the rest of India. The grim statistics of illiteracy, poverty, and disease were shameful compared to conditions in neighboring provinces. The immeasur-

able differences were even more disheartening; the lack of pride and the superstitious mind and society, at a time when British Indians were speaking of the rights of man and human justice.

In most of the states, the prince, his family, and a small circle of aristocrats owned most of the land, the sole source of wealth. The peasants were chattels, well conditioned to the subservience demanded by landlord, revenue agent, merchant, and prince. Yet within a lifetime they would be asked to vote, to support and understand the radical ideas of the new India.

Some rulers kept their religion pure, their small lamps of learning bright, their personal and court life spotless as an example for their people, but even enlightened paternalism is not an ideal preparation for democracy. In some of the states where there was a spirit of progress, a sound economic life, and an enlightened prince, movements for responsible government were aided by the growth of local bodies but such cases were in the minority.

An assessment of the regimes in the princely states must emphasize the severe limitations of their governments. The barren fields of Khairpur would have been barren regardless of the prince. The villages of Kalat were isolated not because of the government but because of the mountains. Given the very best of governments and wholehearted devotion, many state administrations would have been sorely tried in curing the endemic social and physical ills.

By 1930 the state peoples were being asked to make independence and democracy a reality. The nationalism of Indian unity caught many rulers unaware and they sensed a threat to their snug berths. They cast about for help, first to their ancient protector and then to their fellow rulers in the princely order. Most of all, however, they braced for the flood of the new India.

The Muslim League would be the ally of even the devil if need be in the interests of the Muslims. *Mohammad Ali Jinnah, to the Annual Muslim League Convention, 1936*

II

Patrons and Patriots

The revolutionary Western experience, having first smashed what it contacted throughout India, soon generated its own local variants. As market economics upset the old order, scrambling classes and castes, and as ideas carried in the English language mocked old truths, India began to seethe. In 1885 Allan Octavian Hume, a British reformer concerned with the "moral and material" progress of the Indians, organized, with government permission, the Indian National Congress.

The new India was creating its own leaders, however, and although they were cast in a British mold, they were of the subcontinent's peculiar soil. The Congress, a mixture of British and Indian likenesses, was an apt vehicle for their needs. It became a point around which the stunned Indian peoples could rally. Mr. Hume's mild reform group had, by the turn of the century, lost its timidity and gained self-confidence at the expense of its former patron. Europe's myth of invincibility had been shattered by Japan's victory over Russia in 1905, and World War I offered the Indians a chance to test their weakened overlord.

While the Congress outwardly became more Western and less Indian in its outlook, techniques, and organization, its leader, Gandhi, seemed to be the epitome of rural India. That he was an English-trained lawyer, a cosmopolitan world traveler, and a master politician notwithstanding, he became the half-naked symbol of a struggling people. Progressive nonviolent noncooperation became the revolutionary strategy of Indian nationalism.

The Indian National Congress was permeated with the nineteenth-century liberal spirit. Its xenophobia was subordinated to the goal of an independent Indian society in the future. The confrontation between the British and the Hindus was never one of bitter hatred because the English had only displaced the Mughuls, also alien rulers, and had brought to Asia the model for the future. The ideal state and society, to Congress leaders, was a social democracy and a secular state. Gandhi's unique contribution was to undergird the western blueprint with a moral order capable of restraining radical secular demands while integrating the idea of modern government with the traditional Indian heritage.

While many specific details of the proposed Indian state awaited long debate and discussion, it was immediately clear that the princes would not be tolerated. Even a cursory reading of Indian history reveals how treacherous and burdensome were the principalities to the central government. The extent of the communication and transportation revolution made all-India rule possible, and to the Congress, desirable. As the Indian revolution progressed, the princes found themselves increasingly abused by the growing modern segment of Indian society.

Communal politics

Although the Muslims hated the British for offenses past and present, they had little desire to trade British for Hindu rule. The implications of a unified democratic India included majority rule, dooming the Muslims, therefore, as a permanent three-to-one minority. Some began to sense submersion and integration, the antithesis of their semitic creed. The leadership of the community, first in a whisper and later in a scream, charged that the program of the Congress would destroy Indian Islam, its credo, culture, theology, and unique destiny.

The Muslims had not deeply imbibed European culture because they considered their own its peer. Islam was little affected by its sister faith, Christianity, much to the consternation of the missionaries. Neither had the Muslims become involved in the new commercial life brought by the British. This lack of involvement in the new politics restricted the Muslims' understanding of what might be expected when India modernized, and few leaders could understand or believe in secular platform of the Congress. It seemed to many of them to be a Hindu conspiracy.

The fear of the Congress initially troubled only a few upper class aristocrats in the United Provinces and some scattered Bengali intellectuals but it matured into a break with tradition. The Muslim League, founded in 1906, was the first attempt by the Indian Muslims to utilize a British-style party to advance their interests. Its demands were hardly more than those of a religious trade union—more jobs, better educational facilities, increased status. Led by Agha Khan III, the League was a clique rather than a movement but it was the beginning of modern Muslim politics.

As World War I had weakened the British, its Middle East theater of operations aroused the traditional-minded Indian Muslim community, hitherto a silent host. The victorious allied armies which destroyed the Ottoman Empire camped in the court of the Caliph, symbolic leader of Islam. Whether the caliphate was, in theological fact, the papacy of Islam was unimportant because the Indian Muslims clung to it as a symbol of their strength outside India. India was the farthest continental expansion to the east of Islam, and the faith had known danger there. To Muslim frontiersmen, the Caliph was the symbol of a hearth, a spiritual homeland from which he had once known and might again expect succor. Thus when allied arms defeated the Central Powers, the Indian Muslims organized the Khilafat movement to save their faith.

The Khilafat leadership realized that it would need support from other quarters in India to bring the government to respect its demands. They allied with the Indian National Congress to evolve a cooperative anti-British strategy and from 1916 to 1924, Indian politics were singular in aim. The small pro-British Muslim League maintained an embarrassed passivity.

The overripe fruit of the Ottoman state fell of its own weight and the Turks abolished the caliphate in 1924. The Khilafat members, politically sensitized, were shocked and benumbed. In confusion they searched for a new mission. Many of the more westernized members stayed with the Congress to work for an independent India while others flocked to the Muslim League. The new recruits to the League had little in common with its aristocratic membership except Friday prayers but they knew they did not want a trade union. After a period of depression and quiet, the heady transfusion of Islam galvanized the League into a Muslim movement. Fezzes mingled with felt hats, mullas consorted with Cambridge dons, the search

was on for the future of the community and communal politics
became a reality.

The British response

The British were more than disinterested spectators. During
the war they had exhausted their energies in the fields of
Flanders but with the armistice and the "Indian summer of
empire," the professional rulers returned to their work. The
genius of the British in India was in the proper assessment of
the foe, and the foe in 1919 was the Indian National Congress.
In a return to the tactics of the East India Company, the
British began working out an alliance against the Congress.

During World War I the princes had supported the war
effort with men and money and their loyalty was sure. Why
not continue to use them as a counterfoil to Indian politicians
and why not at least wink at Muslim parties? The personifica-
tion of the strands which the British were weaving together
was Agha Khan III. As a favored son of the King-Emperor,
he was appointed a member of the Legislative Council in 1902
and was elected president of the Muslim League from 1906
to 1912. He was made an Indian prince (without territory)
in 1916. In the informal and subtle personal politics of the
interwar period, the Agha Khan, at home in all but the Congress camp, was to play an important role.

Although the princes and the Muslim League were light-
weights in a struggle between giants, their entry into the ring
was disconcerting. The growth of competing nationalisms and
local patriotism in India muddied the clear vision of the subcontinent's future. While the League and the Congress both
espoused a liberal creed, their differing interpretations gave

rise to a "two nation" theory and Indian conflict became implicit.

From the British point of view, a divided house was in keeping with every dictum of colonial rule. Yet there were serious differences within and between the governments in Delhi and Whitehall, as to the honorable course for British policy. Divided loyalties often pitted Englishmen against one another over a particular problem and even the occupying power found itself increasingly divided.

Enhanced princes

While the rise of Muslim nationalism was viewed as helpful to imperial planners, the Muslims were distrustful of British motives. The princes were more reliable and were therefore encouraged to organize and strengthen themselves. In 1916 Lord Hardinge had convoked the first of several annual conferences of rulers, describing them hopefully as "helpers and colleagues in the great task of imperial rule." [1]

The first reinforcement of princely power was the Imperial Service Troop Plan, which allowed the state governments to raise, equip, and train sizable battalions under British officers. These soldiers were available for combat under the Union Jack in case of imperial need. At home, the princes found security in their forces as nationalism began to erode state frontiers. They were also allowed to pass "Regulation against Disaffection" acts, which prohibited the formation of nationalist groups within state boundaries.

A second major support for the rulers was the Chamber of Princes, established by a royal proclamation in February, 1921. Its membership was drawn from among the more important

middle-sized states but it had no authority to bind the princely
order. A standing committee of its notables conducted its light
load of important business while both the large and the small
states took cognizance of its debates. The Chamber, powerless
in princely India and mocked in British India, found itself
increasingly involved with British-princely relations. Years of
confinement to their narrow persons had focused the rulers'
interest exclusively on their egos, honors, and purses. The
Chamber, representing no real interest group, pursued these
phantoms while around them raged the real storm.

The solid protection the British gave their princely allies was
legal. The Government of India Act, 1919, gave full support
to princely independence following the recommendation:

The Princes should be assured in the fullest and freest manner
that no constitutional changes which take place impair the rights,
dignities and privileges secured to them.[2]

The 1919 constitution was an expressly transitional award, however, and as early as 1927 its revision had begun. The Butler
Committee, which studied the relationship between princely
and British India, concluded:

In view of the historical nature of the relationship between the
paramount power and the Princes, the latter should not be transferred without their agreement to a relationship with a new government in British India responsible to an Indian legislature.[3]

These conclusions, which seem in many ways absurd, were
part of the extraordinary treatment given to the rulers in British
law. They were, for example, given sovereign immunity in the
courts of the United Kingdom when in India the Viceroy had
but to ring his bell to have their sceptres. The Congress bitterly
cited the support of the princes as another example of "divide
and rule" colonial duplicity. Nevertheless, the Simon Commis-

sion accepted the findings of the Butler Committee and recommended that the two Indias continue their separation.

Under the new constitution, the affairs of the states were transferred to the Crown representative, a "second hat" of the viceroy, because it was reasoned that the princes were in alliance with the British Crown and not the Indian government. The 1935 act also made it possible for the rulers to affiliate with the elected assembly but when every prince refused to do so, no one was surprised, even though they were offered tempting terms; 40 percent of the Upper House and 33⅓ percent of the Lower House membership.

The same act provided that British India should become a federation in which the provinces would have considerable power exercisable by popularly elected legislatures. The viceroy's prerogatives were restricted by a council in which Indian votes were given increased weight. After a series of abortive meetings in which the Indian politicians refused to accept the act, it was imposed and the first elections were called for 1937. Notwithstanding their previous position, the Indian parties decided to seek election.

The Congress victorious

The elections of 1937 were heroic in scale. Indian students traveled in villages they scarcely knew existed, begging rural India to vote for a new nation. The vernacular press enjoyed an unprecedented flowering. For the first time in centuries, perhaps the first time ever, the people of India were asked for more than submission; they were asked for consent. The Muslim League did not broadly contest the elections, relying instead upon understandings with the Congress that coalition minis-

tries would be formed in provinces having large Muslim populations. When the avalanche of support for the Congress was
tallied, its leaders surmised that there was no Muslim vote and
refused to honor the communal claims of the League.[4]

The wrath of the spurned, jobless politicians and the increased suspicion of the Muslim community toward Congress
leadership wrecked future possibilities of League-Congress cooperation, particularly in the United Provinces. The decision
to scuttle League politicians was the first deliberate step to
weaken and divide the Muslim party because the leaders of
the Congress saw its religious mandate as reactionary. Religion
as a basis for the political organization of India was impossible
because of the broad range of belief and the innumerable faiths
and sects. If the League's claim was accepted, a unified India
would be impossible and without Indian unity, independence
was unthinkable.

There were practical reasons as well for destroying the League
as a competing elite. In 1937 the Congress leaders could nip
communalism in the bud, they believed, because the League
would have to overcome the British, the Congress, non-League
Muslim politicians and the princes. The elections of 1937 had
shown the Muslim League to be a "paper party." How could
it hope to threaten the Congress with its new success when
even the British began patronizing it?

The Pakistan movement

Perhaps the Congress assessment of the future would have
been correct had it not been for Sir Muhammad Iqbal, a Muslim philosopher-politician and Mohammed Ali Jinnah, a shrewd
lawyer-politician. Iqbal might have been a pillar of Indian
unity and modern secular politics because his education in

England and Germany had exposed him, in unusual breadth, to the Western tradition. Instead, however, he reacted to this experience by returning to his own faith with rekindled vigor. "Yet I love the communal group, which is the source of my life and behaviour and which has formed me what I am by giving me its religion, its literature, its thoughts, its culture . . ." Making obvious the political importance of his message, he concluded: "The formation of a consolidated Northwest Indian Muslim state appears to me to be the final destiny of the Muslims, at least of Northwest India." [5]

Iqbal's mind was well ahead of his fellows in 1930 but as the months passed, the idea of a Muslim state took shape. The electoral debacle of 1937 brought it to the fore and produced a leader with a mandate. Mohammad Ali Jinnah, a gaunt and astringent lawyer from Bombay, left the Indian National Congress and his post as "ambassador of unity" and took charge of the League. Jinnah coined a slogan for the party: "Faith, Unity, Discipline." He would see to the last, but the party needed articles of faith and the Muslims needed unity.

Pakistan, a symbol as universal as the Khilafat movement had found earlier, became the ideology of the Muslim League. Born of Iqbal's dreams, Jinnah's politics, the Mughul past, and a Cambridge student's lexicon,[6] Pakistan was to be a Muslim national homeland in India. At first the idea was viewed as foolishness, but by 1940 the Muslim League had translated it into a hard political demand. Pakistan became a gospel, the very soul of the Muslim League, the faith for which Muslims were to die, and the prime reason for their unity.

In every part of the subcontinent, Pakistan was discussed. It came to imply not only exhilarating power and majesty to Mr. Jinnah and his lieutenants, prestige to his few financial backers, better days ahead for the lower-middle-class Muslim,

and utopia to the tonga-walla, it came to mean for Indian Islam
the sole escape from the fruitless subsistence of India.

Balkanization and the princes

While leaders of the Congress first laughed at the notion of
Pakistan, they later argued seriously that while Indian society
was plural, it was not contradictory. Unity in diversity, the
stock-in-trade phrase of the federalist, was implied in every
statement. But the advancement of the Pakistan idea brought
sponsors and converts. The prospect of the "Balkanization" of
India was a welcome one to the princes. Large states might
become independent while smaller principalities might federate
with like-minded neighbors.

If the principle of the League's demand for separatism was
confirmed, the princes might be delivered from the hands of
the Congress and continue to enjoy their comfortable lives.
Nor was this solely a calculation based on jaded excesses; it
was an attempt to assert a traditional society over a modern
one. Many rulers came to believe that their states were more
reflective of the Indian soul than would be the artificial trans-
plant of the West. They also realized that the Muslim League's
leadership was very much like that of the Congress except that
it was much more in need of support. Cooperation seemed
to be suggested.

For his part, Mr. Jinnah was careful to avoid antagonizing
the rulers. In the interests of the over-all policies of the League
he could not openly ally with the princes, but an informal
understanding might both weaken the Congress and expose
new sources of support for the League's perennially empty
coffers.

The seemingly desirable arrangement was not contracted,

however, because few princes believed that the League would succeed and few found solace in its platform. By 1939 Mr. Jinnah's party did not control any provincial government and was clearly subordinate to the Congress. Any prince, willing to gamble, had to consider the hostility of the Congress and the strictures of the Political Department of the Indian government. League leadership therefore concentrated almost exclusively on Muslim majority provinces in British India, with intermittent contact with Muslim princes. The Nawab of Bhopal, for example, was important because of his role in the Chamber of Princes, just as the Nizam of Hyderabad's wealth was like a magnet to his poor callers. Balkanization remained a highly improbable contingency.

The Muslim League and the Congress meanwhile were arousing individual Indians to political action of every kind. The League sought so awesome a coalition that the British could be intimidated and the Congress stalemated, at least on certain issues. The hot breezes of the summer of 1939 were the harbinger of a political monsoon unique in Indian history but its arrival was delayed by German dive bombers over Warsaw.

The war

The war forced India's politicians to take sides. They could either declare a moratorium on radical politics in support of the Allied cause or be suppressed by the government at the cost, perhaps, of British lives in Europe. Few Indians had the stomach to aid the Nazis but the war was a European affair and offered a fine opportunity for independence. While debates raged the princes came to the aid of the British with money, men, political and moral support, and personal sacrifice. The Nizam of Hyderabad purchased Spitfires for the

Battle of Britain and troops of many states soon found themselves on imperial duty. At home the rulers took the opportunity to tighten internal security and used the war as an excuse to eliminate nationalist troublemakers. It became illegal to "form any organization in the State, whether political, social or religious, without the previous sanction of the Government." [7]

Under Gandhi's whip hand and despite the reluctance of Nehru and others, the Indian National Congress was committed to a "Quit India" campaign, in the face of imminent Japanese invasion. The plan sought the forcible overthrow of the government. Allied troops in Burma and Bengal and Chinese troops supplied from India would have been isolated and destroyed by the movement had it been successful. The government replied to violence with violence and for several weeks Delhi was out of touch with forces in Bengal, Bihar, and eastern United Provinces. But with the princes' wholehearted cooperation, their own drastic action, and the Muslim League's "benevolent neutrality," India was saved for the British for four more years. The Congress leadership paid for its action by imprisonment.

The Muslim League, like the princes, found itself in a good bargaining position during the war. About 40 percent of the Indian armed forces were "Mussalmans," a fact not overlooked by Mr. Churchill [8] or Mr. Jinnah. The League had no love for the Axis cause and, in 1942, independence would have come too soon for Pakistan to be established, had the "Quit India" scheme worked. Hence, support for the British was both moral and expedient. The removal of Congress politicians from high places and the League's opportunities to fill them further enhanced the party's fortunes.

By the beginning of 1943 the princes and the League were

relieved of Congress pressure and allowed time to build their strength. The war artificially inflated the role of the leaders of the Indian parties and states. Mass activities were halted and leaders were considered representative of their communities and interests. The future of independent India was made during the war, since independence was granted quite soon after the armistice. Mr. Jinnah the lawyer, Mr. Nehru the lawyer, and Lord Mountbatten the soldier would settle things at a table. The masses would be used but not consulted.

The retreat of the League from its popular orientation had a not altogether constructive effect. If Pakistan, as a demand, had been defined in debate and discussion throughout India, it would have come to mean certain distinct things. Surely the existence of separate autocratic states within Pakistan would have been repudiated. Choudhary Rahmat Ali, for example, specifically condemned Mr. Jinnah for trafficking with the princes or assuring them autonomy in Pakistan.

It is essential to record that, while they are always ready to recognize all legitimate rights, whether of private individuals or of princes, the Paks absolutely reject and repudiate the sweeping and senseless statement of the President of the All India Muslim League accepting in the name of the Muslims the principle of the sovereignty of the Princes . . . for it would be, first, to renounce all Pak claims to Kashmir and Kachch and other states which are integral and inseparable parts of Pakistan.[9]

Even if the League had entrusted the ideal Pakistan to the gentle care of the Muslim intellectuals, they would have had to resolve the inherent conflict between seventeenth-century personal rule and twentieth-century democracy. Instead, Pakistan was kept in the pocket of negotiators, to be shaped on the bargaining table. At any given time, it meant and stood for the total power which the League possessed vis-a-vis the other parties

The bargaining table

The princes were one of the groups at the negotiating table and the League cooperated with them, regardless of its conscience, in the interest of its community.

Jinnah moved toward an alliance with the Princes. He told the Jam Saheb of Nawanagar that he would readily consult the Jam Saheb as Chancellor of the Chamber of Princes about any constitutional proposals on the understanding that the princely order would not cut across him.[10]

At this stage the alliance which had been postponed because of the League's uncertain future became attractive to the rulers. There were three classes of princes, none of which would suffer if Pakistan became a reality. The nearly six hundred princes whose lands lay outside the Muslim majority area might go free or might retain some power if Pakistan became independent. In any case, Pakistan posed no threat to them. The second group of sovereigns, rulers within the Muslim majority areas, were courted by the League, introduced into its innermost circles, and proffered tolerant friendship and aid. The third group, composed of a few Muslim princes ruling Hindu populations, could hope for independence and if Pakistan succeeded, it would be a powerful ally with which to confront the Indian government.

Underlying the League's strategy was the calculation that the rulers as a group were capable of plunging the subcontinent into civil war and chaos. They could so weaken the Indian government that the Muslims could attain their objectives. From its formation, the Muslim League operated as a quasi-governmental body making decisions based on its community interests. To court the princes and the British was in the Muslim interest, no matter how repugnant the alliance to the broader meanings of the Pakistan movement.

The Cripps Mission, which had come to India with the grudging acceptance of Mr. Churchill, had offered India Dominion status after the war if it would cooperate with the allies. The Congress answer was the "Quit India" program but the Cripps proposals carried two pithy recommendations. The first was that Pakistan might be possible if certain regions wished to secede from the Indian Union. The second was that there was no thought of a successor state composed entirely of states. The scuttling of princely India had begun, a fact that did not go unnoticed in Patiala or Hyderabad.

The Muslim League leaders realized that they could hope for Pakistan only if they controlled provincial governments in Muslim majority areas, and they devoted every waking hour to the task. They also thought of the dimensions of their territory. Two groups held the key to the size of Pakistan: the princes and the Sikh community. The violence of communal politics and the suspected orthodoxy of the League forced the Sikh nation out of any proposed Muslim state.[11] The only other option available was to expand by the inclusion of state territories. A dilemma faced Mr. Jinnah who, intent on protecting his coreligionists from persecution and yet dealing with their persecutors for a larger prize, was torn between inconsistency and imprudence.

The Congress perceived the League plan and gave the states urgent priority. The growing strength of popular movements within the states effectively limited the sovereign's choice. If he played favorites, even in matters not relating to the state peoples, he could expect internal difficulties. The favored communal group would try to buttress the state administration but in almost every state the prince knew that his inevitable fate lay with the majority and their masters, the Indian National Congress. Nonetheless, the Muslim League held in public that a Greater Pakistan was inevitable, and printed, on page one of the party paper, a map of the projected dominion.[12]

It is interesting to note that every state with a Muslim ruler in western India was shown within the general outline of Pakistan and that the tribal states of the frontier were not indicated in any manner. Since the map was primarily a provincial recreation, the exclusion of Kashmir can perhaps be understood, but it is clear that the League did not expect a partition of the Punjab and therefore served notice on the states of the eastern Punjab. Yet Jinnah, the month before, had said: "For the

THE PROJECTED DOMINION

Dawn, September 3, 1944

present the Pakistan issue does not react on Their Highnesses who are free to introduce Responsible Government in their States." [13]

Early in 1945 the progress of the war assured the Indians that they could intensify politics once more. After two years with the field to itself, how had the League fared? The Unionist ministry still held the Punjab, the Khudai Khidmatgar party was in control of the North-West Frontier Province, and Baluchistan was still a British preserve.[14] Sind's government was unstable and the British were equivocating on the tribal peoples' right to participate in the forthcoming elections.[15] But, all things considered, the Muslim League had used its time well. It had made some strategic converts and had become much more muscular, as the coming months would prove.

The princes had already lost the battle. The Chamber of Princes was shot through with communal alignments and the states themselves were increasingly dominated by popular groups. No major party placed its trust in the haggling rulers. The world as well as the Indian people knew that the subcontinent's history after the war would be written by Nehru and Jinnah. Only the terms were in doubt.

We want a Muslim party. We want a unified Muslim organization, every member of which is ready to lay down his life for the survival of his race, his faith and his civilization. *Mohammad Ali Jinnah, quoted in* The Memoirs of the Aga Khan

III

Desperation Politics

Although the allies had broken the momentum of Axis expansion and had begun the inevitable march on Berlin and Toyko, they were weary, exhausted by the anemia of war. The British realized that the empire in India could not continue after the peace except by utilizing means which they despised. The decision to grant independence was made at the time of the Cripp's Mission and the obvious next step was a relaxation of political restrictions in India so long as the war effort was not maimed.

Upon their restoration to public life, Congress leaders realized that the power balance in India had shifted during the war and that the Muslim League was a more formidable opponent. They plunged their party into a new campaign to win support and the League responded in kind. Both parties soon found themselves in a hyperpolitical struggle of such bitterness that violence came to play an increasing role.

The future of 400 million people was to be decided in less than two years after the end of the war. It was the compression of time which plagued the League, frightened the princes, and led the society into torment. The future was clouded as well by the approaching end of the wartime economy, the return of military personnel, and heightened industrial unrest. Those who knew India feared that there would be many nights of the long knives.

Into this setting came the Cabinet Mission, to relieve Britain of the burden of an Indian settlement, yet keep the subcontinent in the war against the Japanese. Independence was coming but the war effort, of which the princes were an important part, had to continue. The secretary of state for India, Mr. Amery, made it clear that the proposals of the Cabinet Mission would not affect the relationship of the princes with the Crown Representative. He was perhaps thinking of the anonymous ruler who said: "We fought and sacrificed our blood to win power and we mean to hold it. If Congress wants to rob us, if the British should let us down, we will fight." [1] The firm guarantee was weakened by Lord Wavell's note that this was true so long as the political offer to the rulers from the nationalists was "unreasonable." But who would judge reasonableness?

In May, 1946, the plan of the mission was revealed by the Labor government. India was to be an independent dominion in the Commonwealth composed of three regions which might, after British withdrawal, secede from the national government of India. These provisions made Pakistan possible and yet saved the British from granting it. It doomed the states by ignoring them. An interim Indian government was to be formed immediately and a constituent assembly convoked to draft a new constitution.

In answer to the anxious appeal of the princes, a memorandum was submitted to the Chamber of Princes on May 12, 1946.[2] Its essence was that paramountcy would end with British rule. The treaty obligations of the rulers would not be transferred to the Indian government but neither would the Crown continue to guarantee the independence of the states. The announcement left open only two possible choices, accession to the successor government or independence. The latter was plausible only for very large states or princely federations and the nature of the state economies was such that the thought of doing without British services, of "going it alone," had little administrative appeal.

Although Jinnah had previously demanded the simultaneous independence of Pakistan and India, he viewed the Cabinet Mission proposals as workable and, what is perhaps more important, as a device which would give him more time. The Congress decided after considerable debate that it could not admit the option allowing the provinces to act separately. Even before the rupture over the proposals, Jinnah determined that the continued independence of the states, at least until independence day, was necessary if the Islamic Dominion was to be created.

His reasoning must have been that the states burdened the Congress, that they were of some aid to the League, and that some of the rulers might want to accede to or ally with Pakistan. As well, the creation of a legitimate constituent assembly would imply that the rulers had to deal with it and might be extinguished, as a political factor, before the Muslim League had won its demands.

The Congress had no intention of waiting for Mr. Jinnah's plans to mature, and in his presidential address to the All-India States Peoples' Conference Mr. Nehru branded nonacceding princes as hostile. A stigmatized ruler could hardly expect cooperation within his state from the local Praja Mandal (Indian state popular party). Sir Stafford Cripps was queried, in May,

1946, about difficulties which might arise from popular rebellions against princely rule.

Question: If the subjects of a State revolt for the establishment of self-government, will the Interim Government help the ruler of that State to crush the revolt? Or will it help the nationalist cause? [3]

He replied that it would be a decision for the Crown representative, but no Indian prince missed the significance of the question. The pressure was on and the British were equivocating. The Muslim League was at best a weak champion. By July the princes accepted the plan as a basis for negotiation.

Hitherto the political demands of the Indian parties were extreme because there was little chance of their fulfilment. In mid-1946, however, demands came to involve specific issues and gross ideologies gave way to minute details. The first meetings between the Congress negotiators and the princes were unproductive because the nationalists demanded representation by elected officials from the states. The princes held that theirs was the sole political voice of their states and began padding their privy purses and recruiting larger guard forces.

The All-India States' Muslim League, a poor cousin of Mr. Jinnah's British Indian party, attempted to enhance the voice of state Muslims in the negotiations and called for acceptance of a five-point program. The program included demands for separate electorates for religious communities with the states, minority safeguards, the prohibition of regional princely confederations, an end to communal rioting in the states, and a condemnation of the Maharaja of Kashmir.[4] It met with little success.

In July elections were held for the Constituent Assembly. The Congress won all but nine of the general seats while the

Muslim League captured all save five of the constituencies reserved for Muslims. Both parties confirmed their popular strength. An organized minority was pitted against an organized majority in a situation in which one party's loss was the other's gain.

Emboldened by electoral successes and infuriated with the British and Congress "tampering" with the original Cabinet Mission plan, the League repudiated the plan and reverted to its previous policy. A policy of active agitation was begun. An all-Indian "Direct Action Day" was staged to show the Congress and the British that the Muslims would have their homeland even at the cost of civil war. The scarcely disguised passions of the religious-cum-political street mobs erupted in unprecedented bloodshed. Calcutta was beyond civil control for some time. The hard-pressed authorities, themselves divided and tired of war and the thankless lot of the referee, faltered. Civil war became the journalists' prediction for the immediate future.

There is little doubt that Mr. Jinnah was ready to risk chaos to have Pakistan. His view was that from the Motilal Nehru report to the Cabinet Mission plan, the Hindu majority had shown little regard for minority rights. They had not tried to ease the fears of the Muslims. Such distrust was inevitable in the subcontinent where there was no buffer, where the deprivation of one person allowed another barely to survive in the zero sum game of Indian existence. Other factors in the radical policy decisions of the League included five crises troubling its leadership: the Punjab, the North-West Frontier Province, Kalat, the interim government, and the British who were impatient to stay on.

The Punjab

The Punjab was the heart of Muslim India although the United Provinces was its head. The great monuments of the Mughul past and the Aligarh Muslim University served the Urdu speakers of the Ganges valley. The fertile lands of the Indus, however, which earned the Punjab the title "Breadbasket of India," provided the numerical strength of the Pakistan movement. Unfortunately, the province was also the "Ulster of India" because of its divided society. The Land of the Five Rivers was run by rural oligarchs who inhibited the urban elite from bringing social and economic change to the province. Every shade of heterodox religion found adherents and there was little internal cohesion. The Muslims and Sikhs comprised the majority of the hard-working peasants while the Hindu minority was found generally in the cities. The Punjabis were classified as "martial races" and British army recruitment centers dotted the plains. Little was done to disturb the peasantry which produced such virile troops, and it was charged that the British purposely kept the province backward to ensure a steady flow of trusting manpower.

The provincial government was controlled by a powerful political machine supervised by Sir Sikander Hyat Khan, a wealthy and not overly scrupulous boss. The Unionist party, as it was called, was a multi-communal organization with rural strength whose influence reached into the neighboring Punjab states. Its directors frequently served the rulers as advisers and ministers.[5] The Muslim League considered the party heretical since it cooperated with the Congress. The Congress also judged it harshly because its program was patently reactionary. Further, it was the vehicle for Punjabi interests which were shared neither by the League nor by the Congress.

If Pakistan was to be born, the Muslim League had to dis-place Khizr Hyat Khan, the chief minister of the Punjab, and establish a League government in the Muslim heartland. A weather eye was kept out for any dangerous developments in the Punjab states. A "Direct Action" campaign to topple the government was launched on January 29, 1947. It was the largest demonstration of its type to date and included para-military Muslim League national guardsmen. The Punjab gov-ernment countered with a suspension of civil liberties and imprisoned provincial League leaders. Mass protest demonstra-tions followed and on February 26 the government resigned. Violent politics had won the day.

The victory of the Muslim League over law and order in the Punjab and its subsequent difficulty in replacing the Union-ist government with loyal League politicians revealed the de-gree to which the Sikhs and Hindus of the province were disturbed. They saw the victory as a triumph of militant Islam. Communal outbreaks, once sporadic, became more frequent and the division of the peoples of the Indian Ulster became more pronounced. As families left Lahore and Amritsar, their places were taken by terrorists from all parts of India. Sir Si-kander might well have wondered why the League was anxious to inherit such a tinderbox.

The North-West Frontier Province and Kalat

The North-West Frontier Province was an embarrassment to the League. With a population over 90 percent orthodox Muslim and a heritage second to none in loving a good fight, the Pathans were following the "Frontier Gandhi," Abdul Ghaffar Khan, down the Congress path. Perhaps this was be-cause they hated the British so thoroughly and thought the

Congress a proper instrument of their longstanding vendetta. In any case, Pakistan was impossible without the Frontier Province because the British would not allow the Khyber Pass to be separated from a successor government capable of defending it. Moving in from the Punjab, the League organizers led by Abdul Qayyum Khan, a convert from the Congress, began following the Punjab pattern, and considerable attention was directed to the warlike tribes of the Afghan frontier country as well as to the four princely states of the region. Ghaffar Khan saw the challenge clearly but, mistaking both the proper aid and the correct moment, invited Nehru (rather than Gandhi) to tour the province with him.

On the day before the visit *Dawn* did its part by printing gory pictures of Pathans dead in communal rioting throughout India and Nehru's arrival was not without incident. There was little need for last-minute propaganda, however, for riots broke out and after several narrow escapes and one death in his party,[6] the leader of the Congress left the province. By December, 1946, the Muslim League was strong enough to call for a plebiscite on the issue of Pakistan. Once more the politics of violence had carried the day. In subsequent weeks the League could not displace the Khudai Khidmatgar-Congress government of Dr. Khan Sahib, but it was clear that when the crucial plebiscite was held the Pathans would choose Pakistan.

The methods used by Indian politicians in 1946 and early 1947 reveal how unsettled the future of the subcontinent was. The League support for the princes and its extralegal techniques in the North-West Frontier Province and Punjab testify to the tentative nature of Pakistan. This gives some small circumstantial support to one of the more interesting bazaar rumors of the day.

It is said that Mohammad Ali Jinnah and the Khan of Kalat

were friends. As must have been the case with more than one Muslim prince, Jinnah enjoyed the warm hospitality for which the rulers were famous. As politics became more bitter, the worn leader must have enjoyed the autumn respites of the cool hills of Baluchistan. On one visit, the story goes, Mr. Jinnah asked the Khan if, with Kalat's long and isolated coastline, he could procure and import arms secretly. The Khan nodded. Mr. Jinnah wondered if, under desperate circumstances, the Khan would undertake to join the Pathan tribes in the north in an insurrection should the Pakistan demand be refused. Again the Khan agreed. The third condition of the rumored arrangement was purported to be the designation of Major General Iskander Mirza, an experienced frontier officer, to coordinate the military aspects of the rebellion. "The Hindus and the British will see that we mean to have our independence," concluded the League leader as he left the Khan.[7]

There is not the slightest proof of this conversation and in fact it is universally denied by Pakistani leaders. Yet it illustrates the tension and grit of the Muslims, so close to independence and so far from it. The June 3 Plan and its grant of Pakistan never put to the test the rumored rebellion.

The interim government and British impatience

A second all-India Direct Action Day forced the Congress to concede several points to the League's interpretation of the Cabinet Mission plan, and Liaquat Ali Khan, chief lieutenant of Mr. Jinnah, entered the hitherto boycotted interim government. The League refrained from taking its seat in the Constituent Assembly, however, charging that the Muslims should have their own body for Pakistan.

Joining the government under these terms complicated Indian politics because the League ministers in the cabinet would not accept majority votes as binding, yet they could not be dismissed. A miscalculation in high Congress circles resulted in the award of the finance portfolio to Liaquat Ali Khan, who then hobbled the government with its own purse strings. Meanwhile, the half-empty Constituent Assembly was preparing to meet the rulers to arrange for their accession. The Congress was forced to turn all of its energies to this task in the light of League policy, and Princes' Row in Delhi was ablaze with late evening lights. The pressure was high because every state acceding to India before partition would be denied Pakistan and would strengthen the "bandwagon" approach of the Congress.

On February 20, 1947, Prime Minister Attlee, assessing the dilatory negotiations, the extreme stands, and the smoldering dangers in India, announced that the British would withdraw from the subcontinent no later than June, 1948. His speech was calculated to shock the Indian parties into a realization that compromises were necessary. The Prime Minister also announced that he was sending a new viceroy, Lord Mountbatten, to bring fresh ideas to the settlement of outstanding disputes.

Within three months after his arrival in India, the new Viceroy had announced and put into operation plans for independence, partition, and accession. Indian independence was guaranteed, Pakistan was granted and the new order was to be established 10 months ahead of schedule, by August 1947!

The grant of Pakistan needed clarification. Its territorial frontiers had never been concretely assigned and the very idea of Pakistan was a bitterly contested issue which had not been worn smooth by years of negotiation and understanding. Once granted in principle, it was a raw wound rubbed with the salt of communal disorder. The Muslim League wanted a large and viable state in which the Muslims would be a majority but not the sole residents. Yet the chapters of violent politics had forced all but Muslims from its embrace. Therefore, the Punjab and Bengal would be divided by district on the basis of religious composition and the Pathans would be given a chance to vote yea or nay to Pakistan.

Lord Mountbatten's program for the princes was to advise them most strongly to seek immediate accession with one of the two successor governments, such accession to be governed by contiguity of territory and, to a lesser extent, community of religion. This approach, seemingly the essence of common sense, did not provide for border states, states in which the ruler intended to assert his independence, or states in which the ruler and his subjects were of different minds on their future. In short, it did not remove the problem of the princes from contest between the Congress and the League.

While the new Viceroy hurried the princes to their inevitable fate, sometimes with the carrot and other times with the scarcely concealed stick, the interim government was paralyzed by the League, which wanted to keep the negotiations well stocked with issues and allies. The Constituent Assembly could not be stalemated, however, and Sardar Patel and V. P. Menon, outstanding talents with the hard and the soft words, respectively, took charge of the negotiations with the rulers.

With Bhopal leading an illusionary "Third Force" and with the troublesome giants of Hyderabad and Kashmir standing warily by, Liaquat Ali Khan sought to assure the princes of the League's support and delivered a speech of historic importance, in which he stated:

The Indian States will be free to negotiate agreements with Pakistan or Hindustan as considerations of contiguity *or their own self-interest may dictate, or they may choose to assume complete and separate sovereign status for themselves.* (Italics added) [8]

This was the culmination of the policy which pitted the rulers against the Congress. That it was made counter to the spirit of Lord Mountbatten's directive reveals the conscious support which the League was now proffering to Hyderabad and every state in the subcontinent. The announcement practically accused the Congress of spinelessness, but little thought was given to the power which the League might be asked to use if it was to act as guarantor for the rulers.

Even assuming that the statement was bluff, it allowed Kashmir and Hyderabad independence until after the British departed, at which time the larger dominion had every advantage. On every specific issue of partition except the disposition of the states, Jinnah labored to make Pakistan complete before independence, so much did he rely upon the British and so little did he trust the Congress. But the latitude which he allowed the princes in the interest of strengthening his negotiating hand put them outside frontier security. The bird came home to roost not only with regard to Kashmir and Hyderabad but with regard to some of the Muslim rulers who later acceded to Pakistan. The bluster that Pakistan would safeguard the independence of states acceding to it became a sword which cut the new Muslim government more than India.

In all probability, League leaders, who were not alone in their opinion, thought that India would be extraordinarily weak at the time of its independence and that Pakistan could, if the case demanded, secure Kashmir by force. There was considerable faith in the Nizam's ability to defend Hyderabad

against such a divided India long enough, at least, for Pakistan
to stabilize its territories in the west and east.

Meanwhile the courting of non-Muslim princes proceeded
apace. "Tempting concessions were being offered the rulers to
inveigle them into joining Pakistan. The League leaders were
concentrating in particular on some of the border states." [9]
Specifically, Jodhpur and Jaisalmer were courted by the League.
It is said that Jinnah offered their rulers a pen and a blank
piece of paper and asked them to write out their demands,
which he would accept. Of equal note was the pledge that
the states, as states, would be independent in Pakistan.

Real estate was important, however, and after the communal
fires were ablaze in Lahore, Hindu and Sikh princes and advisers would not resist internal pressures, abetted by the Congress, against their affiliation with Pakistan. Besides, who knew
whether Pakistan would last for more than a month? Better a
small but secure allowance than a short-lived paradise, mused
the rulers. But Kashmir and Hyderabad stood separate.

It is probably true that the Muslim League's entire state
policy pivoted on Bhopal, Hyderabad, and Kashmir. The border states would have been a bonus, but they were clearly outside the main thrust of League actions. The difficulty was that
the magnitude of the communal war repelled the border states,
enervated Bhopal, alienated Kashmir, and isolated Hyderabad.
But the fruit of the discord was yet to fully ripen.

The interim Pakistan government

Following the announcement of the June 3 Plan, a Constituent Assembly of Pakistan was organized, and the government hastily set to work on plans for the division of the assets
of the Indian Empire. In a questionable decision, Jinnah de-

cided to become Pakistan's governor-general, thereby personally offending Lord Mountbatten, the savant of princely affairs. The Pakistan Constituent Assembly, acting as the federal legislature as well, nominated a panel composed of the leading members of the chamber to supervise state negotiations.[10]

The States Negotiating Committee established under the Indian interim government was divided into two sections. Sardar Abdur Rab Nishtar and Ikramullah headed the Pakistan section, although Jinnah was personally in charge.[11] The princes could find their place in the new order by either executing a standstill agreement which postponed the day of reckoning, or by acceding to the Dominion in the fields of defense, foreign affairs, and communications. Both agreements merely substituted Indian for British authority, and neither option committed the rulers to introduce responsible government. Section 3 of the sixth article of the Indian Independence Act allowed, however, that the original terms of the Instrument of Accession might be altered by mutual agreement.

Pakistan's Constituent Assembly approved two forms of an Instrument of Accession, the longer of which was deemed proper for more developed states while the shorter applied only to the tribal states of the western frontier. To both forms was appended a list of subjects in which the Dominion legislature could act in the states. The central government was limited not only by the subjects reserved for the ruler but also by the interim constitution of the country, the Government of India Act, 1935 (as modified), which specified the place of the states in the federation.

As independence drew near, almost all of the states acceded to India. The so-called safe states of the League, those enclosed in the Pakistan territory of western India, had Muslim rulers, some of whom had been of aid to the League in their struggle. These were the only states presented with the League's Instruments of Accession. As August 15 came, however, no prince had acceded to Pakistan.

THE INDIAN PRINCELY STATES, 1947
Based on a map published by George Philip and Son, Ltd., London.

During the prepartition search for aid, the rulers had been cooperative. From members of the Kalat and Bahawalpur governments it is gathered that personal contributions were given to Jinnah after an appeal had been directed to them. Although state funds were guarded against political dispensation, the rulers had their personal and landed fortunes. The Wali of Swat told of an appeal prior to the Pakistan referendum on the frontier. "I gave them 100,000 rupees," he said.[12]

The Agha Khan's interest in a separate Indian Muslim homeland was remarkably consistent. His early contributions to Fazl-i-Husain in the Punjab and his active participation in the Muslim League through 1936 reveal a pattern of support which surely did not end with his retirement from public politics. As partition approached, he announced his support for Pakistan and suggested that his followers move from Bombay to Karachi. Taking the place of fleeing Hindu merchants, they were not unimportant.

The Nizam of Hyderabad was by all accounts the most promising donor and also the most disappointing. The Nizam, careful to the point of penury with his great wealth, thought that his resources would be needed if he maintained his independence. On two occasions he deputed subordinates with cash to Pakistan, but the results were rather unhappy. As well, there was a personal conflict between Mr. Jinnah and the Nizam, and the ruler offered more support to the All-India States' Muslim League and the All-Indian Muslim Conference before it than to the League.[13]

In general, the relatively minor financial aid from the princes to the League came late in its struggle. The middle class bore the load until the events of 1946–47 brought increased prospects of success. More important, the princely gifts were part of *quid pro quo* politics. If the mutuality of the obligation was not explicit, it nonetheless put the League in the debt of the contributors. Jinnah's uncompromising support of princely independence, a partial discharge of the debt, would not satisfy the princes who acceded to Pakistan.

The Indian princes were no doubt attracted to the League's tolerance and conservative economic stance but the Congress was able to exert local pressure and to use Lord Mountbatten's royal suasion well. The flexibility and range of choice of the rulers were illusory—the true determinant lay, as it always does in politics, with power and the overwhelming proximate power dictated terms to the rulers. Communalism underwrote political reality, but was no substitute for it.

Mountbatten's miracle was that after he had precipitously advanced the fact of British withdrawal by almost a year, he was able to move most negotiations at a pace which would allow his timetable to be met. The negotiations which he could not prod were those of the states, unsettled on the very eve of independence.

The only trouble that could have been raised was by non-accession to either side and this was unfortunately the very course followed by the Maharaja. *Lord Mountbatten, June 29, 1948*

I V

The War for the States

As the long special emigree trains began to transfer whole populations through the latticed fields of the Punjab, their cars were sometimes halted by murderous gangs who turned them into human slaughter houses. Peasants numbly walking to their new homeland were hacked to pieces. Shops and temples were ravaged and minorities through the subcontinent found their very existence threatened. In the midst of the cruel summer, madness was a too-common affliction and whole families were killed.

It was the same, perhaps a little less savage, in Calcutta and throughout northern India. Centuries of an uneasy tradition of coexistence were uprooted in death, destruction, and torture. Police and army discipline shattered on communal issues, and as the British boarded their ships for home, one venerable Muslim officer said, "The British are a just people; they have left India in exactly the same state of chaos as they found it." [1]

The creation of Pakistan implied not only the drawing of administrative lines but also the largest population transfer in modern history. The plan was to keep the army under one command to see that order was maintained, but that arrangement proved impossible. The Muslims of the Ganges valley, descendants of the Mughuls and Kings of Oudh, moved west to the desert nearer the Holy Cities from where their religion had sprung. The East Bengali and Bihar Muslims clung to a delta over 1,000 miles from their countrymen in the west, more Indian than Turk or Semite. In both areas there was practically nothing—an arid marchland and a swampy delta, the promised land of eighty million people.

The Muslim League leadership which had directed the Pakistan movement became the governors of the new state even though they were alien to its territories. Speaking Urdu and English rather than Bengali or the vernaculars of the Punjab or Sind, they were a refugee government. Karachi, a bleached and sunny port on the Arabian Sea, was chosen the capital. Within a year its 400,000 population had been more than doubled and the metropolis was blighted by incredibly sordid refugee hovels. There was no place to live. Even lightpoles along the Arabian Sea were concrete, so scarce were the materials of building and before the Cooperative Housing Society area began to blossom with its daring and fluid residences, new citizens of Pakistan lived and died in the streets.

British military policy had been to distribute, rather than concentrate troops from the same area or of the same religious faith. The mixed battalions were in keeping with the all-India role envisioned for the army, but when a common political authority ended, the result was a lack of effective police action. Less than half of the future Pakistan army was in a position to come to the aid of its government. Those troops posted in Delhi and the Punjab spent sleepless nights and long hours escorting refugees, caring for camps, and maintaining order. Groups of *muhajireen* (refugees), sometimes numbering thirty thousand men, women, and children, walked from East Punjab to Pakistan.[2] Their lines stretching over ten miles, were easy prey for the jackals of the bush, unless protected. Somehow, six and a half million people arrived and subsisted in their new country. But the scars were deep.

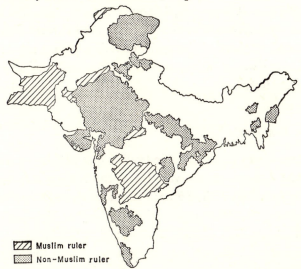

Muslim ruler

Non-Muslim ruler

MAJOR PRINCELY STATES IN INDIA WITH MUSLIM MAJORITIES OR MUSLIM RULERS, 1947

Based on a map published by George Philip and Son, Ltd., London.

As there were few policemen and fewer soldiers, there were almost no workers to care for the haggard immigrants. From behind the walls of purdah, from the Christian missions, from the Red Crescent society came workers ministering to a wounded people.

Nor was all of the tension and trouble confined to the Indian frontier. Afghanistan took the opportunity to bid for a wide belt of territory along its frontier on the grounds that the British title to it was faulty. The Pathans of the boundary region thought they might take advantage of civil chaos in the plains to engage in looting. All the while, most of the hardware of the British army, yet to be distributed, lay behind the frontier of the increasingly hostile Indian Union.

Mr. Jinnah's new government, shorn of every device for social control, faced these problems with dedicated resolve but little else. It supported its army's effort to keep civil order, warned Afghanistan that the country's borders were firm, and demanded its share of the spoils of independence from India. But Lahore was in flames and the states were undecided or, worse, contested.

The first battle

Junagadh was an implausible trouble spot between India and Pakistan. Isolated on the very tip of the Kathiawar peninsula and pock-marked with the enclaves of several other states, 80 percent of its 670,000 people were Hindu. The ruler, Sir Mahabatkhan Rasulkhanji, and the state bureaucracy were Muslim. By sea, Karachi was about 300 miles to the west, but the prince was intent upon acceding to Pakistan. Having consulted with Sir Muhammad Zafrullah Khan, the leading Muslim League constitutional lawyer, prior to partition, he finally decided to appoint a Muslim League politician, Sir Shah Nawazghulam Mustaza Bhutto, as his prime minister.

Such actions alerted the Indian government, which was concerned because Junagadh was the largest Kathiawar state. To the communications of the Congress Sir Shah Nawaz was conciliatory but noncommittal. As August 14 approached, local pro-Indian rulers called on the prince to suggest that he end the suspense. On August 12 the Indian government telegraphed the ruler that his accession had not been received and requested an immediate indication of his intentions, which were revealed three days later when he acceded to Pakistan.

The ruler noted that the state was contiguous to Pakistan via the sea, but gave a more convincing statement of aims when, in his communiqué, he noted that the state had opted for Pakistan "to safeguard its independence and autonomy over the largest possible field." [3] There can be no doubt that the Pakistan government approved of his action, because it was under no obligation to accept a state's accession. Further, the link between the Muslim League and the state cabinet would have precluded so major a miscalculation.

The Hindu population of the principality, chafing under an unenlightened administration, would not stand for such an action. But, more important, the Indian government would not tolerate it, especially with important states still outside the partition settlement. The Pakistan navy hardly had time to land a communications party before it was evacuated in the face of an invasion of the state. The subsequent plebiscite indicated that only ninety-nine persons in the voting population desired accession to Pakistan. The ruler, his advisors, and some traders fled to Karachi.

In the heated legal arguments following the Junagadh battle, one significant question emerged—why did Pakistan accept the accession? The Indian government warned Jinnah of the consequences and asked for immediate negotiations, but the League demurred. Surely no one in the Pakistan armed forces thought that the state could be protected against the Indian army.

The first consideration must have been that the pledge of the British respecting the independence of the states would deter the Indian government from moving. A second factor was probably the view that the Indian government lacked the resolve or the strength to assert its control. Even failing these, the deep involvement of Indian troops and energies in the Kathiawar peninsula was in the interests of Pakistan, straining both on the North-West Frontier and throughout the Punjab. Junagadh could be sacrificed in the interests of weakening the enemy, even temporarily. As a test case, had it succeeded, it might have emboldened other like-minded rulers and signaled a break between the princely order and the Indian government.

Moreover, the League was caught in the web of its own arguments. Liaquat Ali Khan had pledged Pakistan to support any prince's decision of accession. The theory of the ruler's "sovereign will" was put to a test in Junagadh. If Pakistan repudiated it by refusing to accept the ruler's instrument, the argument would be invalidated for the future, at which time Hyderabad might want to use it. The League leaders, accustomed to thinking in terms of the ideology of the Pakistan movement and British rule, had not yet considered Pakistan's territorial interests, which had nothing to do with Junagadh. Further, as a test case, it could not have been more poorly chosen because it was impossible to defend and revealed that the Indian government had no intention of allowing any ruler his independence or accession to Pakistan.

The first test of the British policy toward the states had shown itself to be weak. Yet the lesson of Junagadh might have served to illustrate a mistake which could yet be corrected. Pakistan must have recognized Indian strength and resolve and should have been anxious to settle outstanding disputes. But it was too late; affairs in Kashmir would not wait for reflection.

The Kashmir campaign

No single issue in the modern history of the subcontinent has attracted so much attention as the Kashmir dispute or so much difference of opinion as to its cause. It was almost in-

evitable that this should be true because the ruler and ruled
were of different faiths, the terrain was beautiful and majestic,
and the location of the state was of great strategic importance.

The history of the state added another element which made
conflict unavoidable. Kashmir was "sold" to Gulab Singh in
1846 because the British, who had just disposed of the Sikh
kingdom of Ranjit Singh's successors, believed that its defense
would strain British resources. By the creation of a buffer state
under a malleable prince, they would achieve their aim and
gain booty as well. Using troops from Jammu and calling upon
British aid, the ruler brought the paradise under his heel.

The subsequent history of the dynasty and its rule is anything but happy, and the awakening of the people came only
in 1930 with the return to the state of Sheikh Abdullah, a
recent graduate of the Muslim Aligarh University. By 1932
British troops were called into the state to maintain law and
order.

The tyranny of the state government was so extreme that
outside aid was needed if the Kashmiris were to know freedom.
Sheikh Abdullah allied his followers with the Indian National
Congress, the only strong nationalist party, in 1938. His Jammu
and Kashmir National Conference was organized on the platform of the Indian National Congress: independence from the
British, responsible government, secular politics, and socialist
economics.

As the Muslim League grew in strength and appeal, its leaders organized a Muslim Conference in opposition to the
National Conference of Abdullah. It was not a vital organization, however, and attracted only the conservative and orthodox religious vote in the state. Nor could its members hope
to gain as much power as the National Conference was exercising in cooperation with the Congress. Mr. Jinnah turned his

attention to the state in 1942 and by 1944 had lived there several months. He had first sought to win over Sheikh Abdullah and later organized opposition to him, but all political activity was severely limited by the state's wartime laws.

At the end of the war, all popular parties in Kashmir decided to have done with the dynasty and adopted a "Quit Kashmir" movement aimed at the Dogra Court. The Muslim Conference soon decided to withdraw and follow the "direct action" tactics which had proved successful in the Punjab and North-West Frontier Province. Its leaders were arrested and Sheikh Abdullah's party remained paramount. The state entered the last months before partition in a nervous state of *de facto* martial law.

The ruler desired to accede neither to India nor to Pakistan because the Congress and Sheikh Abdullah viewed his rule as anachronistic and the Muslim League would hardly forget his religious persecution of the Muslims. His own salvation lay only in waiting out the storm and attempting to maintain his independence. Lord Mountbatten, who visited the Maharaja once, assured him that the Indian government did not contest his right to accede to Pakistan. Of course, the Congress used every political strategem to induce him not to accede, just as the League moved heaven and earth to force his accession. In the first week of August, Gandhi visited the state, as did rulers of three Indian states known as friends of the prince. Their conversations are not recorded, but they were not pleading Pakistan's case.

On August 15 the prince transmitted identical standstill agreements to India and Pakistan implying that he desired to normalize relations with both countries. Pakistan accepted the instrument but India did not. Meanwhile the communal holocaust began, and it would have taken a callous man indeed to deliver his state to the blood-letting of the plains. The state government complained that supplies, delivered to Kashmir on the roads which led only to Pakistan territory, were not reaching Srinagar. Of course, they were not reaching Lahore either. Nonetheless, the Prime Minister of Pakistan sent a high-ranking mission to discuss the matter with the state government. At the request of the Kashmiri government which either lost interest or appreciated the difficulties in the Punjab, the discussions were not pursued.

Years of repression and the upheavals on all sides took their toll in Kashmir when a Muslim-led rebellion erupted in Poonch. Self-styled the *Azad* (Free) Kashmir movement, it rapidly spread and was savagely countered by state troops. News of the uprising was circulating in Karachi and Delhi and was warmly endorsed along the North-West Frontier of Pakistan. The armed tribesmen of the region, numbering over 3 million, had posed a threat to the settled districts of Pakistan immediately after partition.[4] They were under the control neither of the British nor the Pakistanis. On October 20 about 900 Mahsud tribesmen entered the state and thereafter as many as 5,000 more [5] entered in trucks, in search of loot, women, and a good fight. They found all.

It should be remembered that at the time the governor of the North-West Frontier Province was Sir George Cunningham, and most of the political officers charged with tribal affairs were also British. The entrance of the tribesmen certainly did not make the Poonch forces rest easier because the tribesmen looted every village, friend or foe.

The invasion and the Poonch rebellion forced the hand of the ruler. He fled his capital in company with Mr. V. P. Menon who had the foresight to require the Maharaja to sign an instrument of accession before the Indian army would intervene on his behalf. He hardly had a choice. Having received his accession, the Indian government airlifted troops to Srinagar on October 27, barely in time to frustrate a climactic victory for the *Azad* and tribal forces. The war for Kashmir had begun.[6]

With Indian army units now committed, the Governor-General of Pakistan called upon his British commander-in-chief, General Douglas Gracey, to order Pakistan troops into Kashmir. In a spirit of moderation, the general counseled Mr. Jinnah to await talks with Field Marshal Claude Auchinleck in Lahore. The conversations are not public knowledge, but Pakistan forces were not committed to Kashmir. As the fall wore on, Indian reinforcements changed the complexion of the war and the tribesmen fell back in their usual indiscipline. The *Azad* forces were more steady but were too few to match a well-led and equipped army. The winter slowed both sides.

In May, 1948, the Indian army launched a major offensive threatening the primary defense lines of the rebels. At this stage the Pakistan regular army, this time with General Gracey's blessings, was committed to buttress the *Azad* lines. A minimum commitment of troops was made because the government feared a full-scale war, in which case the Punjab, which was completely vulnerable, was more important than Kashmir. The military stalemate in Kashmir was frozen at midnight, January 1, 1949, under United Nations supervision.

The truce made, the uneasy neighbors waited for a political settlement. The Indians, holding the Vale of Kashmir and the river sources, everything for which Kashmir is known, were clearly in the winner's box but their hold was made tenuous both by their promise of a "reference to the people" of their status and because of the internal political situation in the state.

There is no way in which the Pakistan government can deny

its legal guilt in the invasion of Kashmir. Persons from territory within its boundaries did invade Kashmir; yet, to label a
frontier-region Pathan a citizen of any country seems legalis-
tic. Surely the Governor of the province and his agents in the
tribal districts feared the invasion, but with so little to restrain
the tribes there was nothing they could do. On the other hand,
the Pathans doubtless had local support and army vehicles and,
at some stage, the help of Pakistan's General Akbar Khan.

The politics of Pakistan in 1947 and 1948 can best be described as confused, and the contradictory aspects of the
Kashmir war illustrate the point. Had the government wanted
an invasion of Kashmir, its regulars could have stiffened the
Azad lines at any time. Clearly the British military advice to
the Muslim League government amounted to a *diktat* to stay
out. Thus military involvement was the last thing the Pakistan
government sanctioned, yet it brought involvement and defeat, and the second battle in the war for the states ended in
an Indian victory.

The end of the Mughul past

Hyderabad state, with a girth of 82,000 square miles and a
population of over 18 million, was the last state outside the
political settlement. Once the Mughul's Deccan province, it
was independent in fact by 1724, although it continued to honor
the Mughul ruler in Delhi as its suzerain. The British found
the Nizam an invaluable ally in the wars against the French
and later against Tipu Sultan. He was, without doubt, the chief
Indian ruler. By 1902, however, the ruler was induced to dis-
band his large army in favor of British protection in the garrison at Secunderabad, six miles from the capital.

With each power taken from the Nizam his titles were increased, so that by the end of World War I he was known as His Exalted Highness, the Nizam of Hyderabad, Faithful Ally of the British Government. The state continued to maintain its own coinage, postal system, and transportation network, and the ruler's revenue made him one of the richest men on earth.

As soon as the British revealed their intention of leaving the country and canceling their treaties, the Nizam questioned whether the "faithful ally of the British government" would also be abandoned. "Yes," was the prompt answer. The ruler therefore decided to reassert the state's independence, even though the nibbling imperialism of British India had land-locked the kingdom.

More than three-fourths of the people of the state were Hindus, but Hyderabad had a unique flavor—not a local patriotism, perhaps, but a local character arising from the efforts of the government to blend north Indian language and outlook with a south Indian environment. This was an imperial task initially, but under the Nizam had become a labor of love. Urdu shared honors with Telugu, and Hyderabadis were pleased to be able to live in two worlds. Nonetheless, few subjects in the state desired continued rule by the state elite.

There was little likelihood that the Indian government would permit a vast foreign enclave in its heart, much less one governed by an autocrat who would doubtless befriend Pakistan. As India put pressure on Hyderabad to accede, a radical Muslim minority became intransigent and began to dominate local politics. The Ittehad-ul-Muslimeen, devoted to an independent Hyderabad in which the Muslims would be supreme, organized a para-military force known as the Razakhars, led by Kasim Razvi, an able demagogue. It increasingly dictated the policy of the state government.

The Indian government did not relent in its effective pres-

sure against the state, but took its crises in order, first Junagadh, then Kashmir, and finally Hyderabad. The Pakistan government was helpless to aid in the rumored build-up of state
forces, and the Indian blockade denied arms from other sources.
The only real support Mr. Jinnah's army could give the Nizam
was to launch a full-scale war which might have been fought
at the cost of Pakistan itself. Pakistan refused, as well, to send
diplomatic aid. Sir Muhammad Zafrullah Khan was asked to
join the state service but Mr. Jinnah kept him in Karachi.
Leaders were seeing their national interest in a more sober
light than in the heady days immediately after partition.

The Indian campaign against Hyderabad reached a crescendo
with charges that the Communists were rapidly gaining
strength and that the Razakhars were violating women and
conducting a reign of terror. The army was mobilized, and
Indian notes to the Nizam were sharp and impatient. As the
end drew near, the state government transferred some securities to Pakistan, but the Nizam never thought of packing his
wealth and fleeing to the new dominion, where he could have
become a great merchant prince. On September 11 Mohammad
Ali Jinnah died in Karachi, and two days later the Indian army
invaded Hyderabad. The troops streaming into the last Mughul
province were, in a way, part of the wake of the father of
Pakistan.

And the last battle in the war for the states came to an anti-
climactic end with the Nizam of Hyderabad bowing low before
Sardar Patel, begging for a pittance of his great wealth. Not
even the state's name would be left in ten years.

The end of the war

The winter of 1948 found the political map of the subcontinent relatively stable for the first time since the British an-

nounced their impending departure. Some of the areas were marked with dotted lines signifying contested areas, but for every dot there was an Indian division holding the disputed territory with real power. The war for the states had not only ended in Indian military victory but had given its leaders enormous self-confidence and satisfaction over a job well done.

The effect of the defeat in Pakistan was no less important but was completely negative. Kashmir, the overwhelmingly Muslim state, the letter "K" in the country's name, was firmly held by the enemy. More than any other single factor, Kashmir would dominate Pakistan's diplomatic, military, and political posture for at least the next decade and a half. Furthermore, the frustration felt by every Muslim in Murree who looked over Kashmir Point to a country which should have been theirs fed rumors of a betrayal by national leaders.

The impoverished refugees, beginning anew, yet brooding over the vivid memories of a flaming home, of a lost relative, of a destroyed life, somehow could see in Hyderabad the end of their dreams, a bittersweet memory of what they had once been.

Where lay the fault? all Pakistan might ask. The answer, too easy in restrospect, is that it lay in seeking both Kashmir and Hyderabad. It lay in a misunderstanding of how the British were certain to act once India became independent, and perhaps most of all it lay in underestimating the Indians. The assumption had been that the division of the subcontinent would weaken India more than Pakistan, an illusion as dangerous as an underestimation of the resolve and courage displayed by the army and government of India. Engrossed in their dreams of an ideal new Muslim state, the leaders of Pakistan forgot that politics are made of deeds, not words, and that power is the final arbiter. Discussions were once held, at a low level, to arrange a Kashmir-for-Hyderabad trade before the war. That this trade was not concluded must be a painful thing to remember in Pakistan.

While both Indian parties may be criticized for legalism, duplicity, and all the dark arts of intrigue, the guilt for the war of the princely states clearly lies with the paramount power whose policy allowed the states false illusions of choice. The power that had beggared every ruling house in India found it necessary, upon leaving, to confess that it was powerless to deliver its creatures to the charge of their Indian brethren. The states were bound to fall because they had been supported by British props. Who would have wept if the Radcliff Boundary Commission had drawn its lines without regard for the various colors on the map?

But the cost of the state problem was not yet fully paid, for both India and Pakistan had to translate their tentative paramountcy into political uniformity, and this would require years of effort and lakhs of rupees. Pakistan, its foreign involvement ended and its cities in ashes, stood teetering on the brink of oblivion, its own princes adding their burden, and the shouts of "we will be back soon" of the Sikhs still loud in its ears; but Pakistan stood.

The Muslim League recognizes the right of each state to choose its destiny. It has no intention of coercing any State into adopting a particular course of action. *Mohammad Ali Jinnah*, Pakistan Times, *July 31, 1947*

V

The Double-Edged Sword

While the novice government at Karachi found itself drawn into external problems rapidly, it soon was faced with domestic issues of more seriousness. Once the refugees arrived, they had to be cared for. Banks and shops had to reopen, the government had to meet its payroll, letters had to find their addressees. But the social order had completely broken down and the government was extraordinarily weak. The Prime Minister testified: "On the 15th August 1947 when the flag of independence was unfurled, our offices had neither chairs, nor pens, nor inkstands, nor paper, nor pencils." [1]

Pakistan, the new nation, also inherited the old problems of its provinces, the divided Punjab, the dangerous frontier, unknown Baluchistan, and the far-off citizens of Bengal. In almost every province there were serious political and social divisions which were now complicated by partition. The heated politics of desperation inhibited internecine struggles in the months immediately preceding independence but they lay so deep in provincial life that their return was assured as soon as the pressure of the great labor subsided.

While crises were developing over Junagadh and Kashmir,

STATES IN WEST PAKISTAN, 1947

Based on a map by the Survey of Pakistan.

others were developing at home with the princely states within Pakistan's frontiers. No ruler had acceded to Pakistan by independence day, and negotiations revealed that some of the princes had taken the League's pledges of independence and tolerance literally. The first home state to show that Muslim League policy was a double-edged sword was Bahawalpur.

Bahawalpur

Lying along the Sutlej River, with its irrigated face toward the Punjab and its arid back to the great Indian desert, was Bahawalpur.[2] The state was saved from an invasion by Ranjit Singh's armies in the early nineteenth century by a British guarantee, and the ruler had shown his loyalty to the King-Emperor many times over. He spent his summers in the United

Kingdom and educated his children in the proper British manner. In the winter season he occupied his palace and displayed his excellent collection of medieval manuscripts and artifacts.

Sadiqgarh Palace, with its massive Austrian chandelier, houses the collection of portraits of the ruler's progenitors dating back to Bahawal Khan, a half-legendary figure who, it is said, chanced upon a lately widowed heiress and founded the state by heroic deed. The chambers of the royal residence served very well for affairs of court but affairs of state were entrusted to the chief minister and the technical personnel of the bureaucracy.

The chief minister of the state was drawn either from the Indian Civil Service or from acceptable Punjabi politicians. The state had received thousands of Punjabi peasants when its expanded irrigation system was brought into use in the 1920s. The boisterous but clannish newcomers posed a threat, it was believed, to the more gentle Bahawalpuris. The division of the population carried political implications because the Punjabis continued to look to Lahore while the state peoples flocked to the ruler's court.

Discretion and political practice forbade the prince to play favorites within his territories, but the breach was not healed. The Punjabi element was able to make its presence felt because it could embarrass the administration and bring the state government into disrepute. Well connected in the province, the Punjabi population could bring the power of the Unionist party to bear on the ruler, who had little choice but to surrender. In any case, surrender was the legacy of most of the Indian princes.

Immediately prior to independence, the control of state governments was a prize eagerly sought by every party. If the Muslim League enticed a ruler to appoint one of its members as chief minister, it could probably lead the state into Pakistan, but the Punjab was not a League province and Bahawalpur was garnered by the Unionist party.

Sir Richard Crofton, I.C.S., the former chief minister of the state, announced his intention of resigning in 1946, and in the ensuing months a list of likely successors was compiled. The final choice of the ruler was Mushtaq Ahmad Gurmani, one of the promising, but junior, Unionist lieutenants. When the Muslim League toppled the government of Khizr Hyat Khan at Lahore, the Unionists in the Punjab states searched for a plan to increase their influence.

In April, 1947, Mr. Gurmani proposed a regional union of Punjab states and toured the neighbors of Bahawalpur. Just as the Muslim League was trying to lure Hindu border states into Pakistan, the Congress was attempting to persuade Muslim rulers to join the Indian Union. The plan for a union of Punjab states would have fitted into the plans of both Mr. Gurmani and the Indian government.

In the early summer of 1947 the Prime Minister of Bahawalpur notified the British Indian government that his government believed that the Sutlej valley should be under one political authority. He feared that if the Indians controlled the headwaters of the river and perhaps even the Sulaimanki Dam, they might reduce the water and Bahawalpur would return to the desert. In fact, this is precisely what happened in the 1950s to require the Indus River diversion project to be begun.

Mr. Gurmani's note made it clear that the state government was acting as an independent agent, and the spirit of independence was conveyed to Sir Muhammad Zafrullah Khan, the League's representative on the Punjab boundary negotiations, in unmistakable terms.

The fact that the terms of reference suggested by Bahawalpur Government are different from those agreed upon by the leaders of the Muslim League and the Congress clearly supports my presumption that we have been regarded as an independent party interested in the partition of the Punjab.[3]

The unwillingness of Mr. Gurmani to take his lead from the Muslim League, even after warnings from Sir Zafrullah that he was playing into the hands of the foe, brought his loyalty to the Pakistan cause into question. Later he refused a post in the reconstituted Punjab government offered to him by Mr. Jinnah and the Khan of Mamdot, and was branded anti-Pakistan. Yet he stayed on in Bahawalpur.

The state's pretensions assumed new importance on independence day when the Amir adopted the title *Jalalat u'l Mulk 'ala Hadrat,* His Majesty the King, a presumptuous styling. Lieutenant Colonel A. S. B. Shah, the secretary of the Ministry for States, later testified to the Pakistan government's reaction.

I had recommended that the Government should not recognize the new title assumed by the ruler. The new title appeared to me to be incongruous because the Nawab had not possessed them before Partition and in the Political Department we were very jealous of the Rulers assuming titles to which they were not justified.[4]

Equally serious was the lack of a standstill agreement between the state and the central government. Two missions visited the state in 1947—the first, under Major Short, from July until September; the second, led by General Iftikhar of the Pakistan army and Mr. Ikramullah, secretary of the Ministry of Foreign Affairs, arrived in connection with very serious communal riots, but the presence of a ranking political officer belied its dual nature.

Ten days after partition the ruler made a statement of his

intentions which was somewhat contradictory. Opening clauses seem to refer to the independence of the state.

The States have once again become fully independent and sovereign territories. . . . These important and far-reaching changes enable us to shape our own destinies and to have a constitutional pattern which will be suited to our needs and conditions and the genius of our people.[5]

The ruler foresaw Bahawalpur's future as an Islamic state, but at the same time alluded to the need for the protection of minority rights, called for religious freedom and justice, and asked for cordial relations with all his neighbors. He added:

In view of the geographical position of my State and its cultural and economic affinities with the Pakistan Dominion, my representatives should participate in the labours and deliberations of the Pakistan Constituent Assembly . . . which will enable the two states to arrive at a satisfactory constitutional arrangement with regard to certain important matters of common concern.[6]

The speech clarified nothing except that Bahawalpur would negotiate with Pakistan as a separate legal entity. The ruler then flew back to England to continue his vacation while his state was in flames and bitter political dispute. The administration was in the hands of Mr. Gurmani, who was yet to play his full role.

No accession was forthcoming by the end of September, and Liaquat Ali Khan told Colonel Shah that there was a "hitch" in Bahawalpur's accession and asked the secretary to try to secure an instrument through the good offices of Mr. Amjad Ali, a friend of Gurmani. In October, after several delays, the reluctant Chief Minister came to Karachi with a signed agreement, which was accepted by the Governor-General on October 5, 1947.

Eleven years later the whole affair was raked up in a libel suit filed by Mr. Gurmani against the editor of the *Times of*

Karachi, who published a letter [7] which was alleged to have been sent to Sardar Patel by Gurmani. It offered the accession of Bahawalpur to India if the ruler of the state would be appointed Rajpramukh of Bahawalpur, Bikaner, and Jaisalmer.

The ruler testified at the trial that Gurmani did not approach him concerning accession to India, that he was in London during the critical months, and that he had been advised to assume the royal title because he had not acceded to either Dominion on August 14, 1947. Some observers expected the Amir to implicate his chief minister because of the personal enmity between them, but there was no way in which the ruler could extricate himself from the same charge since he was obviously free at any time to sign a binding instrument of accession.

The circumstances by which such a letter would get back to Gurmani's political foes eleven years later were so implausible and unsavory that the court was indignant. The letter was ruled a forgery, and the then prime minister, Firoz Khan Noon, was exposed and censured for his involvement. Noon later told Gurmani that he did not think that Gurmani would contest the issue and raise other disputes.[8] Certainly the trial revealed some of the outlines of the delay and maneuvering associated with the accession of the state.

It was pointed out by some that in the period between his alleged treason and the trial Gurmani was the minister for states and could have destroyed all of the official records which might have been incriminating. Others, some in high places, believed that such a letter did exist but that its original was unavailable and the forgery was concocted only to expose the facts. Still another viewpoint was that the whole affair was an inner-Punjab vendetta artificially inflated to national proportions. Perhaps portions of each charge have a degree of truth, for undoubtedly there was a delay in accession and little excuse for it.

The role of the ruler has not been fully explored. It is altogether possible that his was the most decisive voice in Bahawalpur's accession. His minister for revenue and works, Penderel Moon, has written that the spirit of the state administration was one of independence, for:

If we went cap in hand to Pakistan, we should put ourselves at their mercy and enable them to assert the Paramountcy of the old British Indian Government. The Nawab and Gurmani were anxious to avoid this and considered it both possible and desirable that Bahawalpur should maintain a quasi-independent existence.[9]

Whether treason or politics, it was an unfortunate beginning and the first bitter fruit of the League's state policy to be tasted at home. The next challenge to the Pakistan government from a prince came from the remote hinterland of Baluchistan.

Kalat

While treason or intrigue were the judgments of public opinion in the Bahawalpur case, the Khan of Kalat was believed to be seditious. Following announcements that paramountcy would lapse, he sought the return of areas which the British had extracted from him, including the cantonment of Quetta, the Bolan Pass, and some strategic tribal territories. This claim excited both the Congress and the League in mid-July 1946 when it was first mooted. Mr. Nehru said: "There can be no question of the transfer of these lands to Kalat in the existing circumstances, or, as far as I can see, in the future." He explained:

The fact that Kalat is a border State adds to its importance from our point of view as frontiers are always strategic areas. An independent India cannot permit foreign forces and foreign footholds such as Kalat might afford near its own territories.[10]

But the Khan was not turned from his aspirations, especially since Burmah Oil Company was anxious to conclude a prospecting agreement in the Sibi and Bolan regions. Under the Indian Independence Act, these "leased areas" reverted to the princes who rented them to the British government. To forestall this, a special agreement was negotiated in New Delhi in which Kalat was excluded from the category of an Indian state. On August 12, 1947, eight days after the accord, the New York *Times* reported: "Under the agreement, Pakistan recognizes Kalat as an independent sovereign state with a status different from that of the Indian States." The next day the *Times* printed a map of Kalat and Makran as independent states. On the fifteenth, the Khan proclaimed Kalat independent and appointed Douglas Y. Fell, I.C.S., as his foreign minister.

Considerable controversy developed concerning the exact legal status of Kalat. Mr. Trumbull, the correspondent filing the dispatch, had good authority for it [11] and Mr. Gurmani and Mr. Fell support this view, adding that the accord was witnessed by Lord Mountbatten and several high Pakistani officials.[12] Other members of the Pakistan cabinet deny that it was anything more than a standstill agreement, and a letter from the Secretary of the Political Department, Commonwealth Relations Office, to Mr. Fell seems to confirm their argument. The confusion lay in the legally indistinct character of Kalat's sovereignty.

The Khan's view was that even under the British he was allowed unique privileges not unlike those of Nepal's ruler. The 1876 agreement with the British allowed him to send a representative to the Indian court, a right not accorded to the Indian princes.[13] The Khan boycotted the Chamber of Princes for this reason, and this contention might have led him to understand that the government's standstill agreement was a tacit acceptance of the position.

In any case news reports pointed to major difficulties between Kalat and Pakistan. Within the state, the Khan drew succor from the National Party, an organization composed of royalists and Congress members. Two months after partition, the Khan flew to Karachi with his staff and with Qazi Isa, president of the Baluchistan Muslim League. They were met by the military aide of the Governor-General, and the talks that followed were "to discuss ways and means of further cementing the relations between Pakistan and Kalat." [14] The prime issue apparently was the status of the leased areas.

While negotiations were proceeding, various factions in Kalat state were pressing the Khan to maintain the state's independence and to make it a Baluchi kingdom. Pakistan, through Colonel A. S. B. Shah, was seeking unconditional accession with the leased areas out of contention, and various figures in the state administration were caught in a maelstrom of conflicting interests. In December Mr. Fell went to London for both personal and public reasons, and in January Brigadier Purves took command of the military forces of the state. Neither Fell nor Purves thought Kalat was seeking full independence, and opposition to accession to Pakistan was an embarrassment to them.

While affairs in Kalat had every appearance of confusion, the government of Pakistan was indicating increasing concern over Kalat's intransigence. A truly independent Kalat would have implied a united Baluchistan, and Karachi moved to frustrate such a vision. Ever more Baluchi and Brahui tribal leaders indicated, no doubt with a little prompting, their impatience with the Khan's procrastination.

Kalat must accede to Pakistan and we draw attention of the Khan
of Kalat that both on the grounds of geograp'iic contiguity as well
as the wishes of 3,000,000 Baluchis, it should have acceded to the
Pakistan Dominion.[15]

As time passed, Karachi increased the pressure on the Khan.
National officials feared he would indefinitely delay accession
until broad concessions had been wrung from Pakistan. The
government's slow reactions were due to the crisis in the Punjab. As well, the Khan must have been using his friendship
with Jinnah to enhance his position. Within high circles of
the government, Baluchistan was called "the old man's concern." But friendship was worth only a certain amount of time,
and the other Baluch states had begun to play another game.

The Ruler of Kharan at no stage accepted even the titular paramountcy of Kalat, not to speak of its sovereignty. Even the present
Khan of Kalat invaded Kharan in 1939, but the latter at all costs
refused to recognize its lesser status. The State of Kharan has been
independent since time immemorial.[16]

In January 1948, Liaquat Ali Khan met the Kalat Defense
Minister in Peshawar,[17] and negotiations came to a head in
February when Mr. Jinnah traveled to Sibi to address the
Shahi Jirga (Royal Assembly). On February 14 he met with
the Khan, members of the Shahi Jirga, the Khan's *sardars*
(chiefs) and the Executive Committee of the Baluchistan
Muslim League. The Khan noted that he could not accede
without approval by his (appointed) legislature, his *sardars*
asked for guarantees for their prerogatives, and the Shahi Jirga
and the Baluchistan provincial League quarreled about the
right of representing the province after the states' accession.

These conflicting demands moved Mr. Jinnah to assume

personal responsibility for Baluchistan. In a controversial speech he assured all parties of fair and equitable treatment and notified them of their special status as citizens of the Governor-General's Province. The press read into his remarks an implied delay in the grant of full provincial status, one of the famous and oft-repeated "Fourteen Points" of the League. On February 16, he assured his audience that his government had no such intention and that full provincial status was to be forthcoming. Of more significance was his message to the nation (and the Khan) that the ruler of Kalat had summoned his parliament to ascertain their views on accession and that they would reach a decision before the end of the month.[18] This speech apparently was based on assurances given Mr. Jinnah by the Kalat Prime Minister, Mohammad Aslam, who had misread domestic political developments in Kalat.

On February 25 the Kalat National Party successfully sponsored a "no-accession-yet" bill in the Iwan-i-Am (lower house). The party's General Secretary said: "Here is the question of prestige. There are no big points of difference as we are prepared to give all to Pakistan that comes under the subjects of defence, foreign affairs and communications."[19] At the same time, he suggested that no democratic government of Pakistan would seek to impose an unfair settlement on Kalat. What followed was precisely what Kalat feared.[20]

On February 27 the Iwan-i-Khas (upper house) membership was reported unable to reach a final decision on the matter, and instead proposed that the Khan should have three months "in which to consider all aspects of the problem." The imperfect democracy of Kalat seemed to be reflecting the Khan's desire for a delay. Jinnah's patience was finally exhausted. He turned the matter over to Liaquat Ali Khan and one last political offer was made. The Khan equivocated. As a military commander was later to say, he was trying to hunt with the hounds and run with the hare. The Prime Minister ordered the army of Baluchistan to mobilize and immediately recognized the accession of Makran, Kharan, and Las Bela, thereby isolating Kalat from the sea and the Iranian frontier.

The last blow was dealt by the Indian government. At a press conference on March 8, V. P. Menon revealed: "Kalat had approached the Government of India through an agent one or two months ago, but we refused to have anything to do with the State." [21] Upon hearing this broadcast and no doubt seeing the resolve in the government's eye, the Khan of Kalat acceded to Pakistan, asking only that Mr. Jinnah arbitrate the matters in dispute between him and the federal authorities.

What were the matters in dispute? They seem to have been concerned with the leased areas of British Baluchistan as well as the Khan's relationship to the other Baluchi rulers and tribal chiefs. Divided councils within the state and the sharp bargaining of Pakistan inhibited the Khan's accession. Having acceded, he hoped that the government would treat him magnanimously, but Karachi was of a mind to dictate terms.

Throughout the Kalat affair there were sharp differences within the government over the proper posture toward Kalat. Lieutenant Colonel A. S. B. Shah stood for firmness from the first. His political counterparts emphasized the sensitive nature of the state and were prone to recall the Khan's past loyalty. The Khan's advisors in Kalat found it difficult to work with the ruler, especially since he was under pressure from the tribal leaders and Baluchi nationalists to resist control from Karachi. But after accession, Colonel Shah's policies were in the ascendance.

In April, after Kalat's unconditional accession to Pakistan, the Khan's youngest brother, Prince Karim, leader of the Baluchi nationalist movement, recruited a tribal army on the Afghan frontier country. According to Mr. Fell, this was directly contrary to the Khan's wishes, and he issued a firman denying any support whatsoever for this adventure. Nonetheless, the tribal band did move into Jhalawan district.

The details of the ensuing clashes between government forces and Karim's *lashkar* (irregular tribal troops) reveal the various viewpoints of those involved. General Akbar Khan's version [22] inflates the role of his command of forces from Quetta and identifies the forces of Karim as part of a conspiracy of the Khan and his British advisors. In fact, it would appear that these advisors asked for military assistance to stop Karim and had persuaded him to surrender before the 7th regiment encountered the *lashkar*. On June 16, 1948, Karim and twelve soldiers were arrested, the rest dispersed, and the first but not the last troubles in Kalat were ended. Little mention of this affair was made because of the important disputes outside Pakistan.

Chitral

Chitral, northernmost state in the subcontinent, was brought into the Indian Empire in the name of the Maharaja of Kashmir. The administration later passed into the hands of British political officers who were entrusted with the affairs of the other states of the Malakand Agency, but Chitral continued to have a relationship with Kashmir. When the Maharaja made his abortive play for independence in August, 1947, the legal implications were that Chitral and the other vassal states of the realm would be part of the proposed independent Kashmir. The tribal invasion of the state which sought to force its acces-

STATES ACCEDING TO PAKISTAN

	Date of accession		Area
State [a]	Executed	Accepted	(sq. mi.)
Bahawalpur	Oct. 3, 1947	Oct. 5, 1947	17,471
Khairpur	Oct. 3, 1947	Oct. 5, 1947	6,050
Kalat	Mar. 27, 1948	Mar. 31, 1948	30,799
Makran	Mar. 17, 1948	Mar. 17, 1948	23,196
Las Bela	Mar. 7, 1948	Mar. 17, 1948	7,043
Kharan	Mar. 17, 1948	Mar. 17, 1948	18,508
Chitral	Oct. 6, 1947	Feb. 18, 1948	5,727
Amb	Dec. 31, 1947	Dec. 31, 1947	203
Dir	Nov. 8, 1947	Feb. 8, 1948	2,040
Swat [d]	Nov. 3, 1947	Nov. 11, 1947	2,934

The religion of all states is Islam. Khairpur has a substantial Shi'a population; the Mir is a Shi'a Muslim.

[a] Junagadh was subsequently absorbed into the Indian Union although Pakistan's official position is that it is legally part of Pakistan. Hunza and Nagar were not considered to be Princely States.

[b] Brahui is the language of 52 percent of the population. Sindhi is spoken by 30 percent; other languages represented are Pushtu and Baluchi.

sion to Pakistan worked to opposite ends but by November 3, the Mehtar of Chitral telegraphed his oath of allegiance to Pakistan and notified the Karachi government that his state had "no relation of any kind with the Maharaja as he joined the Indian Union without any regard for our repeated requests and in defiance of our strong feelings against the step." [23] Four days later the Amirs of Hunza and Nagar declared their support for Pakistan. Pakistan had not earlier accepted Chitral's accession, though it was tendered, because it did not want to alienate the Maharaja. Ensuing events changed their reticence to eagerness.

In the war that followed culminating in *de facto* Indian control over Kashmir, a nascent claim to Chitral existed. Almost nine years passed before Prime Minister Nehru, before the

STATES ACCEDING TO PAKISTAN (*Continued*)

Population (1951)	Language of Majority	Literacy (percent)	Title of ruler
1,823,125	Punjabi	14.2	Amir, Nawab
319,543	Sindhi	5.5	Mir
282,945	Brahui ᵇ	7.3	Khan
138,691	Baluchi	3.6	Nawab
75,769	Sindhi	2.7	Jam
54,573	Baluchi ᵉ	3.3	Nawab
105,724	Kowar	0.6	Mehtar
48,656	Pushtu	2.9	Nawab
148,648	Pushtu	0.9	Khan
518,596	Pushtu	0.2	Wali

ᵉ Brahui is spoken by 20 percent of the population.

ᵈ The Wali of Swat also administers Kalam district which has an area of 8222 sq. mi. and a population of 9,702. In all the frontier states, only certain districts were enumerated and estimates drawn up for the entire state.

Source: *Instruments of Accession and Schedules of States Acceding to Pakistan, 1949. The Census of Pakistan, 1951.*

Lok Sabha on May 26, 1956, stated that his country recognized no change in the status of Chitral.[24] He correctly held that since 1876 the State's suzerain had been Kashmir but added that he was unaware of any normal accession to Pakistan. This ignored the formal instrument of accession executed on October 6, 1947, published on November 3, 1947 and accepted by the Governor-General of Pakistan on February 18, 1948. Whether it was legal is a separate question.

Swat and Dir

One of the problems which vexed the central government soon after partition was Afghan hostility. The common frontier of the two nations has a history of dispute and war which did not end when the British battalions pulled back from Fort

Jamrud. Part of the frontier touches Dir and Chitral and gives them a strategic position. When Pakistan sought to conclude agreements with the frontier princes, the tension created by Kabul was an impediment to diplomacy. The federal authorities moved very slowly, settled for a reconfirmation of obligations which had been executed with the British government, and did little to further disturb the rulers.[25]

Between Swat, Dir, and Chitral is the district of Kalam which was claimed by all three states. Chitral claimed that the people of Kalam paid tribute to the Mehtar and were related to the Chitrali tribes. The Nawab of Dir pointed out the ethnic and tribal similarities between his people and the Kalamis and the Wali of Swat contended that since the valley of the Swat river is a natural commercial unit, he should have jurisdiction over the region. The British kept the area independent as a buffer between three often-warring states.

The Wali confides that a British officer told him that on the eve of independence when the British left and before the Pakistanis entered, he could seize the region. To that end the ruler bought the claim of the Chitral Prince, but the Nawab of Dir would not sell. The trouble was, the Wali added, that there was never a time when there was a lacuna in central authority.[26] The ruler's troops occupied and claimed the mountainous country but the Pakistan government refused to accept its legality.

Aside from the Kalam controversy, both Swat and Dir did little to present problems to the new nation but the seeds of future conflict lay near the surface of their relationship. The Kalam affair and the whole Pukhtunistan controversy would embroil the diminutive states.

By the end of March, 1948, the states were no longer a dominant factor in interdominion affairs and normal accessions were in the hands of the central government. At best the new relationship was little more than a reestablishment of paramountcy over the principalities. Neither India nor Pakistan was willing to allow the rulers to continue to inhibit change in their states, however, and thus began the long process of reform, liberalization and education.

PART TWO

State Modernization

Should the States have an autocratic or a democratic form of government? I wish to make the States as democratic as Pakistan itself, and I am glad the rulers also agree. But, as the States are not used to elections and representative institutions, we should not proceed hastily. You know to what a pass our own democracy has come. *Liaquat Ali Khan, address to the first session, Pakistan Muslim League, February 20, 1949*

V I

Dilemmas of Reform

A year had passed and Pakistan stood. Civil war had ended, foreign wars were stalemated, Lahore was quietly nursing its near-mortal wounds. Six million refugees huddled around their homesteads while the nation faced an uncertain future.

Upon the death of *Quaid-i-Azam* (great leader) Mohammad Ali Jinnah, the effective leadership of the government passed to Liaquat Ali Khan, who turned his attention inward to the problems of the bereft nation. The tasks lay ahead: creation of an efficient bureaucracy and army, formulation of a foreign policy to set a counterfoil to India, drafting of a meaningful constitution.

Yet the mission of the Pakistan Movement was deeper, broader, and more fundamental than the organization of a government or the restoration of the *status quo ante bellum*— it was to restore the pride, vitality, and strength of the Indian Muslims. The community had paid a grim price for the chance to control its destiny and Pakistan's leaders carried a proportionately heavy responsibility to history.

But how could the reformation be stimulated, especially in the absence of the supreme arbiter, Mr. Jinnah? Liaquat Ali Khan, trained in the law, experienced in the party, adroit at institutional maneuver, but lacking in dramatic appeal, decided that the Muslim League would be the leaven and salt of the Muslim renaissance. With the party as the church of the new prophesy of Pakistan, the universal faith of the citizens and democratic leadership would be linked to evolve a political consensus, a constitution. The power of the state would be held in trust by guardians until the party's work was done.

No nationalist movement or party ever faced greater obstacles. The Pakistan ideology, for example, had not only to point to a goal but to integrate a scattered and diverse community. What common plea could ennoble Sind landlords and peasants from Bengal, appeal to hill tribes from the Afghan frontier and industrial workers in Lahore, please anglicized lawyers from Delhi and simple tonga wallas in Karachi?

Many people were awakened to Pakistan in the name of, and for the sake of Islam without agreement as to its spirit or meaning.[1] The westernized party elite, no less faithful to the religion, nonetheless understood it in a modern context separated from the popular view by the cosmic distance dividing the traditional from the modern world. The nation's leaders found themselves with a mandate of religion but the mission of a modernized society and state. The controversy attendant to this dilemma haunted every cabinet and became the troublesome hallmark of the Islamic Republic.

Complicating the ideological tasks of the party and movement was the administrative heterogeneity of the country. The

British left a legacy of governor's provinces, a chief commissioner's province, tribal areas, excluded areas, and princely states, all with unique administrative patterns. And East Bengal, fully half of the country, lay 1,000 miles across the facetiously labeled "Indian Corridor."

Structural diversity reflected the social and linguistic fragmentation of Pakistan. The babble of many tongues gave way to English in councils of state but parochial loyalties had no such universal replacement. In most of Pakistan the Muslim League rolled over local opposition only in the eleventh hour heat of communal war. When external pressures subsided, the westernized elite from Delhi and the United Provinces found themselves in alien territory and the old animosities came alive.

The pattern of conflict was clear—from behind federal guarantees of provincial autonomy, local bosses mobilized traditional, feudal, religious, and linguistic forces in support of their power struggle with the national leadership. By remaining nominally loyal to the Muslim League, they sought only to pervert it, or failing that, to wreck it from within.[2] In the very agency designated by Liaquat Ali Khan to unify the country did the disruption of Pakistan begin.

The focus of conflicting forces in Pakistani politics was squarely centered in the struggle between a westernized, Urdu-speaking urban elite from the Ganges valley and the conservative interests of the Indus valley. Bengali regionalism would complicate politics later. The only hope of the national leadership lay in democracy, in the enfranchisement of groups which might undercut traditional leadership in favor of a new freedom.

Hope for a Muslim rebirth lay in personal reactions to the crises of partition and communal war which flung open the doors of change, destroyed centuries of tradition, and brought millions into Pakistan in search of a new world. In their pain and deprivation many individuals saw their nation as a glorious vision, a holy cause, and a genuine need—they saw it too as their only hope in days to come. But a clear majority of 80 million Pakistanis had not suffered, few understood the significance of their plight, and many viewed change as a threat to their position.

The League was thus faced with a great challenge to broaden its enrollment, educate its members, and liberalize party life. Equally important, the government of Pakistan had to work in conjunction with the Muslim League to associate the people with their state. This was more easily advocated than accomplished because rule in the subcontinent had been alien for more than a century and xenophobia and envy brought all government officials into disrepute. The officials which Pakistan inherited, and to whose credit the state's survival is clearly due, were trained by foreign masters for imperial purposes. Affability and sympathy with the "natives" was not encouraged. As a wag put it, the Indian Civil Service was neither Indian nor civil nor a service. The haughty bureaucrats were similar in outlook to fine soldiers who had been carefully isolated from the virus of politics. These groups, so essential to the health and liberalization of the state, lost respect for the national political leadership in the first years after independence. Association of the people with the administration, the cliché of every prime minister, was postponed.

Added to the burdens and problems faced by the regime was the national enervation in the awful bloodletting of partition. In its wake a moroseness grew, nourished by sorrow for the losses, regret for the violence, bitterness over Kashmir and Hyderabad, envy for the richer neighbor, and fatigue, terrible fatigue. Given the pervasive social anemia, responsibility had to be taken by the few who faced reality. Within months after Mr. Jinnah's death, all the early optimism of the cabinet had disappeared. Political energies were wholly consumed in governmental matters, and the great needs for education, party reform, and liberalization went unanswered. They would later take their revenge.

Illustrative of the dilemma of the government was the problem of the princely states, seriously in need of reform and incapable of supporting it. And to aggravate the embarrassment of the cabinet, state groups began demanding democracy at any cost. Time after time the liberals in the federal government were asked to choose between order and progress.

Radical Reformers

The *Pakistan Times* fired the first shot in the battle for state reform with the banner headline, "Despotic Rule Continues in Bahawalpur." [3] The lead article fixed the blame for continued state autocracy on the Muslim League which had kept aloof from state problems in undivided India, thereby "encouraging" princely intransigence. The 1939 reform movement, for example, was stifled by wartime regulations which continued even after partition. Reform leaders in Bahawalpur were quoted as demanding civil liberties, responsible government, freedom of the press, the release of all political prisoners, relaxation of firearms regulations, and the abolition of a particularly onerous court. The reporter left little doubt that Karachi by its inaction condoned the repression in Baghdad-ul-Jadid.

The cabinet paid scant attention to the report, considering it as part of the drumfire of harsh criticism from the paper, but it recognized that the forces of change at work in the states made government involvement inevitable. This involvement was hastened when the All-India States Muslim League announced that it would consolidate state reform groups under its aegis.

The States League was organized in undivided India to meet the need for a Muslim organization in the princely states. It supported Muslim minority rights, Muslim princes, and, in the case of Kashmir, the Muslim majority against the maharaja. Its leadership had little experience extracting reforms from Muslim princes because of the united front policy of prepartition days. As well, the Nizam of Hyderabad offered not inconsiderable support for its war chest in the interests of strengthening his regime.

Following Pakistan's independence, the Working Committee of the party decided to follow the precedent of the Muslim League and divide the party on dominion lines. On February 6, 1948, the Indian membership was cast loose despite their pleas for support. Party leadership then announced that it had received petitions from several Pakistan state groups and was appointing a "good-will mission . . . to study the condition of the common man." [4] The fact-finding body also was charged with the recruitment of a membership in the states on the basis of a new program.

The platform adopted by the party was initially quite liberal, a fact which did not go altogether unnoticed in the state capitals and feudal manors of West Pakistan. To build support in the states by means of an ultraliberal program was clearly utopian, or, at the very least, a long-range project. Every indication, however, was that the impatient leaders of the party had no intention of supporting prolonged agitation. In fact, they soon recruited membership under the broad banner of opposition to the rule in the states rather than any proposed constructive changes. In Khairpur, for example, the party affiliated, as a branch, the Zamindars' Association. Its small land-holding membership was powerful because it could paralyze the state administration, but it was certainly not an organization of "common men." In contrast to the stated aims of its parent, the Khairpur group sought only the abrogation of the regulations prohibiting associations, a revision of the electoral laws to include the middle class, and representation in the Council of Administration.[5] In the frontier states the party enrolled persons not opposed to autocracy as such, but to the rule of a particular dynasty.

The hastily raised coalition which comprised the local strength of the party branches gave it some membership but proved its program a sham. In the interests of gaining power quickly, party leadership ignored the positive duties of educating the states' masses which would not only have given the organization greater strength, but would have served constructive purposes as a vehicle for state modernization.

The central government was increasingly concerned with the governments of the princes, as were the reformers, but it did not necessarily share the latter's program for change. Under Liaquat Ali Khan's direction, the government contacted the leaders of the state League and on May 26, 1948, a joint meeting was held to discuss the need for a coordinated policy.

The conclusions reached at the meeting were not made public before the first annual convention of the party in Karachi in June, 1948. Over five hundred delegates from the Indian and Pakistani states confirmed the bifurcation of the party on dominion lines and then adopted a constitution for the All Pakistan States Muslim League (APSML). Its preamble called for immediate responsible government in the states and the spirit of the proceedings and resolutions was marked by radical demands. Members of the Constituent Assembly, among

them Mian Iftikharuddin, said that the princes need not even
be recognized, despite the treaties they had signed, because
they were merely a residue of British imperialism.[6] In this spirit
the delegates petitioned Sardar Abdur Rab Nishtar, the federal
government's representative at the convention, to adopt policies
leading to self-rule.

The weeks following the close of the sessions marked the
zenith of the States League's power. The consolidation of the
antimonarchical elements in the states endowed its leaders with
great influence further enhanced by the continuance of the
Muslim League's longstanding decision denying membership to
state subjects. Almost by default, Manzar-i-Alam, the energetic
young president of the APSML, found himself the symbol of
reform in the states.

In response to the pressure generated at the convention and
within the cabinet, the government announced the establishment of a new Ministry of States and Frontier Regions. To
add moment to its creation the press communiqué noted that
"The affairs of the new Ministry will be under the direct control and guidance of Mr. Jinnah." [7]

The Governor-General's personal control of the portfolio,
itself an unprecedented act in Commonwealth history, was
both an acknowledgment to the princes that the man who had
guaranteed their future in Pakistan was personally in charge
and an assurance to reform elements in the states that they
would be accorded fair treatment in Karachi. Only the founder
of the country could have assumed such contradictory roles.
Within two months after his assumption of powers in the
Ministry, however, the supreme arbiter was dead. His contracts
were honored but the spirit of the times was for change.

On September 25, 1948, two weeks after Mr. Jinnah's death,
the Prime Minister, the President of the States League, and

the Amir of Bahawalpur met to consider political changes in the state. Immediately thereafter federal officers were sent to Bahawalpur and Khairpur to implement the first stages of constitutional reform.

Riding the crest of government support and public concern, Manzar-i-Alam demanded the dismissal and trial of M. A. Gurmani who, he charged, "had tried to crush the States' Muslim League and the Muslim League National Guard, terrorized by imprisonment and created impediments to accession." [8] Whether he was speaking for his local supporters or the federal government is not clear, but in response to the demands, the ruler dismissed Gurmani and issued a firman (royal decree) establishing responsible local government. He also announced that the state administration would be reorganized on the pattern of the Punjab. The right of the universal franchise was granted and the prince conveyed his desire to consult with elected officials to "extend popular association with the administration." [9] This was an almost revolutionary position for the ruler who had, according to one of his ministers, "expressed the wish that only refugees from Princely States should . . . be received and settled in Bahawalpur, since these, being accustomed to personal rule, would more readily accommodate themselves to our conditions and develop a loyalty to the ruler." [10]

The changes in Bahawalpur were the first step in political reform and were an exercise in cooperative pressure by the States League and the central government. Yet the viewpoints of the two groups were initially different and were increasingly antagonistic. Unintentionally, the Pakistan Muslim League and the States Muslim League came into conflict over the priority and speed of internal political reform in the states.

Although Liaquat Ali Khan inherited Mr. Jinnah's portfolio

of state affairs, his other duties precluded an energetic concern with their problems and ministry officials, never unimportant, increasingly took charge. When Mr. Ikramullah moved to the Ministry of Foreign Affairs, Lieutenant Colonel A. S. B. Shah, a strong personality who later served his country well in high positions, took charge. His view toward the princes was one of unyielding hostility but he did not envision immediate self-government. His advice was to remove the princes from politics while transferring royal powers to an administrator who then might dispense them to "in-training" politicians.

Many members of the cabinet agreed that the most pressing need in the states was for stability—indeed it was the most immediate need throughout Pakistan. The assignment of competent new residents to the states and policy coordination in the national interest was therefore a primary task. Lieutenant Colonel (later Sir) A. John Dring moved from the Frontier Province to replace Mr. Gurmani in Bahawalpur. Colonel Dring was charged with the delicate mission of leading the ruler of the state to relinquish increasingly broad powers to the central government, a step to be followed later by their progressive dispensation to responsible local parties. In such gradual conservative change was the embodiment of Pakistan's state policy.

Gradualism was an anathema to the States League which would languish if it could not deliver power into local hands. Its leaders repeatedly expressed dissatisfaction with the limited scope of the Bahawalpur changes, with the "bureaucratic mentality of the States' Ministry of the Pakistan Government," [11] and with the fact that only Bahawalpur was involved in reform efforts. Such opinions were certain to alienate the central government and the APSML was in no position to incur the wrath of the cabinet.

The States League was weak after the division of the party and the withdrawal of support from Hyderabad state. There were few capable organizers, limited resources, and a negligible membership. Inasmuch as sensitive political opinion in the states was only beginning to develop and the rulers maintained a check on radical political action, the party could hope to succeed only with government patronage. But, reflecting either the pressure of local leaders or his own impatience, Manzar-i-Alam soon became the focus of conflict between the federal government and state reformers.

The dilemma of the cabinet was clear. It believed in reform [12] but thought it necessary to wait until the government was on more secure footing and until local politicians were trained for their responsibilities. Liaquat Ali Khan attempted to set a schedule for change which would make the states self-governing federal units of Pakistan at the time of passage of the constitution. The States League could not wait and Manzar-i-Alam decided to seek the affiliation, en bloc, of the States League in the Muslim League. In his statement he noted that the action was necessary, because

the peoples of the states are still groaning under the yoke of bureaucratic rule . . . Once we are represented in the Pakistan League as a unit and through it, in the Pakistan government, we are likely to have a stronger voice in matters affecting the states' people.[13]

He noted that the Praja Mandals in India had been accorded similar privileges and, in his indiscreet style of politics, charged repression to the princes and national bureaucracy while implying that the cabinet was irresolute.

Chaudhury Khaliquzzaman, president of the Pakistan League, scornfully noted that group affiliation had never been allowed and that it would require a major amendment to the party constitution. However, the Working Committee of the Muslim League was scheduled to consider the request in March. On April 4, 1949, the committee, which had earlier sanctioned individual memberships for state people, blandly revealed that supervisory committees were being established with authority to create "organizing committees for the States which have acceded to Pakistan and for the tribal areas of the North-West Frontier Province." [14] Thereafter the end of the States League was only a matter of time, and, as it turned out, of negotiation.

But the States League leaders could not endure a silent death and on the day of the League announcement, Manzar-i-Alam vented his spleen.

It is surprising that responsible statesmen have given expression to reactionary views regarding constitutional reforms in the Pakistan States. They propose to delay the establishment of fully responsible government in the States till the Constituent Assembly frames a constitution for the whole Dominion.[15]

He reminded the nation of the stand of the party against zamindari (a system of land-holding by landlords) and jagiradari (a system of land-holding based on land grants), a position which could have held little fascination for the strong conservative wing of the West Pakistan League, the "Nawabs, Noons, and Knights." [16]

The Working Committee of the APSML said that they would contest the decision of the Pakistan League and drafted a manifesto charging that the issue of the backwardness of the states was a "trumped-up charge" to serve vested interests, that the Amir of Bahawalpur had introduced reactionary changes in the administration, that the Ministry of States and Frontier Regions needed complete reorganization, and that a committee would be appointed to draft a "Charter of Rights for the Tillers of the Soil and the Oppressed Women of the States." It warned the Pakistan League that its own strength was failing and that the exclusion of the States League would further enfeeble it.

The caustic Muslim League reply to the many charges of the States League was carried as a *Dawn* editorial on April 6. It ridiculed the notion that any party, especially the "come-lately" state group, had a right to group affiliation. It suggested, quite properly, that Manzar-i-Alam and his lieutenants sought only to preserve their own position and cared little for the welfare of the state people. The President of the Pakistan League made it clear that it would not simply ignore the rival group. "Shorn of its appendages, the resolution amounts to starting a parallel organization to the Pakistan Muslim League in the States which have acceded to Pakistan." [17] The reverse may have been more true but by June the Bahawalpur and Khairpur branches of the States League would become branches of the larger party.

Two days after the arrival in Bahawalpur of the national party's top leadership, a spokesman announced the establishment of a Muslim League branch in the state. The Pakistan Muslim League agreed to no longer discriminate between members from the states and those from the provinces. The Bahawalpur States League was to be reorganized by a plenary conference in which the outstanding state figures would be represented and all former members of the States League were to resign and cooperate with the reorganization committee led by the Khan of Mamdot. Newly elected members of the state Majlis and local bodies were to sign the Pakistan Muslim League pledge.[18]

Six days later, the Khairpur League sanctioned a similar agreement after "heated discussion." State politicians feared that they might be denied a separate League branch and find themselves part of the surly politics of Sind. Their spokesman told newsmen that the membership of the Khairpur party had voted to join the Pakistan League on the assurance that the state would have an independent provincial League branch.[19]

With its only significant divisions detached, Manzar-i-Alam's States League ceased to be a factor in Pakistani history and the initial adventure in radical, albeit insincere, reform was closed. Dissent was once more confined within the Muslim League caucus and once-vocal state politicians found their futures dependent upon their loyalty to the central government rather than their agitation in the states. The sole expedient option was support for the doctrine of gradual change.

The painless demise of the All Pakistan States Muslim League and its tearless wake revealed its shallow contact with the people it claimed to serve, its inability to articulate and work for the true needs of the state peoples, and its utterly bankrupt tactics. Nonetheless, even a demagogue can be useful if he sets a problem in bold relief and arouses a people to its responsibilities. The States League scored some impressive victories—a ministry for the states, preliminary reforms in Bahawalpur, the liberalization of certain civil rights in most of the principalities, and the first serious legislative debates on the future of the princes. The gift of the party's last breath was the integration of the state peoples into the Pakistan Muslim League, a privilege they had been denied for the first two years of independence. All these victories were won from central or state authorities, however, and they might have been forthcoming regardless of APSML pressure. Within the states the party had done little to further political awareness or modernization.

Unfortunately, States League members in the states held an ultraparochial outlook. Rather than seeking ties to national interest groups or organizing state masses in support of their candidacy, they sought only to replace the prince with an aristocracy. Surrounded by giant provinces, local elites saw in political autonomy their easiest route to power. Rather than risk election, they desired guaranteed seats in the legislative assemblies on the basis of their traditional position of supremacy in the states, guarded as they were by feudal and economic advantage.

The tasks of educating and assimilating state peoples into national life was thus made more difficult because the central government had no intermediate level with which to link the common people and the Pakistan dream, no vehicle to undercut the territorial strength of the traditionalist opposition to a modern Pakistan. The reorganization of the Pakistan States Muslim League branches had little practical effect in the modernization of the states, and only complicated government negotiations with the princes. It also eliminated the hope for a functioning opposition to the state oligarchs by imposing the one-party system in which the traditionists gained control.

The evolution of federal policy

Whereas the States League had championed, for its own survival, the immediate enfranchisement of state politicians, the cabinet faced the state problem in its broader context. In a torn country which had yet to bind up its wounds, the compelling need was for recuperation, not more surgery, for the reinforcement of civil authority rather than its derogation. The liberty to own firearms, one of the reformers' demands, was set in the context of the prevailing crisis and could mean only a more grave deterioration in civil order. In short, the Dominion was husbanding every small contribution to its strength, and the ability of the government of Bahawalpur to finance part of the defense force of Pakistan was far more important than the Amir's arbitrary powers.

Another problem faced by the cabinet was the promise of the past to respect the letter and spirit of the instruments of accession of the rulers. The federal government legally could control only foreign affairs, communications, and defense. Informal pressures could be, and were brought on the sovereigns to modify their administrations, but state political life was beyond their ken. The philosophy of the princes, not unlike Calhoun's notion of the concurrent majority, empowered the rulers to stalemate government policy in the states unless their agreement was won, forced, or bought.

Underscoring the legalism of the government position was the simple fact that Pakistan stood in the shadow of Kashmir. With the world looking over its shoulder, Karachi was very correct with its own "lesser allies" and there were fresh memories of the embarrassments of Bahawalpur and Kalat. In the Constituent Assembly the Prime Minister defended his policy of gradual change not only by reference to internal conditions and legal arrangements, but by allusions to India's marching troops enforcing their will on defenseless rulers. One had to practice at home what was being preached abroad.

Perhaps the most compelling reason for the stance of the cabinet was the almost hopeless underdevelopment of the states. As Mr. Gandhi said of Saurashtra state in India, "How are we to manage these States. Where are the political leaders to run them and the manpower?" [20] The state elites were ambitious but as time would show, had not the slightest training or ability in the public arts—indeed, they lacked even *noblesse oblige.*

In addition to the general characteristics of all the states which inhibited the modernization of their societies were local differences in development, size, literacy, and leadership. Even though the reformers frequently granted that developments in Dir need not proceed at the same pace as those in Bahawalpur, change in one area implied change in another; provincial status for one put the government under stress to grant provincial status to all. The princes, informed of their brethren's rights and responsibilities, demanded the same or more in return for their continued cooperation.

Liaquat Ali Khan stated his personal convictions in the Constituent Assembly on March 5, 1949. Aware that state and national reformers were unwilling to accept continued inaction in Karachi, he carefully noted that there were three closely related, but quite separate issues involved in state policy. Constitutional change redefined the nature of the legal relationship between the federation and the principalities. Without constitutional change, progress in other matters was impossible. He added:

The Rulers are being advised to act constitutionally and to introduce immediately, in consultation with the Government of Pakistan, such constitutional reforms as will enable the States to take their place within the constitutional policy of Pakistan by the time that the constitution has been framed.[21]

The second concern of the federal government in the states was princely representation in the Constituent Assembly. A select committee of which the Prime Minister was chairman would make recommendations allowing the assembly to seat spokesmen of the rulers who could then contribute to the drafting of a constitution acceptable to all.

The third broad field in which the federation was concerned in the states was political and administrative change. Liaquat Ali Khan explained that the most pressing need was for administrative reform and announced that the chief ministers of the states would be appointed in consultation with the central government. State structures were to be revamped on provincial lines but their final nature would be established only after the Constituent Assembly had completed its deliberations.

Political change was more complicated because of differing local conditions which called for diverse techniques, institutions, and paces of change. The government, he continued, had actively stimulated the introduction of some representative institutions in Bahawalpur, Khairpur and, to a lesser extent Kalat but he admitted that no long-term policy had been formulated.

Two months later the New York *Times'* correspondent in India and Pakistan, Robert Trumbull, discussed some of the reasons for Liaquat's policy, stating: "The policy of the Pakistani States' Ministry is to keep some of the autocratic rulers strong instead of weakening them as India has done." Especially along the frontier, he continued, the government walked lightly because "If their iron-handed authority, so hard won, were weakened now, the jealous tribes and sub-tribes would be at each other's throats after years of peace." The unique aspect of the policy of Pakistan was: "The states are being 'assimilated' rather than absorbed into the rest of Pakistan by gradual processes geared to their varying degrees of advancement." [22]

The problems of Pakistan's states would have sorely taxed the liberal spirit of any politician and that it destroyed such convictions in many men is not surprising. Pakistan's existence had to be placed before Pakistan's democracy. The raw new politics of representation had to be integrated into the national political pattern in such a way that they did not destroy the forum. Yet the philosophy of democracy was sound because the states were most deserving of special priorities in development and education. Without representation and a strong voice in national councils, how could the state peoples compete for the limited resources of the new country? And how would their rural mentalities be stretched into citizenship unless politicians seeking support opened new vistas to them?

Thus every day which passed without a constitution, without the liberalization of the states, was a day lost forever in the essential task of the Pakistan leadership, the reform and renaissance of the Pakistani Muslims. Yet in Liaquat Ali Khan's era the dialogue between reform and retrenchment was inconclusive in a body politic frozen on dead center. The real test was being shaped in the states themselves.

The main task before your Highness henceforth will be the bringing of the administration, judicial and constitutional machinery of your state on a par with the rest of Pakistan. *Liaquat Ali Khan, to the Mir of Khairpur, September 16, 1951*

VII

The Politics of Parity

The first five years of Pakistan's independence were years of emergency government, compulsive reactions to recurring crises of war, near-famine, and disorder. The institutions which existed in the Pakistan provinces before independence were not strong and partition pulverized their remains. The new government had to fill every need, and its frantic totalitarianism was the sole barrier between oblivion and existence. In such a period, the latitude of government servants was unlimited, the discretionary powers of officials unchecked, and national coordination of effort impossible. The interim constitution bequeathed by the British was little more than a paper mask behind which a few hundred men did their best. This was particularly true in the princely states of Bahawalpur and Khairpur.

Over the years these riverine states had weathered and worn as had the Punjab and Sind. When irrigation waters brought the mud of the Sutlej into the fields of the states, it was followed by Punjabi and Sindhi peasants starved for land. The river was the link between the provinces and the states and while there were differences in habit and bearing, education and social welfare, the people of the Indus valley were cut of common cloth.

It was an accepted policy in the States' Ministry to treat the two states in one way and the tribal regions in another. But before modernization could be undertaken, the states had to be brought into the federation of Pakistan as equal partners with the provinces. In the politics of parity by which Khairpur and Bahawalpur lost their uniquely independent status lay the future pattern of change on all levels. The forerunner of political experiment was Bahawalpur, the premier state.

Bahawalpur

The Amir of Bahawalpur accepted Pakistan's paramountcy in its minimum context.[1] Article 7 of the Instrument of Accession specifically excepted the ruler from compulsory participation in any revised constitution while the Government of India Act, 1935, guaranteed his sovereignty within the state. Article 6 offered the only legal bridge to change: "The Instrument of Accession shall not be varied by any amendment to the Act or of the Indian Independence Act, 1947, unless such amendment is accepted by me in an instrument supplementary to this instrument."

But the emergencies attendant to partition voided many legal niceties and a supplementary instrument [2] was executed almost immediately under the pressure of severe communal rioting [3] and the border crisis with India. It defined Bahawalpur's role in the Pakistan defense organization, placed all troops except the royal bodyguard under Pakistan army command and levied a charge for national defense on the ruler's treasury. It also modified the initial instrument by inserting broad clauses on defense and external affairs which tightened federal control. The Prince's obligations were stretched but had yet to be expanded.

Food-grain smuggling also compelled the federal government to act beyond its authority in the first months of independence. Bahawalpur's excess production was used to stabilize the price of wheat under British rule and grain was allowed to leave the state only upon government orders and at fixed prices. After independence speculators in the state expected restrictions to be lifted. The government of Pakistan followed past British policies of food control while across the frontier, India witnessed spiraling grain prices. The forty to sixty miles of desert between the wheat fields along the Sutlej and the high prices of wheat in India were no barrier to enterprising smugglers, and the illicit traffic assumed major importance.

Dawn put the blame squarely on Bahawalpur's government.

Bahawalpur continues to be governed autocratically, and the condition of the people there bears testimony to generations of neglect. Whatever the facade, the administration has been semi-primitive. . . . Since the State's accession to Pakistan, its 300 miles of frontier with India has been neglected and the smuggling of food grains across it has continued almost unchecked.[4]

The more rabid *Pakistan Times* attributed the lack of proper police action to the fact that officials of the state government were in charge of the operation.[5] The desire to check smuggling was understandable, but to accuse the government of being primitive, in one breath, and in the next to castigate it for neglect of a new security problem seems unreasonable (unless, of course, state officials *were* profiting).

The charges gave grist to the mill of the States Muslim League which was pressing for political reforms. Popular agitation, considerable press concern, strong advice from the Chief

Minister, and unmistakable federal resolve led to a conference between Liaquat Ali Khan, the President of the State League, and Colonel Dring, during which a supplementary agreement of accession was signed.[6] It marked the first stage of the political settlement.

Article two was of greatest importance—the ruler agreed to accept a new role as a constitutional monarch, the figurehead of state government. Administrative and political responsibility was transferred to the chief minister, who was made responsible to the prince. Clearly this was not the complete neutralization of traditional rule in Bahawalpur but rather an agreement which set in motion the progressive realization of federal control and later representative government.

The enactment of major reforms before March 8, 1949, the silver anniversary of the Amir's rule, was detailed. The terms of the settlement were not specified but their content was made subject to federal review before their promulgation in the spirit that: "These reforms will, in any case, represent a substantial advance on the District Board and Municipal elections already announced." [7]

Of more substantive importance were the stipulations compelling the ruler to discharge and exile from the state a former finance minister, reduce by half the strength of the royal bodyguard, and place the remainder of the guard under the command of the Pakistan army staff. Bahawalpur accepted an obligation of 100,000 rupees as a nonrecurring defense assessment and 100,000 rupees annual contribution toward defense expenditures and the recruiting and paying of a border constabulary controlled by the central government. State tax rates were to be fixed on levels no lower than those of adjoining provinces, to prevent an investment imbalance.

This broad retreat of the prince was not without its cost. The chief minister was still subject to the ruler's will in most cases and the Amir continued to be important in the state administration. He was allowed the personal right to nominate his representative to the Constituent Assembly, a right subsequently to be very important. His allowances were guaranteed at the high level at which he had previously pegged them, even though the agreement forbade an increase.

In fact, the four-way struggle for power in the states had just begun. Federal authorities, intent on centralizing power, extracted rights beyond those of the original instrument of accession and began humbling the prince as they had humbled the provincial leaders; yet the ruler's power within the state was relatively untouched by federal control. The Amir's alienation of his birthright was effected slowly, and at federal expense, in favor of an appointed civil servant responsible to the ruler but responsive to the federal government. Popular politicians had not even tasted crumbs of the change at the top.

The link between the competing politicians of Bahawalpur and Karachi was the Chief Minister. For three years he would serve as the pivot point in internal and federal politics as he assumed the ruler's authority only to parcel it out to local leaders or the federal government. The process of political erosion over which he presided can be understood in its broadest dimensions. It was a progressive weakening of the Prince and the Chief Minister in favor of federal and local parties, yet the specific balance of power in any given period reflected personal rather than legal arrangements. It was an open secret in Karachi that ministry officials were often piqued with Colonel Dring, as were the Amir and Bahawalpuri politicians, but it would have been a superhuman task to have satisfied all parties.

On March 8, 1949, the eagerly awaited reform plan was made public. A state assembly, the Bahawalpur Majlis, was created with an original strength of twenty-five members, sixteen of whom would be elected. Seven nominees of the ruler and two state officials would also sit in the House. The cabinet of four would include two nominees of the ruler and would be led by the Chief Minister who would, in addition, hold the portfolios of law and order and finance and would be responsible for the subjects for which the federal government was empowered in the state. The cabinet members nominated by the prince were concerned with the aspects of state life which the ruler controlled while the elected ministers had cognizance over politically harmless fields known as "transferred subjects." [8] In short, it was a return to dyarchy.

The legislative scope of the assembly was confined to the transferred subjects but section 14 of the Government of Bahawalpur Act, 1949 specified: "The Majlis shall have power to make laws with respect to transferred subjects but a law so made shall be subject to certification and disallowal by the Wazir-i-Azam." [9] In short, the legislature was not only restricted in its jurisdiction but was denied ultimate authority within its narrow limits.

In reserved subjects, the executive leadership of the state might certify and promulgate a bill "in the name of safety, tranquility or other interests of state" (article 16). The ruler might withhold his assent from a bill (article 17) and the chief minister could promulgate ordinances for six months if the Majlis was not in session (article 21). Almost all the rules of the House were controlled by the chief minister including rules of debate, quorum, questions, and order. It was clearly a tutorial arrangement.

The spirit of the times and the queer "in between" position of the state people is well illustrated in the sophistry of the oath of allegiance of state Majlis representatives.

I, _____, having been elected (or nominated) a member of the Majlis, do solemnly swear that I will be faithful to the constitution of Pakistan and saving the same, bear true allegiance to His Highness the Amir of Bahawalpur, his heirs and successors and the government established by law, and that I will faithfully discharge the duties upon which I am about to enter.[10]

The power of the prince was by no means ended in such a "reformed" government and there was always the possibility that the ruler might find a party desirous of advancing his interests. The state bureaucrats, for example, were as fearful of the merit system and nation-wide recruitment of the Pakistan Civil Service as they were uncertain of their future under state politicians. They offered a ready vehicle for the prince's ambitions. In the midst of the clash between the States Muslim League and the Pakistan Muslim League, Mr. Khaliquzzaman, the League president, warned, "State authorities to desist from harassment and oppression of the voters because it will create a very undesirable situation." [11] Nor would his be the last voice raised against royal interference in Bahawalpur elections.

On May 29, 1949, the Bahawalpur Majlis was convened. The auspiciousness of the event was enhanced by the complete reconciliation between the States League and the Muslim League. In his opening address to the assembly, Colonel Dring said it was the ardent wish of the ruler to make the state a powerful and valuable part of Pakistan and that this was now possible because of the representation of the people in the state's administration. He also warned the representatives that the state was faced with grave problems such as refugee resettlement, smuggling, industrial underdevelopment, and the need for increased grain production.

Syed Hasan Mahmud, Convener of the Bahawalpur Muslim League and leader of the House, replied that his party was determined to "make the experiment of responsible government a success to prove that they deserved full transfer of power within the shortest possible time." [12]

Less than a year later, an *Extraordinary Gazette* announced further domestic reforms. Control of finance and law and order continued to be held by the chief minister, while the previously reserved subjects were transferred to the Majlis. The executive councilors, symbols of the Amir's authority, were replaced by elected ministers. The Membership of the Majlis was expanded by five representatives and the house was allowed to select its own officers, except the chief minister. The ruler sanctioned direct elections based on a universal adult franchise as soon as electoral roles could be prepared following the 1951 census.

Colonel Dring commended the State Muslim League for its responsible behavior in the House and offered a "second stage" of reforms as its reward. Since the Pakistan Muslim League had organized the state, the federal government was ready to see more power transferred to the assembly because of party, as well as administrative, checks on popular action. And even after three and a half years, only twenty-one of thirty members were elected and law and order and finance remained executive functions. *Dawn* greeted the changes with a jaundiced eye.

We regret to say that at the rate at which governmental responsibility is being transferred to the elected representatives of the people of Bahawalpur, there is little hope that the State will achieve democratic parity with the provinces within any reasonable time.

While appreciating the increased scope of the assembly's power, the editorialist noted that "the purse string and police baton will continue to be firmly held in the hands of the European Chief Minister appointed by, and responsible to, the Ruler.[13]

In October, 1950, Liaquat Ali Khan transferred the portfolio of states and frontier regions to Dr. Mahmud Husain, one of the League's few intellectuals. His instructions were to bring the developed states into the federation. The new minister adopted subtle techniques not always appreciated by the old "state hands" of the civil service. For example, he once met the Amir of Bahawalpur, in Karachi for consultations, at the railway station, an unprecedented action when judged by British or former Pakistani practice.

Such innovations were controversial, particularly because both Colonel Dring and the Amir were harshly criticized by the top officials of the States' ministry. Dr. Husain believed, however, that the rulers most desired that appearances be maintained and as long as real power was transferred to Karachi, appearances did not matter. He and his political colleagues were confident that the policy of gradual change, of the slow erosion of princely power, would triumph because time was on their side.

In the early spring of 1951 change was in the air. Within the state Colonel Dring lamented that while the rest of Pakistan was enjoying a prosperity born of the Korean War, Bahawalpur was being denied its fair share of economic growth and was burdened with a heavy defense payment. It was not eligible for federal grants or subsidies. Perhaps the answer might lie in seeking a closer affiliation with the central government.

In Karachi the Amir of Bahawalpur and his retinue were lionized by the capital's society. There were gala receptions for a man previously condemned as a despot, and the Governor-General and the Prince sat together for a formal portrait. The word was soon out—Bahawalpur was to become a fully federated unit of Pakistan.[14] Dr. Mahmud Husain's announcement stressed the importance of the new arrangement which gave the state provincial status. The Governor-General was empowered to extend existing as well as future acts of the federal

legislature to Bahawalpur and the new constitution would auto-
matically apply to the state.

Bahawalpur was relieved of its 100,000 rupee defense contribution and became eligible for development loans and subsidies. The federal government assumed the collection of certain
taxes to which, if they failed to yield 750,000 rupees annually,
the state treasury was to contribute. The dynasty was exempted
from legal suits in the state courts and the Amir's privy purse
was set at 180,000 rupees per year. The Minister of States
hastened to add that the agreement with Bahawalpur did not
establish a precedent for any state except perhaps Khairpur.

With the federal government in a position to radically change
and modernize the states and with a Bahawalpur Muslim
League ready as the vehicle for increasing democratization, a new
Government of Bahawalpur constitution was promulgated on
March 1, 1952.[15] The 49-member assembly was to hold all the
powers of a provincial assembly. The ruler through his advisor
was entrusted with special responsibilities for the prevention
of grave menaces to peace and tranquility and for safeguarding
the state's financial stability. "Amir's Rule," the state version
of provincial governor's rule, could be assumed if the sovereign,
through his advisor, was satisfied that "government cannot be
carried out." The imposition of Amir's rule was made subject
to the concurrence of the central government as was the power
to "divest the Majlis of certain powers."

The assembly might approve or refuse a financial demand of
a ministry but it was not allowed to vote on estimates of expenditures charged to state revenues. The Amir was empowered
to promulgate ordinances when the Majlis was not in session
although they might be canceled by the assembly. The Majlis
was to meet at least once a year.

The structure of the new government was not materially different than that of the provinces except that the Majlis might be stripped of certain powers. The other unusual aspect of the act concerned the hereditary "governor" whose prerogatives were exercised by a minister, and the rights and privileges guaranteed to the royal household.

Dawn's editorial on March 10, 1952, saluted the new act as "in line with the democratic traditions of the provinces" and said of the other rulers, "they have had enough time. The process of gradual reforms no longer holds good." The paper could have extended its praise to the officials who patiently extracted the last powers of the ruler and to the equally patient liberals in the state who had cooperated in earlier experiments of limited representative government. But as for the democracy of Bahawalpur, only time would tell. The teacher had led the students but now the students would have to lead their people.

Khairpur

The second "progressive" state in Pakistan carried a staggering burden of poverty, illiteracy, and ignorance. Each year after harvest the roads of Sind and Khairpur are filled with landless laborers, the *haris*, seeking a new field and a new master. The system of pirs, Muslim spiritual guides used generally in the mystic Sufi brotherhood, is widespread and their religious level uneven. Although the Indus and Sutlej slide together to nourish Khairpur's fields, the state is bleak and disquietingly isolated.

In the summer of 1947 affairs within the state had added to human misery. The ruler was deranged, the administration repressive, and the tensions of impending partition everywhere felt. The state groups made "common cause in demanding the change of the present administration which is not in keeping

with the modern democratic times." [16] On July 20, 1947, the
ruler was finally declared insane and a Council of Regency was
established to govern during the minority of the Mir's son. The
court circular noted that there had been some hope of the re-
covery of the Prince's health but that since partition was so
near, the council was organized to guide the state.

Khairpur's accession was delayed but there seems to have
been no conspiracy. Apparently the council was awaiting an
opportunity to seriously negotiate with government agents who
were attending to more important needs. [17] Mr. Gurmani, having decided to join Pakistan, stopped in the state and "persuaded them to sign the Instrument of Accession on behalf of
Khairpur State with Pakistan." [18] Mr. Gurmani and the President of the Khairpur Council of Regency presented their instruments to Mr. Jinnah on September 5, 1947.

While Khairpur presented a set of problems similar to those
of Bahawalpur to the federal government, its size and revenue
possibilities were quite different. Whereas the government's
first interest in Bahawalpur was the expansion of federal authority in the state, its concern in Khairpur was less clear.
Perhaps, as several high officials thought, the state should be
merged with Sind in which case federal status would be unnecessary.

The relative unimportance of the state and the absence of
a determined, bargaining prince allowed Khairpur's internal
reforms to come quickly and quietly. On February 1, 1949, a
supplementary instrument of accession clarified the position
and financial responsibility of the state forces and required
that the chief minister of the state would be appointed only
with the consent of the government of Pakistan. His tenure
was guaranteed by Karachi and he was to be the sole channel
of communication with the central government.

Khairpur did not receive large numbers of refugees initially [19] and the growth of liberal political opinion was slow. On February 14, 1948, however, members of the Khairpur State Muslim League charged in the *Sind Observer* that the Ministry of States and Frontier Regions had shown "indifference" to the state peoples and had ignored Khairpur. Liaquat Ali Khan was asked to reply to these charges in the Constituent Assembly. He denied that the state was slighted by calling attention to government-directed membership of Mohammad Khan Talpur on the state Council of Regency. He added that the federal government had "impressed upon the Council of Regency . . . the importance of introducing constitutional reforms in the State as soon as possible," [20] and added that such reforms were expected very shortly.

The key to Khairpur's development was the Chief Minister, a refugee politician and administrator, Mumtaz Hasan Qizilbash. He was, like the dynasts of Khairpur, a Shi'a Muslim even though the majority of the state population was Sunni.[21] Qizilbash encouraged Shi'as to settle in Khairpur, guaranteeing them his patronage in exchange for their loyalty, which in turn protected his tenure. As well, Qizilbash acceded to the leadership of the reorganized Khairpur Muslim League following the dissolution of the States League in June 1949.

Whereas Colonel Dring was an outsider presiding over warring factions in Bahawalpur, Qizilbash combined them. He was the centrally-appointed minister, the prince in the absence of the minor Mir, the leader of the Muslim League, the resident leader of the Shi'a community and the sole possessor of the powers of government—and happily, he was also an able man. The state's refugee settlement program became a model for the country and won for the minister the confidence not only of the federal government, but of a large segment of the population as well.

The Government of Khairpur Act, 1949, provided for a legislative assembly which was in fact the Council of Regency which exercised the power of the prince. The founding of the Muslim League and the entrance into politics of the Chief Minister made it clear that the traditional elite, however, would be at least partially disenfranchised. On April 13, 1949, members of the State Muslim League demanded new elections to the 15-member assembly on the basis of an adult franchise. Before the year was closed, the Act was amended and Khairpur became the first unit in Pakistan to hold elections on the universal adult franchise.[22]

As long as Mumtaz Qizilbash was firmly in control, the federal government was willing to sanction the liberalization of the internal politics of the state even though it was clear that representative government was a misleading term to use in describing the rule of the Chief Minister. Yet the state lagged behind in constitutional evolution.

On September 16, 1951, Mir George Ali Murad Khan Talpur celebrated his eighteenth birthday and was invested with "full powers" as the Mir of Khairpur. The pageantry was witnessed by the Prime Minister who heard the young prince subscribe to the "golden rule" of politics, "government of the people, by the people and for the people." [23]

Liaquat Ali Khan replied that the Mir's task was to bring the state into parity with the provinces, thereby apparently indicating that Khairpur's continued separate identity was contemplated. After witnessing a seventeen-gun salute, the young ruler announced that he would return to England to complete his schooling. Functions of the court required the reinstatement of the Council of Regency but it was clear that the power of government rested with the Chief Minister and the assembly.

As power was transferred to the assembly, several of its members became restive with the Chief Minister's rule, a leadership within the assembly and party which was buttressed by federal support and which inhibited local democracy. In the spring of 1952 nine members of the assembly petitioned the central government for reforms, pleading that they should be able to elect their own officers, including the chief minister, and that every bill passed by a majority should become law.

An example of the frozen politics of the state may be seen in the effort of several liberal members of the assembly to effect token land reform. In March, 1953, Jan Mohammad Sandile moved a resolution condemning jagiradari and *kam rakhi* (concessionary rates of land revenue taxes). The government made it clear that such recommendations were unthinkable.

The concessions in Land Revenue have been allowed by the Rulers of the State from time to time in recognition of meritorious service rendered by the person enjoying the concessions or their leaders [applicable to the Mari Baluch tribe.] Some concessions have been allocated in token of charity, for the maintenance of Dargahs. The members of the ruling family are also enjoying some Inams.[24]

Change, therefore, would have alienated clerics, retainers, charities, the Mari Baluch (a particularly troublesome tribe), and the ruling family. Real power was reserved for the executive and the scope and powers of the assembly were very limited.

The great debate concerning Khairpur was not directed at the social system or lack of responsible government, but at its place in West Pakistan. For many reasons [25] the government's final, but hardly enthusiastic decision was to allow Khairpur to become a federal unit of Pakistan with full provincial powers, and on July 5, 1953, the federating Instrument of Accession was published.

On the same day a press communiqué announced the new Government of Khairpur Act, 1953, which provided for the extension throughout the state of federal law and authority, as provided in the interim constitution. The assembly membership was doubled and the special constituency of the ruler was abolished. The Council of Ministers was to be chosen from the assembly but was to be directed by a chief minister appointed with the "consent and concurrence" of the governor-general of Pakistan. The legal leader of the cabinet was therefore neither chosen from the Legislative Assembly nor responsible to it, although the announcement piously noted that "he is expected to cooperate with the elected ministers." [26] The ruler, through the chief minister, had special responsibilities patterned after those of the Amir of Bahawalpur and equally dependent upon the concurrence of the governor-general of Pakistan.

The *Dawn* editorial "Khairpur Reforms" noted sourly: "With this hotch-potch democracy, the claim that this new constitution has brought Khairpur 'in line with the democratic set up in the other provinces' can have no substance at all." [27] But by July 16, 1953 the Khairpur caretaker cabinet led by Mr. Qizilbash was sworn in, while election lists were readied. Sufficient parity was established to entrust the modernization of the two developed states of Pakistan to local leaders, under the watchful eye of the central government.

To sum up, it may be stated that the main problems . . . are two: ignorance and social and economic inequality. Both of these are fundamentally opposed to the two basic assumptions on which a democratic structure is normally built, enlightenment and equality of opportunity. *Concluding statement of a government-sponsored study of Punjab village life,* 1960

VIII

Case History in the Democratic Experiment

Few who heard the historic Christmas Day announcement of free elections, to a sovereign Majlis, could imagine that democracy in Bahawalpur state would last less than three years. Fewer still appreciated the vast liability of the uneducated and oppressed villagers who would fail to understand their role in democratic politics. Pessimism was out of place in the bright and happy throng that received the Amir's announcement as a historical dividing line between the past and the future, as the beginning of Bahawalpur's entrance into the modern world.

For politicians and common people as well, the coming of full representative government in the state seemed to be the culmination of federal policy. The issue which had constantly dazzled the public was princely autocracy and the erosion of arbitrary rule. State politicians had encouraged this focus without referring to the positive aspects of the development of political parties in the state. The whole country found itself with high expectations for the fledgling democrats of the "ex-princely state."

For several intellectuals and many state politicians, however, representative government did not mean democracy any more than it implied state modernization. Their understanding of rural politics and the leadership of the Bahawalpur Muslim League made them gird for an uncertain future. Their insights into the electoral process in a traditional society bear scrutiny.

Party politics

Party organization of a loose nature preceded the grant of responsible government in Bahawalpur. The key figure in the state Muslim League was Syed Hassan Mahmud whose forebears, given their vast holdings, once requested British recognition as an independent state dynasty but were refused. When Indian independence was announced, the aristocrats in the states knew that their chance might come when British protection for the prince was withdrawn. The first timid conversations among landlords, clan leaders, and village headmen began.

Caution was the better part of valor in political affairs so long as Mr. Gurmani was prime minister, for he was a man respected for his use of power, and the prerogatives of the state government under the Control of Associations Act discouraged open meetings. After accession and the unprecented riots, thousands of refugees moved into the state and forever ended the old order. These *muhajireen* had their own notions about government and, camped as they were, soon formed an association.

From these refugees who had given everything for Pakistan and had no intention of living in an autocratic backwater, the

All-Pakistan States Muslim League drew strength. Literate, active, alien, and miserable, they were an obvious source of strength for protest politics. Yet they were in no position to lead for they were too few, too poor, and too rootless to lead a majority which had previously faced a distasteful invasion of Punjabis.

In addition to the rural interests of Hassan Mahmud and the refugee population, there was a third group in Bahawalpuri politics, the "Establishment," the royal court society of Dera Nawab Sahib and London. The state services held their positions with the motto "Loyalty" rather than efficiency, and they were led by the Heir Apparent who, in the first Bahawalpur reform government, was minister for police and jails. Immediately after partition, however, it was Mr. Gurmani who oversaw the smooth workings of the Prince's government.

As it became clear that the Pakistan government was intent on removing the prince from active state politics, the pace of party organization quickened.[1] A meeting of prominent Bahawalpuri leaders was called to determine their place in the rapidly changing state society. There were men in attendance with no sympathy for change and others who had "eaten the bread and salt" of the ruler and would not violate his trust. There was skepticism about the ability of the group to solve the problems of the refugees, the economic development of the state, and the reform of the administration.

Many members at the head table had no answers for the detailed questions but the articulate Hassan Mahmud had given thought to political life of the state and answered many of the queries. At the age of twenty-six, he spoke of a new era, and yet behind him lay the loyalties of the past and the heritage of the land. He was soon recognized as the leader of a rural party as yet nameless. From that time forward, every weakening of the prince was a strengthening of the rural party.

The first goals of the political revolution were realized in 1949 when the States' Muslim League and the federal government forced the ruler to dismiss Mr. Gurmani and to promulgate reforms. State newspapers, springing up everywhere in the new climate of freedom, demanded further reforms, and politicians became more radical. Some agitators miscalculated the bounds of the new freedom and were arrested. The state government solemnly announced:

[It] does not wish to interfere with the individual liberty of any person or political party, but at the same time it cannot tolerate deliberate agitation calculated to interfere with the maintenance of law and order and to obstruct the State in the fulfillment of its part in the structure of Pakistan.[2]

Thereafter criticism of the government was more moderate, particularly when it concerned the Heir Apparent's role in state affairs.

Hassan Mahmud's party was not involved in radical propaganda against the state government and by biding his time, its leader was able to watch with relish as the States Muslim League was wrecked by the Pakistan Muslim League. Reconstruction of party life in Bahawalpur was entrusted to the Khan of Mamdot, leader of the Punjab League, and he recognized the bright young landlord as convener of the Bahawalpur party. Thereafter, the combined weight of the federal government, the state aristocracy, and the liberals of the nation were against the prince. It was hardly a contest.

The choice of the rural party to succeed the prince was a faithful reflection of economic conditions in the state but it was not necessarily the most democratic arrangement. Rural strength meant that the least developed people of the society would be responsible for political choices, and they were not their own masters. The liberal element in the cities found themselves dominated by the landlords claiming to rule in the name of the peasant majority.

The land owners usually welcomed elections, as these provided them opportunities to gain political power. However, there was some ambivalence in their attitude as they regarded it degrading to request for votes from their tenants and *moeens*.[3]

Having organized the landlords of the state, Mr. Mahmud sought out the "number ones," or village headmen, and gave them electoral positions on his party ticket. There was no party program and no working committee to control one-man rule and the real determinants in state politics were the sources of traditional authority, the very same sources which the Pakistan government hoped to discredit. For the outside world, the alliance of the Bahawalpur League and the central government was for democracy but within the state it meant only a new dynasty and the continued isolation and stagnation of the village.

Initially, the check on the unbridled power of Hassan Mahmud was the Chief Minister, Lieutenant Colonel Dring. In the tutorial period the relationship between the party and the minister was smooth and Mr. Mahmud soon joined the government as minister for education and health. He promised the Chief Minister cooperation if more reforms were soon forthcoming and if he would be consulted on government plans. With few exceptions, the politics of 1950 in Bahawalpur were dull, so little friction was there between the House and the Executive.

By January, 1951, the last vestiges of the power of the prince were removed and the League assumed all portfolios except finance, and law and order. The new dynasty would be enthroned in 1952 with the passage of the new interim constitution of Bahawalpur.

The opposition

The Christmas Day announcement of the Amir which promised to enthrone the State League also stimulated the expression of dissatisfaction with the rural party. *Dawn's* political analysts believed that a major opposition party would contest election in the enlarged Majlis and that it would be led by influential refugees, smaller landlords, and some cultivators.

The state press had also become disillusioned with the League leadership and *Sutlej* and *Insaf* editors, in opposition to the party, charged: "There are just three persons who rule over this State and their position is like the Holy Father, the Holy Son and the Holy Ghost." [4] For directly baiting the Chief Minister and the leader of the Assembly, the papers were promptly banned. The Pakistan Newspaper Editor's Association demanded their reinstatement but the ultimate outcome was not entirely in keeping with freedom of the press.[5]

Sardar Mahmud Khan, a spokesman of the opposition group which had come to be called the "Left Muslim League," noted that under the "crippled system of reforms. . . . The Majlis met only nineteen days within three years. Property belonging to the municipalities was sold to friends of the League leader at 1 rupee per foot in spite of public demand for the same land at 17 rupees." [6] He listed four points of the opposition program; self-government on the basis of provincial autonomy and protection from jagiradari power, healthy economic reform, the settlement of the refugees on a generous and equitable basis, and the reform of the Bahawalpur League so that it was con-

stitutionally sound. There were also charges that the Makhdum
(Hassan Mahmud) and the Leghari families had allied to oust
non-Bahawalpuri settlers and refugees from the state.[7]

The Left Muslim League, later the Jinnah Awami League,
was the old States Muslim League reborn. Economic liberal-
ism, refugee resettlement, and radical political reform were the
permanent platform of part of the state's population. The party
was able to recruit other dissident elements but its strength
lay in the refugee community which felt shut off from power
and influence in the government.

Even though the central government could not have mis-
taken the course of politics in Bahawalpur, it was committed
to the support of Hassan Mahmud and the legal branch of the
party in the state. And there was no question that the State
League could capture most of the seats of the House through
its control of the rural vote. Much as it had scuttled the States
League, the national party undertook to bolster its representative in Baghdad-ul-Jadid. The Prime Minister arrived in late
January 1952 to "compose the differences" between sections
of the state party. He was followed by a two member subcommittee of the Working Committee of the Pakistan League,
which was charged with repairing the deep rift between what
were called the parent body and the left segment. In early
February Abdul Qayyum Khan, the strong man of the North-
West Frontier Province, toured the state in support of the
party and in late February M. A. Gurmani, newly appointed
minister for states, announced he would attend a tripartite
conference on the transference of the Amir's powers to the
people. On February 26 he made a special plea to the refugees
not to consider themselves in danger or alienated from the
state, but rather as trusted members of its society.[8]

By mid-March other parties seemed interested in contesting

the state elections. The Jama'at-i-Islami announced it would seek at least four seats in the assembly. Chances for the opposition seemed fair although observers were convinced that the Bahawalpur Muslim League would win a clear majority.

Election techniques

Just as the parties of the state were charged with representing the people, the elections sought to validate the choice and selection of the voters, but in Bahawalpur there were irregularities. The Left Muslim League, which had announced a full slate, withdrew from the election because twenty-five of thirty-seven nomination papers had been disqualified. The Jama'at-i-Islami suffered nine disqualifications out of eleven petitions. Spokesmen characterized the political life of the state in bitter terms.

The pattern of pre-election events in Bahawalpur creates the impression that the Muslim League have adopted the Frontier Muslim League's tried recipe for ensuring success in the general elections . . . by . . . cajolery and threats.[9]

In addition to the disqualification actions which somehow failed to affect the Muslim League candidates, other techniques reduced the chances of the opposition to be elected. Hassan Mahmud knew that the Left Muslim League could count on support in some cities but would need to split the rural vote to make an effective showing. To do this they would have to go into each village, select the "number two" man, and nominate him as their candidate. Hassan Mahmud wisely foresaw their move and persuaded the potential opposition candidates to accept the rival party's nomination but to withdraw on the eve of the election, leaving the League candidate uncontested.[10]

So successful were the manifold schemes of eliminating the

opposition through the electoral process that three days before the election the Muslim League was in control of the House. But on April 28 the Amir, at the request of the Prime Minister of Pakistan, canceled the elections on the grounds that the nomination papers had been rejected by "inexperienced" election officers.

The Prime Minister was challenged within his party to justify the weakening of a branch League [11] and even though Nazimuddin scheduled new elections for May 18, the Bahawalpur League was not mollified. A deputation from the state, after meeting with the Prime Minister in Karachi, complained that "once more, after three years, we have been made to feel that we belong to a State." [12]

The price of Nazimuddin's principled action was an obligation to tour the state speaking on behalf of the Bahawalpur League but ill health postponed and finally canceled the visit. The minister for refugees and information, Dr. I. H. Qureshi, was sent in his stead and toured Bahawalpur from May 5 to May 9. The choice of the Minister of Refugees was looked upon by many as an attempt to appease the League opposition which drew its prime strength from the émigrée population. Six days before the new election, the Anjuman-i-Muhajireen (Association of Refugees) announced it would cooperate with the Muslim League. The royal court also showed an interest in the campaign but was warned to stay out of active politics.

On May 28 it was announced that the Muslim League had won thirty-five seats and would form the government. The chief opposition party, the Left Muslim League-Jinnah Awami League, held ten seats and the Jama'at-i-Islami and independents claimed two seats each. On May 30, Hassan Mahmud assumed the portfolios of federated subjects, finance, law and order, and public works. On June 4, the Amir announced plans for an extended European vacation and the cabinet took office with full powers.

Somewhat later the Election Petition Tribunal of the state considered several cases which shed some light on state political life. The case of Muhammad Abid Hussain versus Ghulam Haider Khan Sahib grew out of charges that the respondent, a first cousin and brother-in-law of Mohammad Rahim Khan Leghari, commissioner of police, had used his influence with the police to interfere in campaigning and to break up rallies, and had paid ten thousand rupees to Makhdum Ghulam Miran Shah to secure the League nomination so that no other candidate could stand from Sadiqabad.[13]

A more amusing case was brought by Nao Bahar Bukhair Sahib against Shamassuddin Sahib of Uch Sharif in which it was charged that Hassan Mahmud and Colonel Magbool Qureshi had forced liquor down the throat of the plantiff until he was intoxicated, in which condition he withdrew his petition in favor of the respondent.[14]

It was not exactly an auspicious beginning of democratic government in the largest, most developed state in Pakistan.

Assembly politics

The most important test of the new order in Bahawalpur was whether the people were served well by their representatives. The tactics of political parties are frequently unsavory but are said to justify their unique morality if they lead to a functioning and responsible system of government.

The assembly followed the pattern of organization and procedure common to the various assemblies in Pakistan [15] and developed many of the same weaknesses. Cabinet leadership was firm because of the overwhelming strength of the majority party and because the Chief Minister appropriated practically every important portfolio for himself. He was both master and dispenser of patronage and his extra-parliamentary control of the party and vast wealth buttressed his political position. A serious problem arose because the Chief Minister was also a member of the Constituent Assembly of Pakistan and was frequently absent from the state. The assembly records often show another minister summarizing the government's position because the Chief Minister was playing the more compelling game of national politics. The implicit violation of the federal division in the dual role of the leader is clear.

The lack of concern for state needs was also evidenced by the pattern of legislation which always followed the example of the central government or the provinces rather than the unique needs of the Bahawalpuri people. This weakness would have been mercilessly exploited had it not been for the weak opposition and the government's control of the police and the press. The general lack of concern for local matters and a preoccupation with national politics was not a weakness characteristic only of the state, however.

The debates in the Majlis never reached a high level but they were relevant to the states' problems. The landlords and refugees found themselves in disagreement on a broad range of policies over which the assembly had control. The debates on land, tenancy, and refugee rehabititation were very lively.[16] And when the government introduced a Bahawalpur version of the Public and Representative Officers (Disqualification) Act (PRODA), the opposition walked out of the assembly protesting actions "outrageous to democracy."

Many of the private member's bills introduced were con-

cerned with Muslim conduct. Bahawalpur's society viewed itself as a model Islamic community and the ruler's staff wore
the fez and were pious in accordance with religious dictates.
As early as 1951 demands were pressed to enforce the Shari'ah
(the Muslim religious law) but the Crown Prince tabled the
measure. Later bills were introduced to enact laws making
prayers compulsory and requiring charity payments for the
poor.[17] Such proposals were unsuccessful and Islam was either
ignored or used for secular purposes. Urdu, the court language,
was replaced as the language of the state statutes by English.[18]

As was common in Pakistan, the sessions of the legislature
were short. Before the 1952 reform and expansion act, the
Majlis had met an average of six days per year. According to
available Majlis reports, it met for nine days in 1953 and for
eleven days in 1954. In this period the House was asked not
only to consider the budget and legislative program of the
government, but to transact its own business, hear private
member's bills and resolutions, and question the government
on the state administration. In the 1954 session 237 questions
were asked of the ministers in eleven days. There was hardly
time for supplementary comments before adjournment.

In the same session the government proposed twelve bills
of which nine were passed and one sent to committee, while a
budget of over sixty million rupees was hastily approved. The
mass of detail, project priorities, accountability of the cabinet,
and private business was compressed into such a short time
that the bewildered backbenchers hardly had time to read the
proposals, let alone return home and explain them to the
ignorant villagers.

Nonetheless, the opposition had the pleasure of abusing the
government publicly once a year. Resolutions were brought

which called attention to social and political ills in the state and the public had access to the debates. The tragedy was that the governing party represented class interests at the expense of the majority and that the debate too often degenerated into an argument between Bahawalpuris and refugees. It is also fair to say, in retrospect, that the time was too short to judge what might have happened when the opposition found its parliamentary legs or when the voters in the next general election would vote for or against the zamindars and jagirdars of Hassan Mahmud. Perhaps, of course, the conclusions of the Chief Minister would have been borne out. He said: "Friendship, connections, associations—these personal things will return a man to office regardless of his public record." [19]

A Punjab village study, in many ways descriptive of Bahawalpuri society, evaluated the reasons given for the voting preferences of the peasants.[20]

Reason	Percent	Reason	Percent
Knew nothing of the elections	33.3	Voted for *syed* (man of noble birth)	4.3
Voted under decision of *baradari* (caste brethren)	13.0	Voted for a landlord, an educated man, or a neighbor	4.2
Voted for the only Muslim candidate	9.0	Candidate said he stood for the poor	10.0
Had good relations with candidate	9.0	Candidate promised help	4.3
Voted as headman of village voted	4.4	Candidate was a capable man	4.2

Over 95 percent of the village population voted, with the women voting as directed by their husbands, but less than 20 percent of the voters defined their relationship with the candidate in nontraditional terms.

In the absence of data indicating the contrary, it seems clear that the Bahawalpur peasant was even more governed by traditional political factors than his provincial counterpart. The majority party played on traditional sources of power rather than create new ones with a program of modernization and social and economic reform.

The assembly's weakness in educating the public and responding to its demands was a foregone conclusion, given the organization of parties in the state. The Chief Minister was alone able to direct the government's affairs, and he was neither disinterested nor concerned with the illiberal spirit of the state. The lack of democracy went deeper than one party or one man rule, however.

The citizen and the state

The modernization of Bahawalpur might have been possible if the agencies of government had been able to bring to the peasant a sense of participation, of involvement in the administration. The heritage of alien rule weighed heavily on the villager who over the centuries had come to view every official as a tax collector or thief. The spirit of local administration is given in one of the conclusions of the Punjab study group.

The behavior of government servants seemed to indicate that they often considered themselves not as public servants but as rulers of the people. They seemed to have no hesitation in exploiting the villagers and abusing their powers. In many cases the attitude of the officers was expressive of arrogance.[21]

Perhaps more tragic, the state residents were often totally isolated, and their contacts with outside authorities were infrequent. Superstition, ignorance, and minute parochial interests were more of a handicap than resentment of the role of government.

[There was] an utter lack of political consciousness. The people have no clear appreciation of their own problems . . . no conception as to what place they occupy in the national framework. The result is that although the villagers invariably submit to authority, they have no faith in those who wield authority.[22]

Yet three years is hardly a grain of sand in the desert of village history, unchanged by British and Mughuls, and by invaders more ancient.

State development

The justification of the Bahawalpur government for its strong leadership was that the state needed economic growth and social advancement before democracy. The state budget rose from 28.8 million rupees in 1947–48 to 64.1 million rupees in 1955–56, and while in the predemocratic period the state treasury received about 5.5 million rupees surplus, later budgets were balanced.

While some of the funds of the state government were diverted to political ends, the interests of the state people were not wholly ignored. Enrollment in the schools increased from 35,000 in 1947 to 125,000 in 1955 and eighty-five percent of the students enjoyed tuition-free study. One hundred eighty adult literacy centers were financed and the libraries of the state received attention. Education expenditures increased fivefold between 1947 and 1955.

Rural education posed a difficult problem because transportation facilities were inadequate and long walks under the desert sun were not to be lightly undertaken, especially since some parents viewed the education of their children as unnecessary. Faced with a serious shortage of facilities, the state Ministry of Health and Education decided to establish *maktabs*, schools in the village mosques. They aimed at "reviving the traditional and time-honored functions of the Mosques for spreading the light of knowledge and imparting instruction not only in the tenets of religion but also in general knowledge, arts, sciences and literature." [23]

Expenditures on public health measures rivaled those of education in their improvement. The total amount expended in 1947–48, 438,000 rupees, was raised to 3,750,000 rupees in eight years. Bahawal Victoria Hospital was expanded to four hundred beds and eighty other "hospitals and dispensaries" were maintained throughout the state. An annual eye clinic ministered to people able to make the trip to the cities.[24]

Within seven years after partition, the state achieved the reputation of being a good place to establish a business. A textile plant, vegetable oil and soap processing firms, and a wool grading and washing installation stood on what previously had been the barren southern tip of the state. Mechanized cultivation was also introduced in the large estates of southern Bahawalpur but these innovations could not fully meet the needs of almost 400,000 refugees while raising the living standards of the rural people.

The hard facts of poverty kept asserting themselves and Bahawalpur's food surplus became unsure as India diverted some of the waters of the Sutlej into her own parched fields. The population increase accelerated, while improvement in the literacy percentage was dishearteningly slow. Meanwhile there were persistent rumors of the worst sort of abuse of state resources on the part of the ministers.

Perhaps, given time and experience, the state assembly could have fulfilled its promise and checked the government while educating the peasantry. Over the years perhaps the ruling elite might have settled into its responsibility to govern, in the name of the still silent people, with less abuse of the state's power. In his 1954–55 budget speech, Hassan Mahmud said:

"I am confident that given a stable government and a stable program, this budget figure will go up to eighty million rupees in the next three or four years." [25] But, unfortunately, the state government would be overthrown by the October *putsch* of the Governor-General Ghulam Mohammad and no assembly would exert pressure on the new masters of Bahawalpur, the civil servants in state employ.

Success or failure?

A regime needs time to establish its worth and style, and normally a judgment rendered before a decade of experience would be patently unfair. Yet Bahawalpur's democratic experiment blossomed in the desert and was burned out and uprooted in less than three years. The assembly was dismissed at the end of October, 1954, as inefficient, corrupt, and tyrannous. Few tears were shed when Hassan Mahmud began an extended vacation abroad and the assembly building was locked.

The record is quite clear in revealing the unscrupulous electoral and party tricks of the state Muslim League and its autocratic behavior when in power, but such judgments are relative. Were these tactics unique to Bahawalpur? They were not. Was the Governor-General's shabby action in dismissing the Constituent Assembly after it had drafted a constitution more moral than the heavy-handed government of Hassan Mahmud in Bahawalpur? On the basis of the record, it would be hard to judge whether state political life was more corrupt than that of the nation or provinces.

A second consideration is the level from which state development began. The League ministry might be condemned as inefficient but that judgment would be dependent upon a level of expectation based on provincial standards. Certainly

Bahawalpur progressed in social and economic development much more rapidly than Baluchistan even though Baluchistan was under central control. The case might be argued that Bahawalpur kept pace with Sind in development and could not, in fairness, be compared to the Frontier Province, which received preferential treatment, or the Punjab, which was the best developed region in Pakistan. It is relatively unimportant that state funds found their way into political rather than public coffers, so long as the government made reasonably good use of the state resources.

Perhaps the greatest failure of the short-lived democratic regime in the state was in contacting and modernizing the society. The government was an elitist group interested in its own preservation and it did not care to become a broker of revolutionary ideas. It must be added that some recent village studies of West Pakistan indicate that this failure in Bahawalpur was not an isolated example and that in fact both provincial and national leadership failed to reach the "grass roots." [26]

In summary, it might be fair to say that Bahawalpur's democratic experiment suffered the same fate as those in the rest of West Pakistan, and where it was particularly weak, it reflected the special poverty and underdeveloped characteristics of the state's society.

In historical perspective, however, the experiment was a great success because it was immeasurably better than princely rule, both in the expansion of public services and economic development, and in its potential value in utilizing the people in the cooperative task of modernizing the society. And it was more successful than the government that followed, which enthroned the class for which the Bahawalpuris had neither respect nor affection, the civil service.

Constitutional reforms exactly on the pattern of the Government of India Act, 1935, are not a feasible proposition in smaller States. In their case special ways and means will have to be devised whereby the people are associated with government. *Dr. Mahmud Husain, to the Constituent Assembly, November 17, 1951*

I X

Watch and Ward on the Frontier

The shale-gray hills of the frontier country, reaching from the flanks of the Soviet Union to the arid Baluchistan-Iran border, are the improbable locale of a romantic tradition like in its heroes and epics to that of the American West. Pathan and Baluch tribesmen, armed and with their own laws, dominate popular literature in Pakistan no less than they did in Kipling's ballads. They are the hungry hostiles, the plunderers waiting in the hills lulling their children to sleep with the familiar strain: "Beautiful are the women of India, and sleek are its cattle." The chronicles of rule in India are searched in vain for a ruler who pacified the tribes, for an era when the people of the Indus plain slept secure from the tribal broadsword.

Pakistan inherited the tribes and the difficult frontier of the Indian Empire under trying circumstances. Mr. Gandhi and Abdul Ghaffar Khan, the most popular frontier leader, campaigned against Pakistan in the name of Pathanistan. The Afghan government put a torch under the tribal cauldron just when the infant dominion was struggling to handle the refugee influx. The tribesmen needed little spurring, and a ranking officer of the Pakistan army would later write; "The firm attitude of the army alone kept the North-West Frontier under control." [1]

Mr. Jinnah's government walked lightly in tribal country. By the judicious use of military deployment, the continued loyal service of British tribal experts, the propagation of Islam as a bond between tribes and nation, and generous subsidies, a tenuous peace was maintained. Later, the government would withdraw its regular troops, with fanfare, from deployment in tribal country and send them to the eastern front, while praying that the frontier peoples would not interpret the withdrawal as a retreat. In the princely states of tribal country the government reinforced the rulers' authority, just or oppressive. Somehow the Pathans were held, although perhaps at the cost of Kashmir,[2] and Karachi was able to press the Khan of Kalat into accession without a major war in Baluchistan.

Accession and uneasy alliance between the tribes and their nation was clearly an interim arrangement. The Pakistan government desired that all of its nationals share in public life and join in the Muslim renaissance. To the need for modernization were added more earthy factors: the insecurity of the frontier with its concommitant need for vast expenditures, and fratricidal combat.

But it was easier to advocate democracy and integration for the tribes than to implement modernization on the frontier. The thought of awarding a ballot to a frontier Pathan or Baluch seemed as ludicrous in 1950 as it would have for the American Congress to enfranchise the Apaches in the 1830s. Equally impossible seemed the weakening of the traditional leaders and princes who were the symbols of the tenuous minimum order which too often disintegrated into the chaos of clan war. The problems presented to the Constituent Assembly in integrating tribes into a functioning democracy seemed overwhelming.

Baluchistan and the Baluchistan states

At the core of the dilemma in the southern districts of the frontier was the relationship of the princely states to the Chief Commissioner's Province, which had been established to ring the Afghan frontier with a military preserve. The sparse population of the states and the settled areas together hardly justified a provincial administration and no one thought seriously that each state should have a legislature, governor, and chief court. Political modernization could only follow some sort of union and as early as April 1948, the government was reported to have desired a "uniform policy" toward the four states.[3] But the Khan's hostility and pressing business elsewhere kept Baluchistan in limbo.

The key to change was the federal government, and, to a uniquely high degree, solely the federal government. The province and states were so underdeveloped and so poor that political parties with a mass following had not been organized. Even the press was limited to one or two sporadic weeklies which were notoriously short-lived and which advertised magic amulets to ward off disease and impotency. Quetta, the only city in Baluchistan, had a multi-communal society before 1947 but many Hindus fled, among whom were several active politicians. With the Congress strength gone, the remaining party was the Baluchistan branch of the Muslim League which was led by the brothers Qazi Isa and Qazi Musa.

The only other parties in the region were in Kalat state where, under the rule of the Khan, his retainers were allowed to form the Kalat national party based on tribal allegiance and loyalty to the ruler. In neither province nor states was there an adequate leaven for the traditional political life.

Qazi Isa petitioned the government to allow the provincial League to organize within the states and bring together all Baluchi politicians. The state elites, however, who watched Khairpur and Bahawalpur, fought inclusion in a large party in which their influence would be negligible. On February 12, 1950, the convener of the Kalat Muslim League declared that his party desired direct affiliation with the Pakistan League rather than a merger with the Baluchistan wing.[4]

The party question was intimately connected with the constitutional and administrative future of the states. If they were allowed autonomous party development it could be assumed that they might be allowed independence from the strategic borderland. In late February, 1950, speculation was ended with the announcement by the Working Committee of the Pakistan Muslim League that its Baluchistan branch would have authority to constitute state Muslim League branches.

The decision, in many ways unavoidable, was apparently taken with mixed emotions. Qazi Isa had rendered signal service in building League membership and aiding the government in the Kalat affair, but his personal or public conduct did not inspire confidence in Karachi and he was never taken into the central government. He was later made ambassador to Brazil, an obvious exile,[5] but in 1950 his was the only party in the province with a chance of success.

At the Shahi Jirga in February, 1950, Liaquat Ali Khan stated the goals of the central government in Baluchistan as to "bring Baluchistan and the four States, whose accession to Pakistan I welcome, to the same level of administration as the rest of Pakistan." [6] But so few were the changes actually introduced from either central government or popular pressure that the status of Baluchistan was unchanged. A minor prince was sent to the capital to speak for the Baluchi rulers because the brooding Khan would not go to Karachi and the provincial Muslim League atrophied with the skeptical mandate of the central government.

As late as three years after partition, the Khan of Kalat asserted that he was in full control of his state.

There is no truth in the news that was broadcast from Kabul that the Khan of Kalat has been deprived of his powers . . . I am the Khan of Kalat with full powers and there has been no interference in my State on behalf of the Pakistan Government.[7]

It seems likely that the Khan was overstating the case in answer to Afghan charges but the statement illustrates the external forces which, with the tribal nature of the state, inhibited political and constitutional change.

In the fall of 1950 the government turned its attention to the region by appointing a Reform Committee on Baluchistan with a mandate of "recommending administrative and constitutional changes in the existing administrative and constitutional set-up of that province with due regard to the political, social and economic conditions prevailing therein." [8] The previous March it had been announced that Mohammad Zarif Khan, the chief minister of Kalat, would be replaced by the former private secretary of the Prime Minister, Agha Abdul Hamid.

Eight days after the new minister had taken his post "a reliable source" informed *Dawn* in some detail of the impending political changes within the state. There was to be a bicameral legislature composed of the Dar-ul Khawas (House of Nobles) with a membership of the Khan's forty-six *sardars*, and the Dar-ul Awan (House of the People) with fifty-five elected representatives. The cabinet of six was to include two members each from the houses and the remainder from the royal court. The chief minister of the state, appointed by the ruler in consultation with the government of Pakistan, was to lead parliament and the cabinet. The Khan was to become a constitutional figurehead.

In addition to the cabinet, there was to be a council of outstanding men selected from both houses by the chief minister to advise him on important issues. This State Advisory Council was an attempt to create a nucleous of able men not limited in their power to the check-and-balance system of the constitution. It was clear that without disciplined political parties, the elected representatives in the assembly would be so heterogeneous that they might not be able to organize their efforts. The powers of the *sardars* and Khan were so allotted that traditionalists could manipulate the state government insofar as the patience of the chief minister would permit. The Advisory Council might both advise the minister and interpret government policy to the two houses of parliament. Its long term aim was to breed cabinet-level competence among the state politicians.

As a settlement, however, the Kalat scheme attracted much abuse. The Khan, after his abortive schemes for independence, was generally despised by the press, and the nation's editors ridiculed the presumptuousness of a bicameral legislature and the restricted powers of the elected assembly. Dr. Husain admitted that the settlement was not complete, arguing: "Here [Kalat and the Baluchistan States] we have not yet tried democratic systems of government or to be more exact, advised these States to establish a democratic system of government." [9] He added that it was not constitutional or political reform which was imperative but rather social and economic development.

As well, a definitive Baluchistan provincial settlement, which might affect the princes, was soon to be recommended.

The Baluchistan Reforms Commission released its report on November 17, 1951.[10] Its members considered the four divisions of Baluchistan, the Chief Commissioner's Province, the leased areas, tribal areas, and states. In general, the recommendation was that all settled districts comprise a Governor's Province, allowing, however, for extraordinary powers for the governor until the region's population and economy justified more normal institutions.

The report contains many insights into the problems of democracy for a tribal area. The admittedly token attempt made by the advisory council with a budget of 24,000 rupees over one year was not a success. Nonetheless, the Husain statement called for a Governor's Province without tampering for a time with the sardari tribal system.[11] In short, the traditional political order would not be disturbed but the structure of administration would be expanded. There was a clear acknowledgment that this would entail heavier subsidation but the commission believed that Baluchistan development would proceed faster than with existing fragmented and powerless governments.

As for the states, the governor of the province was to have special powers for "the protection of the rights of any Pakistan State and the rights and dignities of the ruler thereof." [12] But the report fell on deaf ears.

The Baluchistan States Union (BSU)

The novelty of the tentative Kalat constitution and the Baluchistan Reform Report had hardly worn off before new proposals for the Baluchistan states were mooted. On March

21, 1952, the press learned "that the possibilities of forming a union of the four Baluchistan States are being explored at high levels." [13] Plans were revealed for a union legislature of twenty-five members, most of whom would be elected, while tribal chiefs would be nominated.

Comments were soon forthcoming on these rumors. Qazi Musa, leader, in his brother's absence, of the somewhat tattered Baluchistan League [14] welcomed the announcement but warned that if the proposed union was to be a "political tool, it will fail in its purpose." Once again, the more important controversy was the part which the states might play in the region. "Political circles here link the grant of autonomy to Baluchistan with the fate of these [Union] talks. They think Baluchistan is not likely to get reforms before the settlement of these four States' future." [15]

On April 11, 1952, the States Ministry announced that the Baluch princes had signed supplementary Instruments of Accession accepting federation, and further: "This Instrument is being made in contemplation of joining the Union of Baluchistan States; and that after the formation of the Union the Instrument may be amended by or on behalf of the Council of Rulers of said Union." [16] On the day of the signing of the Covenant establishing the BSU, *Dawn's* hopeful headline read "End of Feudalalism in Baluchistan." The press communiqué was much more subdued, noting that the union government was to have a common executive, legislature, and judiciary, but it said nothing of democratic reform.

The Union was primarily a constitutional change precedent to broad political change. The state union administration was to be directed by a wazir-i-azam (chief advisor) who, while appointed by and responsible to the Council of Rulers, could not be dismissed without the permission of the Pakistan government, which also approved his nomination. The Council of Rulers was to be led by a president chosen for four years, in rotation among the rulers, except that the Khan of Kalat was guaranteed the post for his lifetime.

The legislature was to be composed of twenty-eight elected representatives and twelve appointed *sardars*. There was to be one member for each 20,000 constituents while the *sardars* were to be allotted to the states on the ratio of eight for Kalat, two for Makran, one for Las Bela, and one for Kharan. The Kalat chiefs were to take their seats in rotation, their nomination dependent on their position as one of the twenty-four *sardars* of the state.

The cabinet of the BSU, to be chosen from the assembly, was to have no more than five members of which two might be nominated members. The cabinet was to act as the advisory body of the council of rulers, and the appointment or dismissal of the ministers was a prerogative of the princes. However, the central government's approval was necessary for each appointment and dismissal, which transferred real power to the chief minister.

The wazir-i-azam, in addition to his cabinet leadership, held the key portfolios of law and order, finance, economic development, and services, and was the agent to the governor-general for the administration of federal matters.

Upon the accession of the Council of Rulers of the Baluchistan States Union to Pakistan as a federated unit, its princes were charged with drafting a detailed constitution for the union which would meet federal approval. The assembly was to be called immediately. As usual, the *quid pro quo* nature of the concessions was revealed in the privy purses of the rulers; Kalat, 425,000 rupees; Makran, 200,000 rupees; Kharan, 61,000 rupees; and Las Bela, 170,000 rupees, all tax free. The khan-i-azam and vice-president of the Council of Rulers received in addition a sumptuary allowance. It was an expensive settlement.

Dawn's editors took little time to react to the BSU government which they characterized as inhibitory to the development of responsible government. Equally interesting were the views of the Khan of Kalat, who viewed the union as the restoration of his rightful patrimony and a reversal of earlier government policies. Both the press and the Khan failed to assess the importance of the chief minister and the federal status of the union, and while the Khan kept more power than the Amir or Mir along the Sutlej, he had less than he thought. The weakness of the award was that it ignored Baluchistan and full development.

The country soon found how divided the BSU's rulers could be in matters in which their "former" state interests were involved. In November, 1952, an area demarcation conference was called which foundered on political shoals. The rulers agreed that their areas were the most backward in Pakistan and therefore deserving of the greatest help, but they were not ready to cooperate with each other in development. Some promising reforms were planned: standardization of weights and measures, establishment of schools and literacy centers, ending of special taxes on new wells, potatoes, and onions, the purchase of several mobile dispensaries, and agricultural seed improvement. Yet the tribal system remained, a factor which undercut any effort on the part of the government to modernize Baluchistan. Once more Pakistan was faced with the choice between order or progress; once more it chose order.

The first elections in Baluchistan were scheduled for the BSU assembly in 1954, but much was to happen before then and Baluchistan could but watch. And the States Union, whatever its promise or problems, unified only one part of the barren hills. Baluchistan still stood before the bar, awaiting the decision of the bickering judges who were unable to put together what had been broken apart a century before.

The North-West Frontier states

The widely spread *sardari* system (government through tribal chiefs) gave Baluchistan the reputation for being a well-controlled tribal region. The Pathans were not the Baluch, however, and they lay on the frontier rather than behind a provincial wall. Their arms had already drawn blood in Kashmir and the Afghans were inciting them to another jihad, this time against Karachi and Lahore.

The princes of the North-West Frontier realized the strength of their position. Even Mr. Jinnah was conciliatory when he arrived in Peshawar, and his statements to the Pathans promised continued support of government subsidies in return for pledges of loyalty such as were given to the British Raj. He also mentioned renegotiation of amounts and obligations but the wizened old *maliks* (tribal leaders) knew that if the amounts were adjusted, it would be upward. This is not to question the tribal sentiment for the new Islamic state which was Pakistan's strength; but the tribes live on subsidies and have, therefore, a very lively mundane interest in them.

Law and order were the prime requirements on the frontier as in Baluchistan, and Dr. Husain, in discussing the Pathan states, noted:

We have dealings with one single individual who looks after law and order and who practically does exactly that same thing in the States which all the maliks do in the tribal regions. So here at the moment we are not thinking in terms of establishing a parliamentary system of government on western lines.[17]

Somewhat later in the year he confided that "The more important considerations—are security of borders and requirements of watch and ward rather than constitutional reforms." [18] These comments, denying the efficacy of democracy in the frontier states, came not from a bureaucrat or politician interested in autocratic power but from one of the true liberals of the Muslim League. He knew something about the internal politics of the states and of the considerable differences between them.

Swat   Some fifteen miles north of the customs post guarding the entrance to Swat state is the capital, Saidu Sharif. Along the well-paved road paralleling the clay-green Swat River are battlements, their memories of the wars of the state's unification not yet faded. The first ruler, whose rule justified his local title, Badshah Khan (Great King), handed down the mantle to his son Jahanzeb whose task was to ride the tiger of state politics built on group conflict.[19]

As in most underdeveloped states, power and wealth in Swat derive almost exclusively from ownership of the land. The Pathans are perhaps one-quarter of the population, yet they control all of the land. Local landlords have political as well as proprietary rights, and district capitals are actually Pathan manors. Before the coming of the elder Wali, the barons of the state were constantly at war.

With a heritage of religious authority and favorable external circumstances, the imaginative prince imposed his paramountcy on the miniscule multi-state system, balancing and counterbalancing various factions which he could then control. The state militia is under the command of local squires but its mobilization is periodic; the state police however, are controlled by the ruler. The division of the instruments of violence find their parallel in revenue collection which is auctioned to local nobles subject to appeal to the Wali.

The two routes to power—through the land or through the ruler—are thus separate but coordinate. The Wali, at the apex of the appeal system of the state, keeps local khans as divided as they were when his father systematically allied with one to overcome the other. Because practically everyone in the state is involved in the often rough contests for power,[20] political feelings are bitter and the Wali's ability to bring about radical social change are limited.

So far as Karachi was concerned, Swat government was the Wali and little mention was made of modernization in the state. The ruler had sponsored truly dramatic development of communication facilities and had not ignored the social needs of his people. The irony of state development is that what the people possess is either given to them by the prince or maintained for them by the landlords, while their personal plight is desperate. One can see a half-starving child next to a new hospital, or a UNICEF jeep speeding on its errands of mercy along a wide, new road. The paternal state has suddenly blossomed, incongruously, in the land of famine.

Nonetheless the Wali, in domestic administration, accomplished as much as the Pakistan government might have, and probably more. The customs post on the frontier marks the beginning of the "hard rupee" zone of the country where labor costs are low (there is *corvee*) and products are inexpensive. Since the Wali's privy purse is paid in inflated Karachi rupees, public works and social services are only half as costly to organize and maintain. Central control would have implied all-Pakistan labor codes and wage rates and would have entailed shouldering the expensive political headaches nicely balmed by the ruler's system.

Nor would it be fair to ignore the administrative and judicial efficiency for which the state enjoys a fine reputation. In many disputes, the litigants are brought before the ruler, he hears their stories, and immediately delivers a binding judgment. Common, equity, and religious law are merged in one judge with the result that some of the shortcomings of the Western judicial system—technicality, delay, and high cost—are overcome.[21] Similarly the administration of the state is well organized, with telephone lines stretching from one end of the state to the other. And an almost physically impossible one-lane road etched out of the granite mountains inches up from Bahrein to Kalam, bringing a part of the subcontinent penetrated only in individual cases into the stream of its history.

The Pakistan government stayed aloof from Swat politics for seven years following independence. When its officials did venture into the state, they were cautious. The problems implicit in democratic reform were obvious—where loyalty is a prerequisite to law and order, how can an opposition be tolerated? When the social fabric of the state is stable only at the cost of economic inequity in favor of a warlike minority, how can majority rule function?

The 1954 political settlement reflected the central government's desire for constitutional but not political uniformity. The Swat Interim Constitution Act, 1954, and the Supplementary Instrument of Accession provided that the state should henceforth be a federated unit of Pakistan. Within the state an advisory council was established with a membership of twenty-five of whom fifteen were to be elected. They might advise the Wali on general policies of administration, development and legislation, finance, the implementation of specific policies, and such other matters as the ruler might care to refer to them. *The Khyber Mail's* editorial endorsed the philosophy of the changes but added, in effect, that the prince knew best and the council should follow his lead—not that they had any choice.[22]

Kalam, the contested district north of the state, was recognized by the Wali as part of the tribal area under the central government's control, but he was empowered, as agent to the governor-general, to administer it. Not surprisingly, the agreement defining Kalam as federal territory also specified the ruler's privy purse at a generous figure. The weak domestic reforms, high privy purse, and *de facto* control of Kalam testify both to the high regard in which the federal government held the ruler and to his strong position in bargaining. And although absolutely no change was made in autocratic government or social exploitation in Swat, the country might point to the surface uniformity of its democratic institutions.

Dir   In neighboring Dir state, Karachi could not claim even a veneer of liberalization. Like Swat, Dir is organized on the exploitation of the masses by the Yusufzai Pathans except that while the Wali of Swat is not himself a member of the Yusufzai tribe, the ruler of Dir is. To stabilize state government, the ruler's clan was given tax-farming rights, freedom from taxes, and maximum personal liberty, all guaranteed by the state government in return for support.[23]

The hold of the Nawab is made more tenuous than that of his fellow monarch in Saidu Sharif by the presence in the heart of the state of the Sultan Khel and Panjad Khel Pathan tribesmen, who refuse allegiance to the ruler and live as their brethren in the tribal areas, free from governmental control. Constantly at war with each other, they met the Nawab's attempts to subjugate them with unity. The prince, however, controlled the three most important districts of the state; the capital area which fronts on the Afghan border, Jandool in the southwest which is a fertile area, and the southeast border area with Swat.

The Nawab of Dir was, from the beginning, the most difficult frontier prince with whom Pakistani officials had to negotiate. With his state astride the Afghan frontier, the ruler knew his position was extraordinarily strong and he never failed to show it. He would not even leave the state to confer with officials in Karachi.

In the case of Swat, the federal government held its tongue because social services were being expanded, the Wali was a personable and effective leader, and the unsavory aspects of state politics were kept neatly filed in state closets. In Dir, however, the ruler had more kennels than hospitals and on more than one occasion publicly stated that since education would bring an end to his rule, he would not build schools. Popular parties were inhibited not only by the lack of social consciousness in the state but by their repression by state authorities. The head of the Dir Muslim League was assassinated in 1952 and a purge rid the state of like-minded reformers.

In 1954 when the frontier states were being brought into the federation of Pakistan, the ruler of Dir would not accept more than his original accession subjects. It was to take thirteen years before the government overcame its trepidation in Dir and then internal affairs were not its primary motivation and the modernization of state society, not its aim. The First Constituent Assembly did not intervene in Dir.

Chitral   Chitral was in many ways less sensitive than either Dir or Swat. It had formed a legal part of the Maharaja of Kashmir's empire and was involved in the legal aftermath of the war for the state but it was isolated from the cease-fire line by Pakistan territory. In any case, it is difficult to reach and only a seasonal jeep road connects it, through Dir and the Lowari Pass, with Pakistan.

The social structure of the state also differentiates it from the free Pathan states which border it on the south. Like the Kashmiri fuedal system of a century ago, it possessed a professional bureaucracy loyal to the ruling family and empowered to see to a firm justice based on detailed historical obligations. A symbolic pillar inscribed with the rights and duties of each village in the state is found both in the village and in the great hall of state in the capital.[24]

After the state had acceded to Pakistan, the young ruler's eye spotted a lady who, unfortunately, was betrothed to the Heir Apparent of Dir. The Mehtar won her hand with the result that a small war broke out between Dir and Chitral. The Pakistan army stopped the fighting, as the British army had done before, but the Chitral dynasty was denied the use of the only road connecting the state with Pakistan.

The Mehtar piloted his own plane but the Pakistan government thought it best that he leave the state for his own safety and for the tranquillity of the region. The administration of Chitral was entrusted to a Council of Elders presided over by a Pakistan political officer, an action unthinkable in the other frontier states. One may only guess that the Prince welcomed a chance to leave his isolated state in the mountains for the bright lights of Lahore where he was trained to "improve administrative skills."

By the beginning of 1953, however, there was a growing concern in the state for the prolonged absence of the ruler. On January 4, 1953, the *Khyber Mail* printed a letter from the wazir of the Ittihadi Jamaat (Unity party) of Chitral demanding the Mehtar's return. On January 13 the Chitral State Muslim League passed a resolution noting:

We, the inhabitants of Chitral State, hereby bring to the notice of the Pakistan Government the fact that owing to the continued absence of His Highness the Mehtar, we are experiencing numerous troubles and difficulties.[25]

The government's policy was made plain in a semi-official statement to *Dawn's* Peshawar correspondent who "reliably learnt that the Mehtar of Chitral . . . will only return to his State when the Government is satisfied he is fit to shoulder the administration." [26] The Mehtar's disability for administration grew largely from his predisposition to sowing wild oats rather than from his skills, and Karachi had no desire to have a playboy sovereign in the Afghan frontier region.

There were, however, two strong groups in Chitral that wanted his return. The royalists wanted the rightful ruler on the throne, no doubt for very good reasons of their own, and the state Muslim League saw his reinstatement as a prerequisite to responsible government. On March 3, 1953, the leader of the State League once more demanded that the ruler return to stimulate responsible government. In April the federal authorities recanted and announced that Chitral would become a fully federated unit of Pakistan and that its ruler would return to preside over the association of the state administration with the people.

The announcement spiked the equally interesting rumor that the government was contemplating a frontier states union on the model of Baluchistan. The difficulties in establishing such a union, considering the feuds and bad blood between the dynasties, are apparent, but perhaps the more important consideration was that regional unity would eliminate the possibility of playing the states against one another. The British policy had been to keep Kalam as a permanent issue on which to divide the princes so that they would not look for other foes. There is little doubt that, in some degree, this policy was adopted by the States' Ministry of Pakistan.

The Mehtar's arrival in the state on April 11, 1953, was

cause of state-wide celebration. The state became a federal
unit of Pakistan and the following fall the Interim Constitution Act was published.[27] It established the pattern which was
followed throughout the area of an advisory council, in Chitral
of ten members, half of whom were elected. The chief adviser,
to be nominated with the consent of the Pakistan government,
was to preside over the council and administer the state in the
name of the ruler.

Council members were to enjoy tenure for three years and
were restricted to advisory powers in matters of administration
and development. The important restrictions on the administration's authority were vested not in the council but in the
central government. The ruler was to give due weight to his
advisers but if he chose not to accept their judgments he was
required to submit the question to the central government,
whose decision would be binding.

While the checks on autocratic government far exceeded
those of the other frontier states, the settlement hardly established representative government. The Mehtar believed that
the concessions to popular government were quite adequate
and all of the five appointive members of the council were
chosen from the royalist group, to the consternation of the
Muslim League. As the *Khyber Mail* noted: "The Mehtar was
also quoted as saying that the people of the State were not yet
fully capable of accepting a greater degree of reform than had
been given in the 1953 constitutional act." [28] But unlike the
other states in the tense region, the beginnings of liberalization were present in Chitral.

Amb   The smallest, least significant, and most retrograde
state in the region was Amb. Created by the British as a favor
to a particularly important Black Mountain tribe in an era of

tribal war, the state rested on little more than legal props and was a guise for a particularly unsavory form of landlordism.

If any principle was uniform in the first decade of state assimilation in Pakistan, it was that state territories were inviolate. Contracts and treaties had to be honored. Yet on February 16, 1949, the North-West Frontier Province Legislative Assembly, whipped on by Abdul Qayyum Khan, the chief minister, passed the following resolution to undercut the rule in Amb:

This assembly recommends to the provincial government to recommend to the Governor-General of Pakistan through proper channels to amalgamate the feudal state of Phulra with its dependencies with the administrative territories of Azad district and create a new tehsil or tehsils as the case may be.[29]

Phulra had been separated from the political control of Amb and given to one of two competing brothers during British rule, but was considered an "excluded area" in which the dynasty held more than property rights. Provincial politicians were forbidden to legislate for the region. Upper Tanawal, a similar region, in which the ruler of Amb had interests, was appropriated in 1950 and by 1953, when reforms were promulgated in the state on the model of Chitral, the Nawab of Amb ruled roughly 15 square miles.

The state advisory council was to have four members of whom two might be elected. A wazir, appointed with the approval of the central government, was charged with state administration and the revenue and police were separated from court personnel. Amb became a federated unit of Pakistan but little progress was made in liberalizing its depressed cultivators, and given its hopelessly small size, development was impossible.

The pattern which emerged on the North-West frontier was quite different than that of Baluchistan or the riverine states because of the strategic and social conditions of the Afghan frontier. Order, watch and ward, control; all these needs came before liberalization and presented the constitution draftsmen with a heterogeneity mocking national unity.

PART THREE

The States and the Federal Problem

The legal aspects of the relations between the acceded States and the Federation of Pakistan in the future constitution is said to have turned out to be "a major political question." *Dawn, June 22, 1954*

X

The Constitutional Morass

While the real tests of Pakistan were taking place in the villages throughout the country, public attention was misdirected to the constitutional debates. Brilliant sallies, incisive retorts, imaginative proposals on the floor of the assembly dazzled the press while tardy school construction and the plight of cultivators was scarcely mentioned. Attracted by the unique, the international community puzzled over Pakistan's "Islamic state" theories and listened eagerly for what it believed to be the inevitable quarrel between Bengal and West Pakistan. Religion, language, foreign relations, and electorates, these were the issues which danced as mirages before an expectant but distracted nation.

The essential problems facing Pakistan were no different than those faced by all newly independent countries which are economically and technically underdeveloped. The common task is to utilize the power of the state in the interests of the nation, for the government to act as a catalyst in the process of modernizing a society. No matter how imaginative the constitution and ideology of the state, it must serve specific social purposes. These were unique in Pakistan only in their magnitude.

It was perhaps inevitable that a people heir to the Mughul past would seek escape in the romance of an attempted return to the past, particularly in the absence of a strong positive ideology. The concern with Islam, begun in an effort to awaken a particular people to their earthly plight and not their theology, became an obsession, a neo-orthodox and finally heterodox monster, the self-same creature the Muslim League leadership had hoped to slay. Human misery, ignorance and superstition, isolation and social decay were the true enemies of Pakistan and its promise was in a program to overcome them.

The tragedy of the constitutional morass was that the politicians chased the vivid butterflies of largely irrelevant controversies and allowed religious elements to move among the people with a confusing doctrine, while at the same time largely delegating the real problems of government to the civil servants. Both the ideology and the politics of the nation required fertile imagination and dramatic appeal, the forte of the popular politician, yet the Muslim League failed to move out of its embattled fortifications in Karachi. In the growing divergence between the political and administrative leadership of the country and in the progressive confusion and obfuscation of the Pakistan vision, lay the seeds of the nation's future agony.

The immediate series of issues upon which Pakistan's democracy foundered concerned the federal structure of government which had been bequeathed by the Government of India Act, 1935. Federal politics are territorial politics par excellence, and the need in Pakistan was for a national purpose. The federal protection given provincial and state leaders was particularly serious in Pakistan because of the almost complete lack of political consensus. The story of the first ten years of

Pakistan is essentially of the rivalry between conservative or parochial provincial elites and a more liberal but baseless central government. Within five years after independence, the founders of Pakistan were in full retreat before provincial politicians, and in all of these disputes the princes were not unimportant.

States and the federation

After the princes (with the exception of the Nawab of Dir) accepted the federation of their states and agreed in advance to the provisions of the future constitution, they were swept into the national political struggle. Their future, being decided by an ever more divided Constituent Assembly, was unsure and the flux of events spun them, like colored chips in a kaleidoscope, first into one constitutional pattern and then into another.

The beginning of the protracted search for a constitution was the Objectives Resolution of March 12, 1949. In addition to an ingenious phrase linking government and God, the document provided:

These territories now included in or in accession with Pakistan and such other territories as many hereafter be included in or accede to Pakistan shall form a Federation wherein the units will be autonomous with such boundaries and limitations on their powers and authority as may be prescribed.[1]

A committee of more than two dozen leading figures then set to work on a complete basic constitution in consonance with the Objectives Resolution.

Perhaps it was too well written, promising, as it vaguely did, an Islamic state, a democratic state, and a federal state. Transmuting an autocratic secular political tradition into a democratic polity imbued with religious values in a near-starvation society was a formidable task and perhaps even an impossible one.

The Basic Principles Committee submitted its blueprint for the future constitution on October 7, 1950, and it was immediately apparent that the country had been promised too much. Offered to the public by the trusted successor to the father of the country, Liaquat Ali Khan, it was nonetheless immediately attacked from every side. The most strident criticism came from East Bengal, the economically impoverished but politically sensitive wing of the country, which was restive because of continued political slights and the alleged disparagement of the language and culture that had produced Tagore.[2] The breakdown of social communication began to undermine the tenuous unity of the nation and, while the interim report was being recommitted to the committee, political agitation increased to a deafening pitch.

Hopefully the national leadership would have understood the increasingly weak position of the government and undertaken a renewed commitment to popular politics. Their prime efforts, however, were committed to day-to-day government business and the search for a quick remedy for the constitutional fever. Party affairs received less rather than more attention as the alienation of the government and the people proceeded apace; at the end of the trying summer of 1951, the last link between the Muslim League and the popular imagination was severed by the assassin's bullet which felled Liaquat Ali Khan.

The death of Liaquat paralyzed the country. There was no successor who could fill the void he left in the party, the government, or the hearts of the Pakistani people. His demise was more unsettling because rumors linking important provincial politicians to the act were common currency not only in the streets, but in the chancelleries of government as well. In an effort to restore confidence, the gentle Khwaja Nazimuddin moved from the governor-general's residence to the prime minister's post and assumed the onerous duties of head of the Muslim League, leader of the government, and premier national politician, none of which he was capable of handling.

His position was unenviable, as it would have been for any man, given the state of the nation. Provincial antagonisms were assuming great strength and bitterness. The progress of the constitutional and legislative debates was dishearteningly slow, and bad faith had poisoned the proceedings. The country faced economic and food crises and had slipped permanently behind India in foreign affairs. Before Nazimuddin was to be relieved of his pressing chores there would be a schism between the executive and legislature which would claim him as its first victim.

In the autumn of 1952 the so-called final report of the Basic Principles Committee was published. No sooner had it been announced than influential Punjabi politicians swore their hostility to it, and the Bengalis found it not much improvement over the interim report, particularly in the light of the Prime Minister's indiscreet politics. The religiously sensitive public, ever swelling due to the pamphleteering of parties such as Jama'at-i-Islami, had little pity on the secularist liberal spirit of the report.

The federal structure of the state was endorsed in the report and Pakistan was to have a bicameral legislature. The Upper House, or House of Units, was to represent territorial interests. Bahawalpur was to have four seats, Khairpur and the Baluchistan States Union two seats each, and the tribal areas, in which the frontier states were included, five seats. In the House of the People, Bahawalpur was allowed thirteen members while Khairpur received four seats, the Baluchistan States Union five seats, and the frontier peoples seventeen seats.

The controversy arose, according to an influential segment of Punjabi opinion, because Bengal, by weight of its larger population, would be able to assert permanent leadership. Dacca, the supposedly favored provincial center, was unhappy with aspects of the draft including the powers of the Upper House. The report was not a compromise and was repudiated by the major protagonists. The violence of its rejection was evidence of the mounting tension in the society on the eve of the permanent assignment of political priorities.

In order to overcome the strength of East Bengal, which was enhanced by the quarrels among the West Pakistan provinces and states, planners in the Punjab attacked federalism in the Indus valley and suggested unification of the area from Chitral to the sea. As the largest population and territorial bloc in the new province, the Punjab could dominate and thus meet Bengal on equal ground. Initially the idea was not popularly held, nor even commonly accepted in the Punjab.

With the strains of partisan criticism and radical attacks on the report ringing in their ears, the members of the Constituent Assembly left the capital on January 1, 1953, returning to their constituencies to sound public opinion. Apparently no one had thought of an election as a vote of confidence to the members after their now long five-year terms. Instead, politics preceded by the time-honored system of consultation with the feudal barons, parochial leaders, and landlords.

As the government braced in the face of both constitutional and economic crisis, the governor-general of Pakistan, Ghulam Mohammad, electrified the nation by dismissing Prime Minister Khwaja Nazimuddin and announcing the appointment of the Pakistani ambassador to the United States, Mohammad Ali Bogra, as prime minister. The April announcement from Government House said that the action had been taken on the grounds that Nazimuddin had been ineffective in meeting the pressing needs of the country. The removal of Nazimuddin was tragic only in that the Constituent Assembly allowed the Governor-General to dictate terms. Once the integrity of the chamber was breached, regardless of cause, representative government in Pakistan was irreparably weakened.

Equally important in this audacious action was the effect it had on the crystalization of partisan forces not within the assembly but on either pole of the government, legislative and executive. The Governor-General, successful in his gambit, became the focus for those favoring unitary government whereas those politicians favoring federalism were in power in the assembly. The dismissal of Nazimuddin, without a voice raised in honest protest, made the outcome of the struggle inevitable. Perhaps the damage would have been minimized had an illustrious legislator been chosen as prime minister, but the Governor-General appointed his man, a diplomat with no local support and no experience, who had been outside the country in the crucial days of debate.

Without doubt, the Governor-General's action was successful only because the nation was weary of the bickering members of the "Long Parliament," who had gone to Karachi to draft a constitution and had not come back. The devitalized assembly was denied the strength of the new members who, frustrated in efforts to gain power normally, had turned to radical protest. These dissident politicians, especially those in Bengal, were the only hope of the Constituent Assembly against the phantom from the British past, the viceroy/governor-general. They did not recognize their predicament until it was too late and they had lost their honor, their ideals, and the nation's trust.

The story of the ensuing melee has been told often and well and need not be retold in its disheartening detail here.[3] After much negotiation the concept of parity between East Bengal and West Pakistan emerged under the rubric of the "Mohammad Ali Formula," which broke the constitutional stalemate in early October, 1953. The country breathed a sigh of relief as the Constituent Assembly now hurried to the pressing task of debating and adopting a constitution.

Consolidation

While the structural problems of the uniquely divided nation were thought to have been resolved, the settlement ignored the more important tension growing between the honorific executive and the parliamentary leaders. The Governor-General, his power magnified by a close association with the unitary group of Punjabi politicians, began more actively interfering in state business in the interests of a consolidated West Pakistan.

The Mohammad Ali formula was a preliminary grouping of territorial units for the purpose of representation. There were to be, in the House of Units, five territorial groups. The frontier states and tribal areas were to be jointly represented with the North-West Frontier Province while Khairpur would join with Sind. The curious group, however, lumped together Baluchistan States Union, Bahawalpur, Karachi, and Baluchistan province while the remaining units were Punjab and Bengal respectively.

Group Five came under heavy fire in the debates from representatives of the regions so carelessly linked together. How could a politician represent such a constituency, asked Mr. Jaffer, and added: "It cannot be denied, that to be a people of one unit there must be facilities of contact and communications between the various parts comprising the Units." [4] Qazi Isa pledged to oppose the fifth grouping "to the last." The states' power was completely destroyed in this plan for they would share their Upper House votes with either larger and more powerful provinces or among themselves. Furthermore, they would have less than a dozen votes in a lower chamber of three hundred.

Even so, members hostile to the princes or state politicians questioned the separate existence of the states as units of the federation. In October, 1953, M. H. Gazder asked the government why India was able to "wipe out" six hundred states in one month while Pakistan was unable to abolish ten states in six years. He implied, not indirectly, that the government was receiving bribes from the rulers.[5]

Mian Iftikharuddin, member of the assembly in permanent opposition, charged that the groupings had no basis in common acceptance, that the people of the states had not accepted the Mohammad Ali formula but that "landlords and rulers said unity, and there was unity." [6] He added that the central government would have found it difficult to nominate their own favorites if the states were merged with the provinces. These were minority views but the grouping plan provoked a continuing debate.

Despite the constitutional debates which indicated an acceptance of the federal form of government in West Pakistan, unitary philosophies had gained ground and were unready to

admit defeat. The assembly scarcely reflected the true currents
of provincial politics as it moved closer to constitutional passage.

Elsewhere Pakistan was in turmoil. The economy groaned
under the buyer's market following the artificial boom of the
Korean War. The March elections in Bengal left the Muslim
League ravaged and it was barely able to maintain face in the
wave of votes against it. A month later the Ahmadiyya riots
in the Punjab and the subsequent recriminations drew the
nation's attention to the unsavory politics of religious war. The
end of May brought news of four hundred dead in the Adamjee
industry riots and governor-general's rule was imposed on East
Pakistan. The newly elected provincial ministry was dismissed,
to watch with frustration as the troubled assembly tried to
give birth to a constitution.

Baluchistan unity

The final revisions of the Basic Principles Committee Report
were on the anvil, and from a legal point of view one of the
most interesting innovations was the proposed amalgamation
of the Baluchistan States Union and Baluchistan. In many
ways the scheme was nothing more than common sense. Every
mission to Baluchistan had seen its sparse population and ex-
tensive area as difficult to administer and develop, especially
with administrative fragmentation. The country owed the Khan
of Kalat nothing, and the other states were figments of legal
imagination.

The proposed merger before the passage of the constitution
brought new rancor to the assembly, particularly because it
reflected the initiative of the cabinet and not of the assembly.
The reasoning was that if even one state was eliminated, the

constitutional principles of federation and Pakistan's treaty obligations would be brought into question. Perhaps more important, the Basic Principles Committee had not originated the scheme and there is little evidence that they approved of it.

The Khan of Kalat was most angry with the plan and characterized it as a "personal conspiracy against me," [7] but five days later *Dawn* endorsed the plan as the fastest way to overcome feudal society in Baluchistan. In the middle of May the Khan appeared before the Basic Principles Committee and officials from the States' Ministry to plead the strong legal case against the amalgamation. There is no reason to believe that his reception was unsympathetic since the plan had originated with the minister for states and frontier regions, M. A. Gurmani, who was leading the consolidation movement of West Pakistan.

The cabinet let it be known that parliament and the Basic Principles Committee would be met with a *fait accompli*. The press reported: "The decision to remerge Baluchistan States Union in the centrally administered province of Baluchistan is expected to be announced during the third week of this month." [8] Ten days later Mr. Gurmani publicly announced: "[The] Government is convinced that to speed up economic, social and administrative progress in these areas it was necessary to reunite them." [9]

The assembly was not intimidated and on June 22, 1954, the day after Gurmani's speech, a spokesman for the Basic Principles Committee announced that a special subcommittee would hear testimony from constitutional lawyers, the Khan of Kalat, and officials of the States' Ministry. The members of the parent committee called upon the Muslim League party caucus to issue a clear policy statement on the issue but the party was as divided as were government and legislature.

The Basic Principles Committee, having heard the report of its subcommittee, placed the evidence before the Constituent Assembly, although the cabinet was proceeding as though no constitutional issue was involved. The findings of the committee were that the merger of the Baluchistan States Union and the province would not be accomplished prior to the passage of the constitution.

The controversy alarmed other rulers as well. On June 23, 1954, the chief minister of the North-West Frontier Province, Sardar Abdur Rashid, denied that the government planned to modify the status of the frontier states.[10] In mid-June Mumtaz Qizilbash intensified his spirited defense of Khairpur's right to remain a federated unit of Pakistan because of its fine record of political and economic development. The Legislative Assembly of Khairpur passed a resolution in support of his position and invited the federal government to conduct a referendum among the people to confirm their feeling.

The affairs in the princely states paled before the great challenge flung at the parliament by the Governor-General in the summer and fall of 1954. The membership of the assembly seemed out of contact with its nominal cabinet leadership while the involvement of Ghulam Mohammad grew more audacious. On July 31, 1954, the assembly declared that it held sole authority over the states for "framing a constitution for the acceded States which shall be binding and which shall not be questioned in any court of law." [11] Section 204 of the interim constitution empowered the courts to interpret the Instruments of Accession but the assembly resolution removed the legal basis by which the Khan of Kalat would oppose the integration of his state and the province, and thereby supported the cabinet's plan.

On September 2, Qizilbash, probably sensing the dramatic

events which were to follow, canceled his projected trip to London and the meeting of the World Association of Parliamentarians. On the same day the government announced its intention of introducing the amalgamation bill in the opening session of the assembly. The Baluchistan States Union Wazir-i-Azam was directed to report directly to the agent to the governor-general in Baluchistan, rather than the Ministry for States and Frontier Regions, in advance of the passage of the resolution.

On September 12 the Basic Principles Committee met to reconsider its earlier recommendations and two days later the Parliamentary party of the Muslim League met for four hours, resolving differences on various matters, including Baluchistan and the princely states. They concluded: "It is understood that they have recommended Baluchistan as a Governor's province with the BSU merged . . . and to have recommended the continuance of Bahawalpur, Khairpur and the Frontier States with mergers if the States' Legislatures so decide." [12] The government had won the day.

On September 20, 1954, the newly amended Basic Principles Committee Report asked the Constituent Assembly to approve the joint representation of the North-West Frontier Province, tribal areas, and frontier states in the new unicameral legislature. The tribal peoples were to be protected from federal interference and it was argued, as it had been throughout the British period, that certain statutes and procedures were not applicable to certain areas. Tradition could not be flaunted. The designation "Special Areas," to be applied to the Baluchistan states as well, would remove them from provincial codes and practices.

Paragraph 132C of the report provided that the special areas were to constitute parts of the governor's provinces and were to be subject to the executive authority of the governor, but since "these areas will have no representation in the provincial legislatures, the provincial legislatures will not be competent to extend their laws in these areas." [13] The president of the Republic had to approve any governor's action in the areas, but in fact the system was as clumsy as it was backward. Abdul Ghaffar Khan summed it up neatly.

So far as I can make out, the object appears to be to do away with the Tribal Areas and Frontier States as free and independent entities, keeping them at the same time from becoming a full-fledged and integral part of the North-West Frontier Province. This is indeed a strange and unprecedented solution. [14]

Paragraph 132D provided that the president could, after having ascertained the views of the people, or, in the case of the Baluchistan States Union, the legislature, abolish the status of the special areas.

The Report recommended that Bahawalpur and Khairpur should form separate provinces with rights and obligations identical with those of governor's provinces, except that the constitutional head of the states would be the ruler as advised by a civil servant, rather than an appointed governor. Future mergers of the two riverine states were made contingent upon the acceptance of such unions by the state governments.

The compromise scheme which allowed the BSU to have special status though linked with the province averted open conflict between the Khan of Kalat and the federal government. The Union's continued independence was assured by the barrier isolating it from the jurisdiction of the provincial legislature in favor of its own. Unfortunately, the agreement did nothing to modify basically the political and economic structure of the region. The issue was not resolved and the problems of the princely states remained on the surface of national politics.

The apparent calm of the fall of 1954 created dangerous illusions that the deep differences between the political communities in Pakistan were bridged. They were not. Parties in favor of a unified West Pakistan gathered under the banner of the Governor-General while the Constituent Assembly made a last attempt to frustrate Ghulam Mohamad. On September 22, the house passed a resolution making cabinet advice binding on the governor-general, thereby substituting for custom a formal rule which the legislators hoped would not be ignored.

With the constitution at last settled and the drafting entrusted to experts working under a deadline of January 1, 1955, the assembly was adjourned sine die, and the Prime Minister left for the United States. The Governor-General, stung by the assembly's action and encouraged by voices in the Punjab, came back from his retreat in the north and made his bid for power. On October 20, he lifted PRODA [15] prescriptions from four important politicians while the pro-*putsch* elements in Bengal and the Punjab demanded the dismissal of the assembly. Four days later Ghulam Mohammad dismissed the Constituent Assembly as he had dismissed Khwaja Nazimuddin, and announced an end to "parliamentary bickering." Although the constitution was in the hands of a drafting committee, he had the effrontery to charge that the House had not done its work. With a definitive settlement two months away, the future of the states and the nation was entrusted to the new Viceroy and his consorts.

"The mightiest must bow before the law." *Fatima Jinnah, quoted in* Dawn *headline, April 13, 1955*

XI

State Integration and the Constitution

As the nation numbly watched, Ghulam Mohammad instructed Mohammad Ali, the prime minister, to form a cabinet without benefit of parliament. The portfolio of states and frontier regions went to an ex-frontier officer and reputed strong man, Major General Iskander Mirza. Sardar Bahadur Khan and Mushtaq Gurmani, while not included in the ministry, were reputedly awaiting high administrative appointments. Dr. Khan Sahib joined the government on October 29, 1954, and the stage was set for a new brand of politics in Pakistan.

The real excitement of Pakistan had left. The breezes which now blew from the ministries of Finance and Interior were of control, not experiment—of the past, not the future. Reform, liberalization, elections, and democracy were ideas bid to slumber while the controllers reasserted their colonial training. For some, however, dissolution was thought to hold promise. Firoz Khan Noon was riding a tide in the Punjab and H. S. Suhrawardy, in many ways the symbol of the frustrated Bengali faction, characterized the Constituent Assembly as a "Long Parliament" in need of purging by a Cromwell.

General Iskander Mirza offered an inside view of the dissolution. He told a correspondent of the London *Daily Mail* that the new government was "rectifying blunders of political scalawags" and that Pakistan's illiterate people were neither interested nor competent in politics.[1] He discussed controlled democracy and sanity in government in some detail. Perhaps the clearest proof of the lack of political morality in the country was that the Prime Minister agreed to reappointment without a parliament and cooperated with such persons as General Mirza.

The autocratic regime then began to extend its program to eliminate "scalawags." On November 1, 1954, it was announced that the Amir of Bahawalpur had been summoned to Karachi by the Governor-General. On November 1 and 2 talks were held in Government House. In his Lawrence Road home Hasan Mahmud, the chief minister of Bahawalpur, heard Radio Pakistan announce that the Amir, under instructions from the Governor-General, had dissolved the legislature, dismissed the cabinet on grounds of maladministration, and taken full powers under section 74 of the state constitution. The ruler duly announced that his centrally-appointed chief advisor, A. R. Khan, would exercise these powers in his name. With hardly a voice of protest, the nation watched its only true state democracy be extinguished.

Following Bahawalpur's rough treatment, the other rulers saw the writing on the wall. On September 2 they were closeted with the States' Minister and on the next day there were fragmentary reports of the discussions which centered on plans for the consolidation of West Pakistan into one province. When General Mirza was asked if the princes favored such consolidation, he said only that "nothing has been finalized."

The One Unit plan

It was now clear that the dissolution of the Constituent Assembly was in fact a device to reopen the constitutional debates. The way in which the sentiments of Bengal were considered in return for its support for autocracy was only a guise behind which a powerful group worked for consolidation. The history of the constitutional debates on the federal issue make clear a secular trend against provincial autonomy beginning with the federal modifications of 1947 and extending through the grouping plan of the upper house and the amalgamation of Baluchistan. The unicameral legislature plan provided in the final draft reduced state and small province representation dramatically and it only remained to make West Pakistan one administrative district.

Informed sources were quoted as understanding that the dismissal of the Bahawalpur Legislature was a prelude to the merger of the West Pakistan states and provinces.[2] There were to be three stages in the program, the first of which was to "bring around" the governments of Bahawalpur, Khairpur, and the Baluchistan States Union. It was thought that Bahawalpur, Las Bela, Makran, and Kharan had agreed but that Kalat and Khairpur were in opposition. In short, the states with functioning governments were opposed to the plan.

The second phase of the consolidation of the western wing of the country concerned the tribal areas and frontier states. There was no clear plan, the story ran, but the maliks and rulers were being consulted. Chitral was perhaps most vulnerable because the Mehtar had recently died in an airplane crash over Dir, reportedly due to a bullet bought by the Nawab's son in payment of a vendetta *de coeur.*

The third phase of the consolidation plan was to weld together the Indus valley from Chitral to the sea by joining the provinces. Presumably the dictatorship could bring this about in the same manner demonstrated in Bahawalpur.

A week after the dismissal of the assembly the Council of Rulers of the Baluchistan States Union agreed to merge their states with centrally-administered Baluchistan prior to their integration with West Pakistan. The reported issue yet to be solved was the civil list benefits and jagir lands of the rulers. What was not reported was that the Khan of Kalat was forced to grant government demands and that his cooperation was not freely secured to regional integration.

On November 7 the Sind ministry announced its firm opposition to union with adjoining provinces and in twenty-four hours was dismissed for "maladministration." Mr. Khuhro was appointed to form a new ministry with the clear mandate that it should favor unitary government. On November 8 it was announced that Bahadur Khan was the nominee of the government to be agent to the governor-general for Baluchistan. The pattern of increasing control became evident throughout the country.

On November 9 the president of the dismissed Constituent Assembly, Tazimuddin Khan, filed a petition before the Sind chief court charging the Governor-General with exceeding his power in the dissolution action. At the time, this step was viewed as tilting with dangerous opponents and the cabinet proceeded with its own blueprint as to how Pakistan should be reconstructed.

Khairpur, hitherto staunchly in support of federalism, was asked for its decision by the Governor-General's men. A few months earlier, the state assembly had called for a referendum to confirm the peoples' attachment to autonomy but in the shadow of Bahawalpur and Sind, the Legislative Assembly meekly and unanimously voted for the merger of their state into a unified West Pakistan, on November 10, 1954. Their last independent act was to resolve that should the union not be consummated, they should not be merged with Sind. In any event, their prudence was rewarded with continued tenure.

With such "unanimous support" for the scheme the Prime Minister announced on November 22 that a unified West Pakistan would be established. He promised that no section of the new province would dominate, that provincial languages would continue, that special arrangements concerning the services would not be changed, that special benefits would continue to accrue to the backward areas, and that the rights and conditions of all the areas would be safeguarded.[3] Why then, one might ask, was the plan being adopted at such great political cost. The Prime Minister answered that there was a need for administrative efficiency, political stability, and full partnership with Bengal. There was no mention of ending feudalism in the states or of extending democracy to the tribes. It was strictly a federal problem, at least according to the government.

The frontier was proving difficult. The appointment of General Mirza, an experienced frontier hand, as states' minister was initially interpreted as bringing a firm hand to the task of integrating the tribal zones. As time passed, however, it was clear that the government was unwilling to risk tribal war. The Afghans and many politicians in the province intensified their hostile outcries against amalgamation and tension was high. Radio Kabul analyzed the plan as a conspiracy to put the Pathans under the heel of the Punjabis, an idea not totally unrelated to the possibilities.

Incongruous as it seems, with dismissed parliaments and

replaced ministries throughout "democratic" Pakistan, the Wali of Swat announced in December that elections would be held for the State's Advisory Council. There were no reports thereafter that Swat was to be integrated with West Pakistan, and the ruler remembers no entreaties to affiliate this state.[4] On December 14 confirmation of continued state autonomy was announced in an official press communique: "The Northwest Frontier Province states will not be merged into the proposed West Pakistan Unit since they are being treated as Special Areas." [5] The tribal areas were assured the same status.

The intense activity of the unification did, however, lure the Nawab of Dir from his five years of hermitage into Peshawar to meet officials from the States' Ministry. He also agreed to meet the press although his aides let it be known that his visit was to determine the exact constitutional and political status of the proposed unified province. The newsmen were more interested in the domestic politics of Dir. The ruler said: "There was no need for any constitutional reform, or rather any reforms in the State, because conditions are perfectly in order there and the peoples' entire satisfaction does not require any reform." [6] The Dir State Muslim League requested that a commission be sent to verify the Nawab's observations. After the prince had refused, the League leader demanded that Dir be merged with a unified West Pakistan, apparently the worst fate that could be wished for the sovereign.

There was no implication of liberalization in the One Unit plan but the rulers were concerned that they might be brought under provincial rule. Since 1935 the only political authority to whom they reported was the central government, a relationship they enjoyed. In late December Firoz Khan Noon was interviewed in Peshawar and asked if the states and tribal areas would be transferred to the administrative control of West Pakistan. He refused to make comment and thereby heightened local suspicion.

Meanwhile the North-West Frontier Province Legislative Assembly voted for One Unit, and in his regular monthly radio broadcast the Prime Minister revealed that although Punjab had 56 percent of the population of West Pakistan, it would be allowed only 40 percent of the representation in the assembly for ten years. He announced that Mushtaq Gurmani, rumored to be one of the chief architects of the plan,[7] would probably be the first governor of the province. On December 11, amidst the most spectacular intrigues possible, including, apparently, kidnapping, the Sind Legislative Assembly voted 100 to 4 for amalgamation.

Kalat and the Baluchistan States Union rulers had yet to agree to the larger integration of their states within West Pakistan. The Khan was ordered to come to Karachi in December to consult with the Minister for States and Frontier Regions. It is said that the Khan was given an instrument and told that he could leave the room in which he sat, and Karachi, only after he had signed the agreement integrating his state.

The first clause provided for an end to Kalat's political history.

His Highness the Khan-i-Azam cedes to the Government of the Dominion of Pakistan his sovereignty and all his rights, authority and powers as President of the Council of Rulers of the Union, together with all his territories including the territories known as leased areas . . . . the Dominion shall exercise all powers, authority and jurisdiction for the governance of the said Union and territories in such manner and through such Agency as it may see fit.[8]

The subsequent articles guarantee the dynastic rights of succession, personal property, titles, and dignity and the final clause voids all previous agreements. The allowances for the rulers of the Union, and particularly the Khan, show a generous increase to an already generous scale.[9]

	Allowance in rupees per annum	
Ruler	*1952*	*1955*
The Khan-i-Azam of Kalat	425,000	650,000
The Nawab of Makran	200,000	225,000
The Jam Sahib of Las Bela	170,000	200,000
The Nawab of Kharan	61,000	70,000

Even with the rise in allowances, the settlement was one of duress, as subsequent events would show.

With the country formally bound to support the proposal, the Prime Minister announced the formation of a council for the administration of West Pakistan, which would draft the necessary legislation to implement integration. It was composed of the governors and chief ministers of Sind, North-West Frontier Province, and Punjab, and the agent to the governor-general in Baluchistan. The chief minister of Khairpur, advisor to the amir of Bahawalpur and Wazir-i-Azam of the Baluchistan States Union were associated with the Council only when its business concerned their regions. On December 18, Mr. Gurmani was elected chairman of the body.

On February 9, 1955, the steamroller which had flattened every politician in West Pakistan ran into the solid wall of the last remaining independent body in Pakistan, the judiciary. The Sind court ruling on the petition of Tazimuddin Khan held that the Governor-General's dissolution of the Constituent Assembly was null and void and that the appointment of ministers from outside the assembly's membership was *ultra vires*. Mr. Suhrawardy, writing his personal success story at the cost of his future political life, appealed, as law minister, before the federal court, which in mid-March reversed the lower court.[10] The West Pakistan Council returned to its tasks.

By late February, 1955, the administrative plan for the new province and the integration of its former fragments was ready. The rulers of Bahawalpur, Khairpur, and the Baluchistan states signed new instruments of accession which allowed their patrimonies to assume a new constitutional position in an undifferentiated province.[11] The new system was to reorganize the Indus valley into ten divisions with headquarters in Karachi, Lahore, Multan, Bahawalpur, Peshawar, Rawalpindi, Dera Ismail Khan, Sukkur, Hyderabad, and Quetta. The same area was to be further divided into fifty districts.

To improve administration, the district commissioners were given much greater power. The proximity of important administrative centers at the divisional level was thought to make possible a more rapid and equitable system of judging appeals and settling disputes. With the exception of Bahawalpur, however, the centers were not close to the state peoples, who supposedly needed better government more than others. In Baluchistan the Agent to the Governor-General said that the excluded areas and states would continue to be administered under the tribal system with *sardari* rule, tribal levies, and a jirga court system.[12]

The North-West Frontier tribal peoples, both in the tribal areas and the states, were guaranteed the special relationship provided by the Constituent Assembly. The same protection against change was guaranteed.

Having ordered the integration of West Pakistan in March 1955, the head of state and his aides began to draft a constitution to legitimize their handiwork. The Emergency Powers Ordinance was promulgated empowering the Governor-General to make provision for the framing of a constitution, to constitute West Pakistan as one administrative territory, to validate such laws as might have been passed by the Constituent Assembly, and to authenticate a budget.

The central government also revealed its intention to transfer all previously federally-controlled areas in West Pakistan to the provincial government but the Governor-General assured the tribal peoples: "No change, however, is contemplated in the present system of administration in the Tribal Areas." [13] And certain modifications of the Council's original administrative arrangements were made. Instead of ten divisions there were to be eleven and both Kalat and Khairpur were to be divisional headquarters, the states having reasserted their territorial essence if not their princely character.

Having constructed the new province, the government moved to make it politically vital. On April 4, 1955, Mr. Gurmani was appointed West Pakistan governor and Dr. Khan Sahib, a non-Muslim League, non-Punjabi leader became chief minister of the province. This "bureaucrats dream" [14] was abruptly ended as the federal court, invalidating the Governor General's ordinances by the Usif Patel decision, awakened Pakistan to its democratic past and ideals.

Return to democracy?

The federal court decision gave Ghulam Mohammad a simple choice: abolish the court or bow before the law. He considered it carefully, summoned expert legal advisors, held political and military talks [15] and on April 15 bowed before the law. The court had bridged the chasm between a dismissed national legislature and a democratic future.

The Governor-General then began his step-by-step retreat by calling for a "Constitutional Convention" of sixty members chosen equally between the two wings. The provincial assemblies of the Punjab, North-West Frontier Province, and Sind were to nominate sixteen, three, and four members respectively with the remaining West Pakistan members to be appointed at the Governor-General's direction in Baluchistan, Khairpur, Bahawalpur, Karachi and the tribal areas and frontier states.[16] On May 17 the plan for the unification of West Pakistan was shelved until the legal situation could be clarified—it was by no means clear.

Following the Governor-General's order establishing a constitutional convention several suits were brought in lower courts contesting its legality. The federal court stayed all proceedings until it had heard arguments from the government describing the nature and functions of the body. At hearings on April 25 and 27, and following consultation between the justices and officials of the Ministry of Law, the Governor-General amended his earlier order to give the successor body the same powers as the dismissed Constituent Assembly.

Its membership was raised to eighty. The quotas approved under the new arrangement were: Punjab, twenty-one; North-West Frontier Province, four; and Sind, five. The Governor-General would directly appoint one member each from Baluchistan, Baluchistan States Union, North-West Frontier states, Khairpur, and Karachi, and two from Bahawalpur.

This plan was also contested and the government asked the federal court for an advisory opinion. On May 10, 1955, it released a four-point judgment which affirmed the right of the governor-general to dissolve the Constituent Assembly and to validate the laws passed by the Constituent Assembly acting as the federal legislature, but ruled that he could not change the structure of government and could but call a new Constituent Assembly. Moreover, the ruling continued, he might designate the electorate of the assembly but could not name members to the body. Therefore in areas where assemblies were not empowered or where official boards and other agencies of selec-

tion did not exist, the Constituent Assembly alone was to
have the power to determine how these bodies would be represented in the assembly.

Ghulam Mohammad, by now a sick man, continued to follow
the dictates of the court and announced that elections for the
Constituent Assembly would be held on June 21. The court
could only demand a return to the past system which had
proved too weak for its challenge. Indirect elections were sure
to seat the feuding leaders who had paralyzed the government before. The nation desperately needed a popular election
to confirm national consent for the vast changes which were
contemplated in Pakistan's government and which had involved the country in a major crisis.

On June 22, to no one's amazement, a weak Muslim League
majority of twenty-four was elected, indirectly, in West Pakistan while Bengal sent sixteen members of the United Front
and twelve Awami League representatives. None of the parties
possessed the discipline necessary to successfully rebuild parliamentary government in Pakistan.

In late June it was announced that Mr. Gurmani would be
the temporary chairman of the opening session of the second
Constituent Assembly which met at Muree, a cool hill station,
on July 6, 1955. It met not only in the dual capacity of its
predecessor, but with its predecessor's short sessions, dilatory
debate, and aimlessness in the face of edicts issued from ministry offices or Government House.

The states in the second Constituent Assembly

On the third day of the session, Mr. Suhrawardy introduced
a bill for the representation of the states. The rulers were to
nominate members from Bahawalpur and Baluchistan States

Union while the Khairpur Legislative Assembly would select its member. The governor of the North-West Frontier Province would select the tribal and frontier state representatives.

> much as we desire that the representatives should come to this House through the method of election, in this particular case, by Instruments of Accession and an agreement entered into between the Ruler of Bahawalpur and the Government of Pakistan, the Ruler has reserved to himself the right that he be bound by the constitution which may be framed by the Assembly provided that in the Assembly his representative whom he will nominate will participate.[17]

The Law Minister explained that the ruler of Khairpur had demanded no such power and that the Legislative Assembly was therefore free to elect a representative. The nominative powers of the Council of Rulers of the Baluchistan States Union were "in conformity with the agreement arrived at between the Negotiating Committee and in conformity with the resolutions which were passed by the late Constituent Assembly." [18] He noted that the states on the frontier were not grouped but the requirements of the House made collective representation necessary, and he suggested that the provincial governor could best judge how to represent the states.

These proposals were the negation of all the liberalization for which previous governments had worked. Interim constitutions in most of the states allowed the people a voice in their future but only in Khairpur were they actually allowed to speak, and there only after the assembly had perjured itself.

The references to Bahawalpur are a legal puzzle. The initial Instrument of Accession and Supplementary Agreement of December 30, 1948, did allow the Amir to nominate his representative to the Constituent Assembly, but the political evolution of the state did not stop in 1948. The state constitution of 1952 transferred full powers to the cabinet of elected officials and the leader of the House assumed the responsibilities and powers previously held for the ruler by the appointed chief minister. The fiction of representation of the prince was maintained under both arrangements, but it was clearly a parallel to the British cabinet system in which the ruler had no real power.

Furthermore, the Bahawalpur Majlis, as a matter of course, sent its leader to the Constituent Assembly. The Amir, in dismissing the assembly under article 74 of the constitution, was allowed, with the consent of the governor-general, to suspend all agencies of the state government except the court. Therefore the dissolution could be justified under state law, but for the federal government to later claim that the Amir alone had the right to nominate representatives in his sovereign capacity was to mock the whole system. The Law Minister should have been aware that the bill was against the spirit of every decision of the high court since the Usif Patel case.

Mr. Suhrawardy also referred to an "agreement" with the Nawab. The appendix lists every published document defining a relationship between Bahawalpur and the central government. The claim that the Amir held an exclusive right cannot be found in any of these instruments. If an unpublished agreement existed, or if the Governor-General concluded a special agreement on December 14, prior to agreement on the unification of West Pakistan, the Constituent Assembly had a right not only to see the document, but to challenge the right of the cabinet to conclude it without confirmation in the House.

Some members of the Assembly demanded that the Bahawalpur Majlis be reconvened. The demand was refused. An alternative proposal was that the Amir should nominate a panel of prospective representatives from which the Assembly might choose two. The demand was refused and Mr. Suhrawardy saw the bill through its third reading and successful passage.

The government was repeatedly questioned about its actions in Bahawalpur. In September Mr. Suhrawardy said that the ministry of the state was dismissed because the Chief Minister had bribed legislators with factories or industrial shares [19] and that since section 92-A of the national constitution could not be used because of the state's federal position, the Assembly had to be dismissed. This view ignored clause 1 of the emergency provisions article of the state constitution which allowed the Amir to divest the majlis of any powers which were being abused, so long as the governor-general concurred.

In November, prior to the passage of the constitution, drafting experts introduced legislation which would remove what remained of the Bahawalpur Majlis. It stated: "It is now recognized that the Bahawalpur Ministry was not dissolved but suspended so that henceforth the Bahawalpur Legislative Assembly also is dissolved on the enactment date." [20] One would be hard pressed to find a parallel to the end of democracy in Bahawalpur.

But in August, Syed A. N. S. Gardezi and Chaudhuri Abdus Salam (formerly the leader of the opposition in the state) took their oaths, as did Mumtaz Qizilbash of Khairpur, Mir Bai Khan, the Nawab of Makran for the Baluchistan States Union, and the Wali of Swat for the frontier states.

The Constitution

On August 7, 1955, it was announced that Ghulam Mohammad's absence from the country was due to serious illness and that his successor would be the acting governor-general, Major General Iskander Mirza. Mohammad Ali Bogra, so long the middle man in a cruel tug of war, resigned and Chaudhri Mohammad Ali, a civil servant trained in finance, was appointed prime minister.

On the next day, Suhrawardy mooted plans for a 310-member West Pakistan provincial assembly in which Bahawalpur was to have 23 seats, the Baluchistan States Union 7, Khairpur 4, Swat 6, Dir 2, Chitral 1, and Amb 1. In Bahawalpur the nonofficial members of district boards would be polled to elect the provincial representatives, whereas the state jirgas would select representatives from the North-West Frontier states and Baluchistan States Union. The Khairpur Legislative Assembly would nominate the state's member. Surely no democracy in history has been as innocent of elections as that of Pakistan.

One Unit was a continuing priority of the federal cabinet. The state representatives, not unexpectedly, supported the extinction of their states, although for reasons sometimes less than noble. Chaudhri Abdus Salam (Bahawalpur) told the House that all segments of the population approved of consolidation—zamindars because their taxes would be reduced to the level of the Punjab, cultivators because the Punjab would (miraculously?) allow the state more water, traders because they would get more import licenses, and merchants because food grain shipments to the provinces would no longer be restricted.

The final form of the consolidation statute was read in the assembly on August 23, 1955. The draft held few surprises except that the Baluchistan states were were no longer listed as "Special Areas." In the assembly debates the public was given tantalizing glimpses of backroom political deals, however, but they were part of vindictive politics. "A fragmented West Pakistan has really nothing to ask from East Pakistan because the realities of the situation in any conceivable pattern would already have given East Pakistan an inconvertible superiority." [21]

This candid and quite correct exposition of Pakistan's binary federalism was realistic because the national party of the country had broken down under the assaults of both East and West. Having thus developed sectional politics, both wings tried to convert the balance into hegemony. Apparently no one seriously questioned whether a unitary West Pakistan was an answer to either the national, federal, or West Pakistan problems. Neither did they consider the problems of absolute parity and the almost inevitable paralysis which was sure to follow. Once more the politicians had ignored both the national vision and the substantive issues which might have made it a dream come true. In the Götterdämmerung which was to follow, they would receive justice.

In the face of strident criticism from the rump of the Muslim League, now emaciated by the loss of members to the Republican party, the National Awami party, and proponents of unitary government, the last reading of the West Pakistan (Consolidation) Act was scheduled by the Prime Minister for no later than October 1, 1955. By the middle of September it was clear it would pass. The cursory and uninspiring debates which followed saw bargaining for small favors. On September 30, 1955, the Act was passed and six of the ten states which acceded to Pakistan were lost in the mist of history. Their demise was formally celebrated on October 14, 1955, when the Governor-General proclaimed the establishment of West Pakistan.

Following the enactment of the consolidation bill, the constitution was delayed by the nature of electorates,[22] regional autonomy, and the reinstitution of zonal federation in West Pakistan.

The final draft of the constitution made three relationships possible for princely states. The first was the complete integration which was the fate of Bahawalpur, Khairpur, and the Baluchistan states. A second position possible was as a "Special Area" under article 104, which provided that the executive authority of the province of West Pakistan was empowered to act in the area subject to the President's concurrence. The third option, part XII of chapter III, made provision for the accession and inclusion of Kashmir. It also guaranteed the tax-free privy purses which had been granted prior to the constitution provided that such funds would be charged against the Consolidated Fund of West Pakistan. Section 3 of article 202 guaranteed the personal status of the rulers:

In the exercise of any authority to make laws and in the exercise of the executive authority of the Federation or a province, due regard shall be had to the guarantees or assurances given under any such agreement as is referred to in clause (1) [privy purses] with regard to the personal rights, privileges and dignities of the Ruler of any such State as is referred to in that clause.[23]

The constitution was finally ready for a nation weary from the wait on February 29, 1956. On March 5, 1956, Iskander Mirza was elected Pakistan's first president, once more, needless to say, by indirect election. Eight years and seven months after independence, the people of the promised state had their constitution. Now came the task of using it in the interests of the Muslim renaissance.

Attend to your leaders who are wrecking the country. Don't talk of the external dangers. The real danger is within the country. Can't you see it? *General Mohammad Ayub Khan, to Rawalpindi journalists, 1958*

X I I

The Bloodless Revolution

The constitution was no sooner published than it was brought under fire. The politicians who refused to accept consolidation were joined by others who disagreed with the central-provincial division of powers. Criticism of foreign policy mounted as Pakistan and the United States moved closer in alliance. Confusion marked the political scene in both provincial and national assemblies and members found it expedient to shift their support hourly. The press and public gasped at the gyrations of political coalitions while the country's economy sagged and the balance of payments problem deepened. Landlords continued to frustrate change in West Pakistan while the Bengalis were permitted a short but sweet moment of triumph with the shrewd H. S. Suhrawardy as prime minister. After thirteen months he too was scuttled. The frustrations of the politically sensitive redoubled.

The undisciplined politics of the country found examples in three arenas of public life, the federal government and East and West Pakistan assemblies. At every level there were actually two parties, one controlled or strongly influenced by the

President and his aides and one composed of the hopelessly divided and scattered champions of parliamentary government. At every decisive moment, the executive officers of the state intervened to make and unmake ministries, and where they could not, used their powers to dissolve the assembly and rule by edict until their followers could regroup.

The inevitable result of this style of politics was that the president of the republic would one day assume complete control. From the dismissal of Khwaja Nazimuddin in 1953 through the dissolution of the Constituent Assembly and the ramrod politics of One Unit, the chief and determining force in Pakistani history was the Governor-General, flanked by the civil and military services. Astute politicians gravitated toward executive authority while the parliament devoured itself with the blessings of Government House. It comes as little surprise that the Commander-in-Chief of the army was asked to take over the government on at least three occasions, and that he finally did.

As early as 1954, and probably before, letters were circulated among the elite of the country arguing that parliamentary democracy on the British model did not suit the country.[1] Certainly the stresses of Pakistan's politics were subjecting it to a brutal testing. Another view associated with the executive branch of the government was that federalism was not a sound constitutional system for a country with multiple linguistic and ethnic divisions.[2]

Thanks to the hierarchical system of authority and organization possessed by the army, civil service, and administrators, these groups could present their views with consistency and unity whereas the parliamentarians were extremely divided. No party caucus could any longer resolve the differences of wilful men. In West Pakistan, the Republican party and the provincial governor (Mr. Gurmani) were pitted against the Muslim League. When Dr. Khan Sahib was chosen chief minister, the Muslim League asked him to accept party discipline or resign. He refused, and on April 23, 1956, the tiger changed his stripes as the majority of the West Pakistan Legislative Assembly crossed the floor to join the Chief Minister's new party. When the vote of confidence was called, Mumtaz Qizilbash of Khairpur cast the tie-breaking vote in favor of the Republicans. His rewards were soon forthcoming.

Hassan Mahmud, former chief minister of Bahawalpur, returned from his self-imposed but prudent exile in Europe and America and joined the government as minister for local bodies. Later he wrote a book in the party's defense.[3] The Jam Sahib of Las Bela became minister for jails. There was a portfolio for every familiar name in the assembly.

The myth of representative government had long since vanished. The original members of the provincial assemblies, elected in the first instance by no more than 15 percent [4] of the electorate, had erected an edifice on indirect elections. West Pakistan and the nation waited for the first national vote which was continuously postponed. Optimists hoped that by 1958, eleven years after independence, the people of Pakistan might have a chance to judge their leaders. Since the vote was always in the future, representatives had no need to be concerned with their public image and devoted their talents to the "game."

Politics were not dull, whatever else they may have been. On the national stage Suhrawardy and Mirza fought publicly and regularly while in West Pakistan the League was always within a hairbreadth of unseating the government. In both situations business was impossible and intrigue mandatory.

West Pakistan offers an example of the *immobilisme* for

which the French are famous. In March, 1957, the Muslim League was confident that it would be able to topple Khan Sahib's government. On March 20 it pressed a vote on a finance bill which would have censured the government. The floor whips of the Republicans were unsure of their ability to win and directed Hassan Mahmud to filibuster until evening recess. After dinner Governor Gurmani suspended the ministry and assembly. A few months later a new Republican ministry was sworn in, but the assembly was convoked only in September and then its session lasted only eight days.

It was rule, not government. In 1957 the West Pakistan legislature passed seventy-five bills while the Governor issued eighty-nine ordinances.[5] When the routine matters are subtracted from the Assembly's legislation, it is apparent how little the Assembly accomplished in comparison to the Governor. In any case, the Governor controlled the Assembly through the Republican party of which he was the patron. His ability to dominate had nothing to do with the effectiveness of government edicts, however, and the civil order problem deepened.

The pitched struggle in West Pakistan found its most destructive manifestations at the center where, since Bengal had been lost to the League, coalition government was the rule. With two fairly matched parties from both wings, there were multiple options which, in terms of platform, were patently absurd. At one point the central government was faced with the prospect of restoring federal government in West Pakistan because the provincial Republican party ministry, in order to gain the votes of the National Awami party, had reversed itself. The goal of any political party is to stay in power but these serpentine maneuverings were outrageous.

At this stage responsible men in every branch of government rebelled, regardless of their feelings on the unitary province organization. General Mohammad Ayub Khan, a strong advocate of One Unit, instructed the President and the Prime Minister that they were to publicly guarantee the integrity of the constitutional structure at least until after the first general elections.[6] Mr. I. I. Chundrigar, himself no enthusiastic advocate of the plan, was not ready to see it undone under the circumstances because the constitution itself was thus called into question—the result, of course, of the unscrupulous forcing of the original consolidation.

Mr. Chundrigar was aware of the substantial advantages of the plan as well as the passions it engendered. He noted the importance of the Indian government's plans to divert large amounts of water from the eastern rivers. Since the states and provinces were assigned quotas, some of which found marginal use, the national interest demanded reassignment to maintain the highest possible food production.

He accepted the notion that the administrative structure of the different provinces was altogether too heavy and costly and added that better administration would be the result if local favoritism was eliminated. He cited the smuggling operations in Bahawalpur, Sind, and Khairpur as examples of continuing problems which were not met by local authorities. Even in matters where cooperation between the provincial and state authorities was necessary, political rivalries inhibited sensible solutions.

Most important, however, was the lack of control of central government over the units. The federal guarantee might have been productive of political liberty and the growth or recognition of multiple centers of power, but instead it became the screen behind which modernization was inhibited, graft was taken in unseemly degree, and the national wealth was squandered. In short, the most liberal and modernized elite of the nation found its program frustrated at every juncture by the legal fossil of British imperial rule. The only solution was unity and unity was impossible so long as provincial politicians held a veto over structural change. They therefore had to be forced to concede.[7]

The appeal of the arguments is obvious, but as Mr. Chundrigar would have agreed, an early vote after a nation-wide election might have confirmed unity without resort to the intrigues which laid the basis for later disruption. The assemblies, open arenas of political contest, were brought into public disfavor since their bickering was common knowledge, but the game was also played in the ministries and chancelleries of the executive branch. The later hypocritical charges that the assemblies were overcome with factionalism are quite true but the executive authorities were hardly innocent in sponsoring it. People would later say that Pakistan's democracy didn't stumble, it was pushed. It might be added that the bullies then accused the injured party of being clumsy and unsuited to walking.

As the political crisis deepened in 1957, the army found itself drawn into partisan struggles. With the civil service, they watched the fratricidal dismemberment of their country and became increasingly impatient. "Let it [democracy] function in Pakistan, but for God's sake tell your leaders to behave properly. You know their language. I don't." [8] The author of the phrase would soon master "their" language.

State politics

Even after passage of the constitution, the nation morbidly watched the vultures pick it to pieces. Once more the public gaze was taken from the essential life of the nation and its crying apolitical needs. And to judge from the life of the villager, nothing had changed except that perhaps there was a little more graft, arrogance on the part of the administration, and increasing frustration. The "new system" was operating on the old rules.

The North-West Frontier states, even under the 1956 constitution, were autonomous. Dir even refused to send representatives to the West Pakistan assembly and would not cooperate with the old enemy, the Wali of Swat, who represented the four states in the federal capital. In October, 1956, Prime Minister Suhrawardy and Provincial Governor Gurmani were in Peshawar for a meeting of the political agents from the frontier districts. The Prime Minister was asked if the Nawab of Dir had agreed to cooperate with the assembly. The reply that no one had discussed it reflects the continued intransigence of the Nawab.

Kalat, legally a regular district of West Pakistan, proved equally troublesome. It was, as some Baluch political circles complained, totally lawless. "There is still an area of this country extending to 70,000 square miles of West Pakistan where there is still no law, no courts and practically no administration—The Kalat Division, previously known as the Baluchistan States Union." [9] Attempts to tighten administration in the area were often rebuffed. In April 1957, for example, a government official and a local *sardar*, the latter having "had a free hand before the establishment of One Unit," were in a skirmish. The tribal leader, challenged by the tahsildar (officer in charge of a small revenue district), ordered his tribal forces, paid and equipped by the government, to open fire. One policeman was killed and the victorious *sardar* took another policeman to his village and ordered him publicly stoned to death. Shortly thereafter, the Commissioner of Kalat Division decided to establish his headquarters in Khuzdar, Jhalawan, nearer the area of tribal discontent.[10]

Nor was this an isolated example of tribal rebellion. Throughout Baluchistan, particularly in Kalat, there was unrest following provincial integration. So long as the tribes were strongly represented in their own territorial group, they believed that their pleas for aid would not be denied. In this they were joined by many of the provincial politicians denied real power in the final constitutional settlement. It was by no accident that a contemporary book by a Baluch author began: "Let the Baluch people read their history, recollect the past, review the present, resign to unity and discipline and resolve for a glorious and firm future." [11] Less polite tracts were also rumored to be in circulation under the sponsorship of the Khan of Kalat.

Matters were made worse in the face of growing national disunity. In May Dr. Khan Sahib was assassinated and the politics of violence seemed in the offing. The coalition government of I. I. Chundrigar was removed after two months and Firoz Khan Noon took office. Soon thereafter Mr. Gurmani was on trial in a libel suit which named him a traitor to Pakistan and in which the nation's Prime Minister was deeply and criminally involved. In East Bengal during raucous provincial debates, disorders in the chamber led to the death of the Deputy Speaker on September 23, 1958. Abdul Qayyum Khan, the blustering leader of the Muslim League, let it be known that if national elections were not immediately and firmly set, there would be bloody revolution.

Suddenly, in early October, 1958, a rebellion broke out in Kalat. News reports gave the grim outlines of the striking of the green and white national ensign of Pakistan and the subsequent hoisting of the Khan's ancestoral banner over the Kalat fort. The Khan's effort to call upon a tribal rebellion was reported as was his refusal, before open revolt, to come to Karachi to discuss his demands.

The government story is fascinating reading. The Khan viewed One Unit as the arbitrary end of his Baluchistan empire and decided to reassert his independence in tribal war. Prince Karim, leader of the leftist Ustaman Gul party and the Afghan lashkar of 1948, and the Khan's uncle, Sultan Ibrahim Khan, allegedly were seeking Afghan aid in the rebellion. Seditious pamphlets financed by the Khan accused the government of forcing Kalat's accession to Pakistan, which was true, and named both Jinnah and Liaquat Ali Khan as kafirs (unbelievers).

Having laid the popular foundation for his insurrection, he then denounced his loyalty to Pakistan, refused to meet the President to explain it, and resisted arrest with three hundred tribesmen. Supposedly he attempted to lure the arresting party into an ambush but was finally overcome with an armored vehicle after three of his retainers were killed. On October 6, he was taken into custody and divested of all distinctions, privileges, and annuities, and the crown was transferred to his eldest son, Daud Jan, who was home from school in the United Kingdom.

Two days later Major-General Iskander Mirza seized power in a bloodless, quiet revolution because of the "dangers" which he saw confronting the state. He warned: "Another type of adventurer among them thinks it fit to go to foreign countries and attempt direct alignment with them which can only be described as high treason." [12] Surely the Khan was guilty, according to government reports, of high treason, and his rebellion was interpreted by many as the act that brought the government's patience to an end.

Despite the fact that the Khan was immediately arrested, the bill of particulars against him was modified and his imprisonment changed to house arrest in Hazara district. In the summer of 1960 his allowances were restored, and a ceremonial bodyguard assigned to his door rendered salutes and prohibited audiences. In 1962, after the end of martial law, the Muslim League demanded his release, and on November 6, President Ayub restored him to his throne with full privileges.

Sources close to the Khan say that the case against him was a fabrication, that there was no flagpole atop a fort on which to raise a personal flag. In any case, the princes of Pakistan were allowed to fly their personal banners on their homes and vehicles. A second curious discrepancy is that the Khan contends that army units made his arrest at 2 A.M. when he was asleep, that his bodyguard, a detachment of West Pakistan police, opened fire only because the intruders did not identify themselves and there had been tribal disturbances.[13]

The cases of central government and the Khan of Kalat are so divergent and the prosecution of the ruler so dilatory that one must give credence to the rumors that the rebellion was less than it seemed. One story is that Iskander Mirza, poised for the *putsch* of October 8, needed a dramatic example of national disunity to justify his takeover. Another view is that the Noon government was displeased with the Khan's Muslim League politics and was avenging an earlier embarassment when the Khan refused to give damning testimony in the Gurmani defamation case. Final answers to these questions are not likely to be forthcoming for several years. The episode illustrates the mood of Baluchistan, however, and the tension that was all too common in the fall of 1958.

The lessons learned in the dismissal of the first Constituent Assembly were not ignored by the new revolutionaries. The constitution was abrogated, martial law proclaimed, political parties, parliaments, and cabinets dismissed, and the army enthroned. The Supreme Court was specifically prohibited from bridging the gap. Twenty days later the President was sent to London for playing a dangerous game in army politics, and General Mohammad Ayub Khan fell heir to the task which had apparently been his fate since 1953.

The martial law administration

A full or fair consideration of the record of the military government of Pakistan would be out of place here. But unlike some of the West Pakistan regimes, it has made a conscious and well publicized effort to modernize the social, economic, and political life of the country. Having watched government after government wind down the fruitless paths of mystic appeals and passionate issues, its leaders have prohibited the politics of the past, purged the symbols of the previous order, and turned to what had too often been ignored before, the rebirth of the nation.

On October 18, 1958, a land reforms commission was established with a mandate to plan an effective redistribution system. Its report was finished and in the hands of an implementation commission in less than six months. Few changes could have had a more far-reaching effect on the future pattern of Pakistani life. The princes were most unhappy with the reforms because they had been guaranteed jagir lands which must now be surrendered, even though at a fair rate of compensation.

The regime has clearly endorsed the unity of West Pakistan and has frequently alluded to the need for a unitary government embracing both East and West Pakistan. Under no circumstances could one imagine a return to the federal West Pakistan in which the states might once more be autonomous. Further, the latitude of the princes within their areas by means of traditional controls has been minimized by the effective programs of the government to modernize the basis of politics.

The Basic Democracies Program, about which so much has been written, is, in effect, an attempt to revolutionize not only the tenure system of rural Pakistan, but the traditional political structure which enfranchised landlord and headman, to the detriment of both modernization and peasant welfare. In those areas which are much less developed, the government is taking special pains to develop such resources as are available, and to prevent a breakdown of order. In Baluchistan, for example, several tribal leaders were hanged in 1960 for actions in violation of martial law regulations concerning anti-state behavior.

Perhaps the most relevant "reform" of the Ayub regime was in Dir state. The Nawab, who had weathered the strongest and most resolute governments in Karachi and Lahore, finally bowed before the Pakistan government. Throughout the period of independence, the Wali of Swat had set examples of fine development and administration and the central authorities were anxious for Dir to progress as well. As the days passed, the government had increasing cause to "tick him off" [14] but his authority, rather than being diminished, actually increased. By intrigue and war he had managed to impose his rule on the previously independent tribes of central Dir. Mention was made of a tribal rebellion but the Khan won the day.

On September 28, 1960, the foreign minister of Pakistan, Manzur Qadir, charged that an Afghan invasion was expected in the Bajaur area immediately abutting on Dir. In the flurry of activity preceding actual armed clashes the Nawab of Dir and his eldest son, the governor of Jandool district, were charged with "double-dealing" with the Afghan government, and were arrested. On October 11, Prince Khusro, a minor son of the Nawab, was recognized, the government of Pakistan had finally assimilated all of its princes.

It is unlikely that the frontier states will be abolished or the ruler's authority diminished so long as it is used in accordance with the national interest. The observations of Robert Trumbell in 1948 are valid today because tribal organization continues to be the basis for power in both Baluchistan and the frontier area in the Northwest. The task is the same, to modernize the society so that it can be brought into national life as a source of strength for Pakistan.

The fact that the martial law authorities inherited the most developed society in Pakistan's history should not be ignored. The rebellions of the past had been put down just as the budgets of Bahawalpur and Khairpur had been expanded to meet the needs of people in education and social welfare. The Pakistan movement has always been true to its aims of lifting up the community. In spite of the confusions of politics, the greed of the new middle class, and the provincial wars of a divided country, the vision and needs seen by the founders of the country have remained true. The revolutionary government of 1958 disdains the terms, but speaks of a quiet revolution. Its leaders sense that the mission has remained constant, but the execution needs more discipline. The reports of all the reform commissions, the integration of village AID, the Basic Democracy's system, and the constitution of 1962 are the new charters of the Muslims of the subcontinent. More than their predecessors they reflect social reality, but to state the problem is not to solve it and perhaps once more the phrase of Mohammad Ali Jinnah, "Faith, Unity, and Discipline," must be heard, believed, and practiced.

Jinnah . . . solved this particular problem swiftly and well . . . to effect on his own initiative arrangements which were not unsatisfactory to the Princes and made them a source of strength to Pakistan.

Aga Khan III, Memoirs

X I I I

On Treating with Princes

The arrest and deposal of the Khan of Kalat and the Nawab of Dir brought to an end the vitality of the princely order in Pakistan. To be sure, fiefs may remain centers of tribal or traditional culture but the day has passed when edicts from Rawalpindi can be ignored. For the first time in its history the government of Pakistan is supreme throughout its territories. This is a landmark not only in the life of the nation but in the history of the western reaches of the subcontinent.

The process by which successive governments, with remarkable consistency and tenacity, brought this to pass holds some lessons for future generations, but it also presents some difficult questions. The broad perspectives of the problem emerge only now, out of the context of the past fifteen years.

Why could India beggar almost six hundred rulers in a few years while for Pakistan ten princes posed such firm obstacles to modernization? The quick explanation generally heard in Pakistan is that there was no reason to hurry and more pressing problems received priority. For India state assimilation was a *sine qua non* to national life; to Pakistan it was one of many tasks.

More specifically, however, Pakistan's states were extremely resistant to change for several unusual reasons. Initially they were heterogeneous, not only in size and population but in development and administration. A comprehensive state modernization plan on the model of the Indian Union did not fit Pakistan's circumstances. As well, the tribal states of the western frontier presented difficulties not found elsewhere in the subcontinent. The diversity of the units and the general underdevelopment of modern society in them challenged the government's administrators.

Not only were the problems complex but the new nation faced an uncertain future even within the more developed districts. Initially, at least, policy lacked the broadsword of the enforcer and Karachi could not, and dared not challenge governments which were maintaining some sort of law and order merely to create a more uniform or democratic structure. The anemia of the central government was more serious because of the lack of well-developed or even nascent liberal groups within the states which could have aided in the modification of princely autocracy.

A third general limitation placed on Pakistan's government was of its own making. The acting constitution of the country was the slightly modified Government of India Act, 1935, which had been drafted to assure the rulers of tolerant treatment. The legal guarantees of the constitution were protected by the federal court, and defied unilateral abrogation. The protection afforded by the laws was supported by the legacy of the Muslim League's prepartition tactics of alliance and support of the princely order.

Equally important must have been the domestic implications of the international controversies surrounding the Kashmir and Pukhtunistan issues. Pakistan had to be circumspect in its

dealing with local rulers lest world opinion see no difference
between Indian and Pakistani policy toward the princes. As
well the whole argument of the government in the Pukhtunistan dispute was that the Pathans were satisfied with their status
and that Kabul's interests were only irredentist. Every ruler
understood the importance of these restrictions on Karachi
which favored their position.

As the debate over the federal division of powers assumed a
paramount importance, provincial rivalries and interests also
delayed radical change in West Pakistan. Since the ideology
of the state carried with it no injunctions dooming the states,
indeed, generally favored their continuing independent status,
federal authorities were inhibited from reorganizing internal
boundaries pending a final constitutional settlement.

Each of these five broad restrictions upon the central government in itself would have explained long delays in state reform and it was therefore apparent from the outset that the
state policy of Pakistan would be cautious, moderate, and
tailored to the particularities of each principality. Moderation
sometimes proved more a screen than a reality, but it explains
the tolerance with which the Princes were treated throughout
the period.

The tools of diplomacy

The seemingly invulnerable negotiating position of the
princely order in Pakistan necessitated an imaginative diplomacy on the part of the central government. The most important and successful tool in negotiations was money. Prior
to independence, Mr. Jinnah offered tempting terms to rulers
willing to accede to Pakistan, and his successors in Government
House were willing to buy loyalty and reform.

The amount of the privy purse awarded to the petty monarchs was the subject for countless discussions. The prudent prince walked a fine line between surrender and arrogance, and the Amir of Bahawalpur was known as the most shrewd and skillful ruler in the country. He was successful, for example, in obtaining not only a large allowance but the right to convert 40 percent of it to precious sterling so that he could continue his summer residence in England. He was also allowed an unlimited import license to maintain his elegant standard of living in Bahawalpur. Similarly he was allowed: "Full ownership of jewels, ornaments, shares, securities and all private property, movable as well as immovable not being State properties in the date of the agreement. If the item is in dispute, the declaration of the Government of Pakistan is binding." [1]

Allusion has been made to the cost of the settlement in Baluchistan with the Khan of Kalat and his fellow rulers [2] but in gross terms the amounts awarded under the One Unit plan are most illustrative of the price of cooperation. Central government appropriations for privy purses and subsidies increased from 1,798,000 rupees in 1955–56 to 5,600,000 rupees in 1956–57 following amalgamation. [3] And this in a country desperate for development capital and foreign exchange.

A second prerogative power resting with the federal government in its negotiations with the rulers was its ability to recognize or modify titles and honors. In prepartition India, the vendettas arising from protocol within the princely order were the most passionate and bitter in the country. Accustomed as they were to a regal banner fluttering from their cars, homes, and offices and to the salutes of their personal honor guards, the princes would have been distraught had they been compelled to become merely rich commoners. Thus article 3 of the agreement with the Amir of Bahawalpur provided that "His Highness the Amir of Bahawalpur and the members of his family shall be entitled to all of the personal privileges, dignities and titles enjoyed by them whether within or outside the territory of the State immediately before the date of this agreement." [4] The Constitution of 1956 also guaranteed the rights and privileges of the princes.

A third available instrument for negotiation was the power of the central government to make territorial concessions on a *quid pro quo* basis. There is some reason to believe this was the case with both the Khan of Kalat and the Wali of Swat. In both the prepartition and later periods of state negotiation, the Khan of Kalat refused to accept change in Baluchistan unless he benefited territorially. During the tense negotiations of 1948 for the state's accession, his advisors noted that the accession principles were accepted but certain demands relating to Makran had not been.

The Wali of Swat coveted Kalam region north of his state. In 1947 Swat forces seized *de facto* control but it was not recognized. Although the Wali was generally cooperative in other aspects of national politics, he would not accept the obligations of the provincial list of the constitution until he was given Kalam. As a face-saving device, the government kept title but appointed the Prince their executor for the region in return for which Swat became a federated unit of Pakistan in 1954.

A final tool in the hands of the federal negotiators was military force. Despite the lack of evidence that force was used to compel the princes to comply with Pakistan's demands in more than two cases (Kalat and Dir), the army must have been at the bargaining table, sometimes in fact but always in spirit. Initially, the army of Pakistan was thinly drawn over hundreds of miles of endangered territory and the isolated rulers had little to fear. Vulnerability is relative, however, and as the Dominion grew stronger and more confident, the threat of force became an increasingly plausive device. Perhaps the best evidence of its importance was that it did not have to be used frequently.

The spirit of negotiations

The description of a political process so irregular and subtle as state negotiations is made more difficult because no master blueprint guided the policy makers. Individuals were allowed considerable latitude in matching their minds to various state problems and it is frequently difficult to see on what basis a particular program was adopted. Not all of the events of state-federal relations were determined by the personalities involved, however, and deep currents in the society were running to consolidation and central control. These spelled an end not only to the princes who were progressively ushered out of Pakistan's history, but also increased the difficulties for practicing state politicians.

The first master of the state portfolio was the founder of the state himself. There can be not the slightest doubt that he was the most tolerant states' minister in the nation's history for he had personally guaranteed the independence of the princes within Pakistan. The judgment of the Agha Khan as to Mr. Jinnah's solution of the state problem has one significant phrase, "his practical Bismarckian sense of 'the best possible.'" Perhaps in 1947 the best possible solution of the princely problem was a tolerant acceptance of the princes' autonomy within Pakistan but times changed and Mr. Jinnah's political heirs faced new situations.

Liaquat Ali Khan's handling of state affairs was an inter-regnum, unfortunately his trademark. Shifting slowly from the ideology of a social movement to considerations of national interest, he was groping his way toward change while his real energies were committed to foreign and provincial wars. After the Indian army emerged victorious in Kashmir and Hy-derabad, Liaquat transferred the tasks of bargaining to Dr. Mahmud Husain.

The new minister, a tactful but aggressive personality, found himself with much more power vis-a-vis the princes than his predecessors. Popular agitation in Bahawalpur and Khairpur offered him a wedge to force open the closed door of princely prerogatives. By 1950 it was perfectly clear that their rule was over and that their deposition was only a matter of time and circumstance. To the credit of the rulers, they assumed their new status with little ill-feeling. Rather they turned their energies to the preservation of their wealth. Dr. Husain's officials were happy to accommodate their demands since privy purses were paid from state revenues not available to the federation in any case. Perhaps, however, the government was too free with other people's money.

Nevertheless, the changes carried out by the cabinet of Liaquat Ali Khan and Mahmud Husain led to the expansion of central power in the states. The rulers were edged out of power quietly and reenthroned benign hereditary governors, each a Rajpramukh. Compulsive reaction to state crises gave way to reflective constitutional planning although deep differences were evident among policy makers, the broader political community, and the press.

When Mushtaq Gurmani replaced Mahmud Husain as states' minister, *Dawn*, the loyal *vox rex*, branded piecemeal reform no longer tolerable. The era of Liaquat's forgetful tolerance and Mahmud Husain's tact gave way to one of Gurmani's dictations. The government was immeasurably stronger and federalism was being brought into question throughout West Pakistan. The minister himself is credited by many as the prime mover of an amalgamation which would doom the states completely. It is curious that he was appointed to such high office, given his earlier record in Bahawalpur and his reputation as a master of intrigue.

Mr. Gurmani inherited a well-advanced state program. The princes were represented in the Constituent Assembly and the rulers' power had been transferred, in most cases, to a chief minister responsive to government wishes. Only on the frontier did the state tigers still have their teeth, as the Minister reminded the nation in 1952. "Perhaps it is not fully realized that the organization of the Frontier States is very different from those of other states and areas in Pakistan. . . . The Rulers of these States are regarded and trusted leaders of the tribes enjoying their confidence." [5] Elsewhere, however, Mr. Gurmani recognized his strength and ignored no occasion to demonstrate it. The letdown of the rulers could not have been more dramatic, for he rebuffed each in his turn, especially the Amir of Bahawalpur.

The Baluchistan States Union was the first success of the minister who had previously stood against a unified Baluchistan. The ministry practically hummed as its chief made over his ancestral home in a new image, an image ultimately of a unified West Pakistan. By the end of his tenure, the princes had accepted federal status and had become part of the larger political life of the country.

Major General Iskander Mirza became the master of the States' Ministry following the dissolution of the assembly by Ghulam Mohammad. He was cut of the same cloth as his immediate predecessor and his policies aimed at control and direction.

It might be fair to characterize the policies toward the princes in this period as more tolerant than those toward the state politicians. Previous administrations had generally sought power in order to transfer it to local parties. The trend begun with Mr. Gurmani was one of usurpation of the powers previously transferred to popular control. The states could not hope to escape national political aberrations. Fazlur Rahman's description of the politics of the unification of West Pakistan seems an apt description of what happened to the infant assemblies in the states:

You have realized, I hope, the nature of the methods that have been resorted to to secure the support of the One Unit Bill. These methods have been dismissal of ministers, dissolution of assemblies, putting in jail of people. Even criminal cases have been threatened against High Court judges.[6]

The quest for uniformity

The end of the states and the pensioning of their rulers was a predictable event in the subcontinent as early as 1900. Forces at work in the world doomed the small and the backward. Nevertheless, the state problem in Pakistan was conceived as part of a federal structure of government—a notion altogether incorrect. Administrators and politicians were unsatisfied with the complex of governor's provinces, chief commissioner's areas, states, tribal zones, and federal enclaves bequeathed by the untidy British. And since leaders in some of these legally autonomous regions did not have a political outlook similar to that of Karachi, the notion of administrative decentralization was questioned and then rejected.

A broader search for national unity underpinned provincial

reorganization and the abolition of the states just as it dictated
the quasi-federal division of powers in the constitution which
was heavily weighted in favor of the national government. Not
only were the structure and spirit of the localities to be cast
in the image of the central government, but governmental life
was to be fitted to a common pattern. It was assumed that
Pakistani nationality would emerge from political uniformity.
Party life was to be dominated by the Muslim League so that
the political consensus would grow parallel to administrative
forms.

The key to all change in the princely states was the chief
minister. Mumtaz Qizilbash, Khairpur's unique leader, noted
that as long as "the Chief Minister is appointed with the approval of the central government he is subject to their advice
and guidance and they in turn are accountable to the party
which put them in power." [7] This linkage, considered essential
to the health of the state, could not be maintained once the
people of the state came to understand that local authorities
were to serve local interests. It is a measure of the degree of
tension between local and national leaders that the Bahawalpur
Majlis was dismissed, the assembly in Khairpur intimidated,
and the Khan of Kalat forced to accept dictation by the army.

An alternative to the federal pattern inherited in 1947 was
the regrouping of regions capable of independent, solvent provincial development. Amalgamation or union was a necessity
in a country where the population of federal units ranged from
43 million to 9,000, yet any such change was thought to bring
into question the federal principle. What confused the issue
further was that federalism was defended as a guarantee of
civil liberty because of its interposition of an authority between the citizen and the central government. In fact, it was
the opposite.

The logic of increasing central control which is the primary theme of Pakistan's history was also supported by the growth of a sizable middle class whose interests lay in national unity. In West Pakistan at least, the defenders of the federal scheme were largely feudal or aristocratic elements who saw in central control domination by the bourgeoisie of the cities. Only later did the provincial middle class elements begin to see in central control a threat to their limited but secure domain.

Regional amalgamation and the reconstitution of a federal Pakistan were not tried. The case of Baluchistan is a clear example of a region where union was necessary if there was to be any hope of development and social advancement. In India such plans had proven successful [8] but the leadership in Pakistan decided that all of West Pakistan should be integrated regardless of the arguments for linguistic or economic decentralization.

From the beginning of the Pakistan movement its leaders were like those of the French Revolution who were committed to overcoming the society which held their people in chains. It is understandable that as the society rebelled against the social planning of national leaders, and as traditional elements attempted to frustrate change, the government would eliminate the enemy from public life with its superior force.

The dilemma is clear, however. If Pakistan is to become one nation, it requires years of common history and experience under gifted leaders, who, while maintaining a consensus within their own circles, recognize their obligations to the broader public. The only national leaders of Pakistan were, and are, the English-speaking *moderns*, politicians, civil and military officers, and educators. The people of the *mohallas* (city districts) and villages, separated by language, tradition, and standard of living, must be led into a national awareness.

Central officials mistakenly assumed that administrative unity would create social unity. Only politicians, particularly local politicians, possess the gift for leading their people into a new and wider world. There is little populism in Asia but a leader dependent upon the mandate of the masses, no matter what he may think of them, is a force for radical change. And a politician in the subcontinent must have local roots. As Brigadier Nazeer Ali Shah, an aide to the ruler of Bahawalpur, has said: "A patwari born and bred at Bannu cannot adjust himself easily to Bahawalpur's traditions and atmosphere." [9] Not only is radical social change difficult without active support within the body politic but democracy may very well be impossible without it.

The seeding of democracy

An assessment of the politics of the princes in Pakistan is impossible without assuming certain values or priorities. Too often the administrators were faced with the choice either of order or of progress. One can honestly view the dissolution of the Bahawalpur legislature as in keeping with effective and efficient government, the integration of West Pakistan as a rational and long delayed improvement, and the central domination of local politics as furthering the modernizing goals of the Pakistan movement.

On the other hand, these actions were invariably destructive to the growth of democracy and to the local participation of the people in their own affairs. The Basic Democracy plan of Field Marshall Ayub's government is an attempt at local democracy, yet the goals of the central government will almost surely be pitted against the political demands which are generated in the fragmented rural society. And local self-government cannot and will not grow unless it is an avenue of self-expression and power.

Comparisons with India are often hastily made, emphasizing the nation-wide elections of which the Indian Union is justly proud. Ignoring for a moment the enormous differences between the two states and their differing standards of literacy and development, can it not be said that democracy cannot wait for a democratic environment; that it must create one by its own operation? The linguistic unions of the Indian federation are perhaps dangerous blocs emphasizing the lack of a national consensus in the country, but through effective national leadership and party discipline the government has managed to harness differences. There is an absence of information about the transformations in the Indian states under this system, but it deserves a very close examination.

Perhaps in a broader sense both countries are following a common stream of history with the growth, through economic development, increased education, and social mobility, of multiple centers of influence and strength within the society which not only blunt the abuse of state power but act as catalysts in the development of a participant society. No state, no matter what its power, can revolutionize a society without such groups.

If the deep problems, ignorance, poverty, distrust, bigotry still remain and if they can be credited with the failure of democratic government in Pakistan, might it not be possible to view the fifteen years from 1947 as a preface rather than a prologue? The promise of democracy and of a democratic society in the country remains the ideal inherited from the parliamentary system, and Pakistan does not lack a goal.

If the presidential system of government introduced in 1962 furthers the growth of a healthy economic community, eliminates abuses in society, and contributes toward the integration

of individuals in a broader world community, it will be loyal to
the ideals of the founders of the state and to those of its citizens. Anyone who has seen village women bent with the ac-
cumulated weight of superstition and poverty could hardly
wish for more.

Viewing the changes of the princely states, and more importantly, their traditional societies, cannot but encourage the
student of the subcontinent's history. That the past will fall
before the future is obvious but the positive aspects of modern
life have brought and continue to bring millions of people
into the mainstream of modern history. The elimination of
privilege based on hereditary and traditional sources allows the
reclamation of the constructive talents of men and women
which, once begun, goes on under ever increasing prospects of
success. The revolution is more than exciting, it is exhilarating.

Appendix

Appendix: Documents

DOCUMENT ONE
INSTRUMENT OF ACCESSION, BAHAWALPUR STATE

Whereas the Indian Independence Act, 1947, provides that as from the fifteenth day of August, 1947, there shall be set up an independent Dominion known as Pakistan, and that the Government of India Act, 1935, shall, with such omissions, additions, adaptations and modifications as the Governor-General may by order specify, be applicable to the Dominion of Pakistan;

And Whereas the Government of India Act, 1935, as so adapted by the Governor-General provides that an Indian State may accede to the Federation of Pakistan by an Instrument of Accession executed by the Ruler thereof:

Now Therefore,

I, Sadiq Muhammad Khamis Abbasi, Ameer of Bahawalpur State, in the exercise of my sovereignty in and over my said State do hereby execute this my Instrument of Accession, and

1. I hereby declare that I accede to the Federation of Pakistan with the intent that the Governor-General of Pakistan, the Federal Legislature,[1] the Federal Court, and any other Federal authority established for the purposes of the Federation shall, by virtue of this my Instrument of Accession, but subject always to the terms thereof, and for the purposes only of the Federation, exercise in relation to the State of Bahawalpur (herein after referred to as "this State") such functions as may be vested in them by or under the Government of India Act, 1935, as in force in the Dominion of Pakistan on the fifteenth day of August, 1947 (which Act as so in force is hereinafter referred to as "the Act").

2. I hereby assume the obligation of ensuring that due effect is given to the provisions of the Act within this State so far as they are applicable therein by virtue of this my Instrument of Accession.

3. I accept the matters specified in the Schedule hereto as the

matters with respect to which the Federal Legislature may make laws for this State.

4. I hereby declare that I accede to the Federation of Pakistan on the assurance that if an agreement is made between the Governor-General and the Ruler of the State whereby any functions in relation to the administration of this State of any law of the Federal Legislature shall be exercised by the Ruler of this State, then such agreement shall be deemed to form part of this Instrument and shall be construed and have effect accordingly.

5. Nothing in this Instrument shall empower the Federal Legislature to make any law of this State authorising the compulsory acquisition of land for any purpose, but I hereby undertake that should the Federal Government of Pakistan for the purposes of a federal law which applies in this State deem it necessary to acquire any land, I will at their request acquire the land at their expense or if the land belongs to me transfer it to them on such terms as may be agreed, or, in default of agreement, determined by an arbitrator to be appointed by the Chief Justice of Pakistan.

6. The terms of this my Instrument of Accession shall not be varied by any amendment of the Act or of the Indian Independence Act, 1947, unless such amendment is accepted by me by an Instrument supplementary to this Instrument.

7. Nothing in this Instrument shall be deemed to commit me in any way to acceptance of any future Constitution of Pakistan or to fetter my discretion to enter into agreement with the Government of Pakistan established under any such future Constitution.

8. Nothing in this Instrument affects the continuance of my sovereignty in and over this State, or, save as provided by or under this Instrument, the exercise of any powers, authority, rights and jurisdiction now enjoyed by me as Ruler of this State or the validity of any law at present in force in this State.

9. I hereby declare that I execute this Instrument on behalf of this State and that any reference in this Instrument to me or to the Ruler of the State is to be construed as including a reference to my heirs and successors.

Given under my hand this Third day of October, Nineteen hundred and Forty-Seven.

> Sadiq Muhammad Abbasi
> *Ameer of Bahawalpur*

I do hereby accept this Instrument of Accession.

Dated this Fifth day of October, Nineteen Hundred and Forty-Seven.

> M. A. Jinnah
> *Governor-General of Pakistan*

DOCUMENT TWO
SUPPLEMENTARY INSTRUMENT OF ACCESSION,
BAHAWALPUR STATE

Whereas Bahawalpur State has acceded to the Dominion of Pakistan and the defence of Pakistan including that of Bahawalpur State is the sole responsibility of the Government of Pakistan;

And Whereas it is essential to the overall defence of the Dominion of Pakistan that there should be the closest co-ordination between the Governments of Pakistan and Bahawalpur State on matters relating to Defence or having a bearing thereon:

Now, Therefore,

I, Sadiq Muhammad V. Abbasi, Ameer of Bahawalpur State agree that:

1. The Bahawalpur State Forces except the units of my Bodyguard shall be attached to and operate with the Pakistan Armed Forces.

2. The Commander-in-Chief of the Pakistan Army should be the Commander-in-Chief of Bahawalpur State Forces and shall exercise full operational, administrative and financial control over them under the direction of the Ministry of Defence, Government of Pakistan.

3. A sum shall be determined by agreement between myself and the Government of Pakistan and shall be paid by the Government of Bahawalpur every year in two equal instalments to the Government of Pakistan for the maintenance of the State Forces.

4. In order to enable the Government of Pakistan to discharge effectively its responsibility in respect of acceded subjects the following additional clauses shall be inserted in the Schedule of the Instrument of Accession of Bahawalpur State;

(*i*) Under the heading "Defence"—"5. All matters relating to Defence or having a bearing thereon."

(*ii*) Under the heading "External Affairs"—"4. All relations with other Dominions or countries and all matters relating thereto or having a bearing thereon."

5. The Government of Pakistan may entrust to the Prime Minister of my State such duties relating to the administration of acceded subjects within the State as it may deem necessary. In the discharge of such duties the Prime Minister of my State shall be under the direct control of and responsible to the Government of Pakistan and shall carry out its directions issued to him from time to time.

Given under my hand this First day of October, Nineteen Hundred and Forty-Eight.

S. M. Abbasi
Ameer of Bahawalpur

I hereby accept the above Supplementary Instrument of Accession.
Dated this Fourth day of October, Nineteen Hundred and Forty-Eight.

K. Nazim-ud-Din
Governor-General of Pakistan

DOCUMENT THREE
INSTRUMENT OF ACCESSION, CHITRAL STATE
(*short form*)

I, Lt.-Col. His Highness Haji Mohammad Muzaffar-ul-Mulk, Ruler of Chitral State, in the exercise of my sovereignty in and over my said State, do hereby execute this my Instrument of Accession and I do hereby declare that I accede to the Dominion of Pakistan and promise full loyalty to Pakistan.

I accede to Pakistan on the same terms and conditions with regard to Defence External Affairs and Communications as existed between me and the British Government and on the enjoyment of the same privileges I received from the British Government.

Nothing in this Instrument affects the continuance of my sovereignty in and over this State or save as provided by or under this Instrument the exercise of any power or authority and rights now enjoyed by me in regard to the internal administration of my State.

I do hereby declare that I execute this Instrument on behalf of this State and my heirs and successors.

Signed in my presence
S. Mahbub Ali,
P.A., Dir, Swat and Chitral   Muzaffar-Ul-Mulk
The 6th of November, 1948   *Ruler of Chitral*

I do hereby accept this Instrument of Accession.
Dated this Eighteenth day of February, Nineteen Hundred and Forty-Eight.

M. A. Jinnah
Governor-General of Pakistan

Schedule

The matters with respect to which the Dominion Legislature may make laws for this State.

DEFENCE

1. The Naval, Military and Air Forces of the Dominion and any other armed forces raised or maintained by the Dominion including any armed forces raised or maintained by a federated State, which are attached to, or operating with, any of the armed forces of the Dominion.

2. Naval, Military and Air Force works, and the administration of Cantonment areas save and except those belonging to the Federated State.[2]

3. Supply of fire-arms, ammunition and explosives for the use of Military Forces of the Federated State.[3]

4. Export by a Federated State of firearms, ammunition and explosives outside Pakistan.[4]

EXTERNAL AFFAIRS

1. External Affairs; the implementing of treaties and agreements with other countries; extradition, including the surrender of criminal and accused persons to parts of His Majesty's Dominions outside Pakistan.

2. Admission into and emigration and expulsion from Pakistan, including in relation thereto the regulation of the movement, in Pakistan, of persons who are not British subjects domiciled in Pakistan or subjects of any Federated State; pilgrimages to places beyond Pakistan.

3. Naturalisation in the Federated State of persons other than Pakistan Nationals.[5]

COMMUNICATIONS

1. Posts and telegraphs, including trunk telephones, wireless, broadcasting, and other like forms of communication for federal purposes.

2. Federal railways; the regulation of all railways other than minor railways in respect to safety, maximum and minimum rates and fares, station and service terminal charges, interchange of traffic and the responsibility of railway administrations as carriers of goods and passengers; the regulation of minor railways in respect to safety and the responsibility of the administrations of such railways as carriers of goods and passengers.

3. Maritime shipping and navigation, including shipping and navigation on tidal waters; Admiralty jurisdiction.

4. Port quarantine.

5. Major ports, that is to say, the declaration and delimitation

of such ports, and the constitution and powers of port authorities therein.

6. Aircraft and air navigation; the provision of aerodromes; regulation of organisation of air traffic and of aerodromes.

7. Lighthouses, including lightships, beacons and other provisions for the safety of shipping and aircraft.

8. Carriage of passengers and goods by sea or by air.

ANCILLARY [6]

1. Offenses against laws with respect to any of the aforesaid matters.

2. Inquiries and statistics for the purpose of any of the aforesaid matters.

3. Jurisdiction and powers of all courts with respect to any of the aforesaid matters but, except with the consent of the Ruler of the Federated State, not so as to confer any jurisdiction or powers upon any courts other than courts ordinarily exercising jurisdiction in or in relation to that State.

DOCUMENT FOUR
SUPPLEMENTARY AGREEMENT,
BAHAWALPUR STATE

[1. The first article notes the participants; H. H. the Nawab of Bahawalpur, Prime Minister, Bahawalpur, Lt. Col. A. J. Dring, Lt. Col. A. S. B. Shah, Sec'y, of the Ministry of States and Frontier Regions and Mr. Liaquat Ali Khan, P.M. and Minister of States and Frontier Regions.]

2. Constitutional Position of the Ruler.

(a) Henceforth, His Highness' position will be that of a Constitutional Ruler. The responsibility for the executive administration of the State shall rest with his Prime Minister working with his colleagues. The Prime Minister will however keep his Highness in close touch with matters of importance such as questions of policy and higher appointments.

(b) His Highness has agreed to limit his Privy Purse to the amount at present allotted, which will continue to be paid and administered as heretofore.

(c) Having regard to the demands of the day His Highness will announce further constitutional reforms on March 8, 1949, when he completes 25 years of his rule with a view to associating his people closely with the administration of the State. The exact form of such reform which is now under consideration will be communicated to the Government of Pakistan before it is finalised.

These reforms will in any case represent a substantial advance on the District Board and Municipal elections already announced.

3. Khan Bahadur Nabi Bakhsh.[7] It is agreed that in view of his past record Khan Bahadur Nabi Bakhsh will not be given employment in the State and he will not be permitted to enter the State or stay there.

4. His Highness' Bodyguard. It is agreed that the expenditure on the Bodyguards kept by His Highness will be limited to the sum of rupees five lakhs per annum. This additional expenditure will not be included in the sum allotted for Defence. The G.O.C.[8] will be kept informed of the organisation and the strength of the units of the Bodyguards. The G.O.C. will make periodic inspections of the Bodyguard Units and advise in regard to their training. All arms, stores and equipment for the Bodyguards will be obtained through the G.O.C.

5. The Border Constabulary. The establishment and maintenance of an adequate and efficient force of Border Constabulary has been approved by the Bahawalpur Government and the plans will be formulated as soon as possible in consultation with the Government of Pakistan.

6. National Guards. All National Guard Units will come under the G.O.C. who will be responsible for raising, administering and training of these Units. The funds allotted for this purpose will be placed at the G.O.C.'s disposal.

7. Defence Allotment. The allocation for defence in the Prime Minister, Bahawalpur's letter of the 29 December 1948, namely rupees one crore recurring and rupees one crore non-recurring, are accepted by the Government of Pakistan. These allocations are exclusive of non-effective charges relating to the State Forces. The remainder of the article fixes the times and amounts of payments.

8. The S.V.P. Loan. It is agreed that the payment due to Bahawalpur State on account of compensation for the Railway Line which was lifted from state territory during the last war will be adjusted against the scheduled instalments due to the Pakistan Government on account of the Sutlej Valley Project Loan for the years 1947–48 and 1948–49.

9. Customs, Excise and Income Tax, Etc.

(a) His Highness the Nawab of Bahawalpur agrees that the Government of Pakistan will organize and control a land customs line along the Indo-Bahawalpur border and the customs laws of Pakistan will apply to the State of Bahawalpur. The Customs administration will be entrusted to the official appointed by the Government of Pakistan in this behalf. Appeals against the decisions of local customs authorities will be to the Revenue Division

of the Ministry of Finance of the Government of Pakistan. The
incidence of the cost of the land customs administration in Bahawalpur and the allocation of the state's share of the land custom's revenue will form the subject of separate negotiations.

(b) It is also agreed that the Bahawalpur Government will
adopt the Pakistan rate of excise duties and direct taxation.

Sn. 19 January 1949
S.M.K. Abbasi
2nd August 1949   *Amir of Bahawalpur*

Kwaja Nazimuddin
2nd September 1949   *Governor-General of Pakistan*

[There were two enclosures to this instrument. Enclosure A was
the letter of acceptance by the Amir of the terms spelled out in the
above agreement. Article 6 of the Amir's letter is not quoted in the
instrument. It reads: "6. Representation in the Constituent Assembly. I agree that Bahawalpur shall be grouped with Khairpur
and that I should nominate the Bahawalpur representative." It
was signed in December, 1948.

Enclosure B is a letter from Colonel Dring to Colonel Shah
concerning the amount of money Bahawalpur was ready to allocate
for defense. The figures are the same given above in the main body
of the document.]

DOCUMENT FIVE
*SECOND SUPPLEMENTARY INSTRUMENT OF
ACCESSION, BAHAWALPUR STATE*

Whereas by an Instrument of Accession dated the third day of
October, 1947 (hereinafter referred to as the "Accession Instrument"), I, Sadiq Muhammad V. Abbasi, Ameer of Bahawalpur
State, declared that I had acceded to the Federation of Pakistan,
under the provisions of Schedule 6 of the Government of India
Act, 1935, as in force in Pakistan (hereinafter referred to as the
"Constitution Act") and had specified in a schedule annexed
thereto, the matters with respect to which the Federal Legislature
may make laws with respect to my State, and by the acceptance
of the said Instrument of Accession by His Excellency the Governor-
General of Pakistan on the fifth day of October, 1947, the State
of Bahawalpur (hereinafter referred to as "this State") was deemed
to have acceded to the Federation of Pakistan;

And Whereas by a Supplementary Instrument of Accession executed by me on the first day of October, 1948 (hereinafter referred to as the First Supplementary Instrument) which was ac-

cepted by His Excellency the Governor-General of Pakistan on the fourth day of October, 1948, I had specified matters, additional to those specified in my Instrument of Accession, as matters with respect to which the Federal Legislature of Pakistan may make laws for this State, and had assumed an obligation to make payments annually to the Government of Pakistan for the maintenance of the forces of this State;

And Whereas by an Agreement executed by me on the second day of August, 1949, and accepted by His Excellency the Governor-General of Pakistan on the second day of September 1949, I had assumed certain further obligations touching the application of certain Pakistan laws to this State, and the payment of specified sums to the Government of Pakistan for the maintenance of the forces of this State;

Now Therefore, I, Sadiq Muhammad V. Abbasi, Ameer and Ruler of Bahawalpur State, do hereby execute this Supplementary Instrument (hereinafter referred to as the "Second Supplementary Instrument") and

1. I hereby vary the Accession Instrument and the First Supplementary Instrument, in manner hereinafter described, that is to say, for the purpose of specifying the matters with respect to which the Federal Legislature may make laws for this State, the Schedule to the Accession Instrument and paragraph 4 of the First Supplementary Instrument shall be deemed to have been replaced by Parts I and II of the Schedule annexed hereunto (hereinafter referred to as the "said Schedule") wherein are specified the matters with respect to which the Federal Legislature may make laws for this State, with effect from the date on which the Second Supplementary Instrument is accepted by His Excellency the Governor-General (hereinafter referred to as "the said date"), and I further declare that as from the said date, the Legislature of this State shall not have power to make laws with respect to any matter included in Parts I and II of the said Schedule, except as is expressly provided hereinafter.

2. I hereby declare that as to all matters included in Part III of the said Schedule, the Legislature of the State shall have exclusive power to make laws, subject only to the power of the Federal Legislature to make laws in regard to matters included in Part I and II of the said Schedule,

Provided that if any provision of any such law is repugnant to any provision in any Federal law applied to the State under clause 3 of the Second Supplementary Instrument, then if the law of the State Legislature, having been reserved for the consideration of His Excellency the Governor-General, has received his assent, the State law shall prevail in the State, but nevertheless the Federal

Legislature may enact further legislation with respect to the same matter at any time.

Provided that no bill or amendment for making any provision repugnant to any law of the State Legislature, which having been so reserved, has received the assent of the Governor-General, shall be introduced or moved in the Federal Legislature without the previous sanction of His Excellency the Governor-General.

3. I hereby further declare that for the better discharge of the functions assumed by His Excellency the Governor-General in relation to this State, in respect of the matters enumerated in the said Schedule—

(a) His Excellency the Governor-General shall have power, by order, to extend to this State any existing Federal law relating to a matter included in Parts I and II of the said Schedule, with such modifications as may be necessary for the purpose of adapting its provisions to the conditions obtaining in this State; and

(b) The executive authority of the Federal Government shall be exercisable in the State in respect to all matters included in Parts I and II of the said Schedule either through the Ruler or his officers, or directly by officers of the Government of Pakistan, as may be determined by order of His Excellency the Governor-General either in relation to any particular matter or generally,

Provided that any order under the clause shall be made after prior consultation with the Ruler:

Provided further that nothing in this clause shall be construed to confer upon the Federal Government, in relation to any matter included in Part II of the said Schedule, any executive authority in excess of that exercisable by the Federal Government in relation to the same matter in a Governor's Province in Pakistan.

4. The matters included in the said Schedule are as to Part I thereof, the several matters included in List I—Federal Legislative List, as to Part II thereof, the several matters included in List III—Concurrent Legislative List, and as to Part III thereof, the several matters included in List II—Provincial Legislative List, in the seventh Schedule to the Constitution Act on the date of execution of the Second Supplementary Instrument, and I hereby declare that any change which may be made hereafter by competent authority, in the aforesaid lists, in their application to the Federation of Pakistan shall have effect in relation to this State in such wise that the respective parts of this said Schedule shall be deemed to have been modified in like manner as the corresponding list, and with effect from the same date.

5. I hereby further declare that if and so often as any provision of the Constitution Act are altered by competent authority, then the Accession Instrument and the First and Second Supplementary

Instruments shall be deemed to have been modified in accordance therewith, and the said Instruments shall be construed with the altered provisions of the Constitution Act.

6. I hereby further declare that, with respect to all matters included in Parts I and II of the said Schedule, His Excellency the Governor-General, the Federal Legislature, the Federal Court and any other Federal authority established by law for the purposes of the Federation, shall, by virtue of the Second Supplementary Instrument, but subject always to the terms thereof exercise in respect of the State as from the said date the functions vested in them on the said date by or under the Constitution Act in respect to the said matters:

Provided that in respect of any matter included in Parts I and II of the said Schedule which was not specified in the Schedule to the Accession Instrument or in paragraph 4 of the First Supplementary Instrument or in paragraph (9) or the Agreement executed by me on the second day of August, 1949, the exercise of functions by any such authority, other than His Excellency the Governor-General and the Federal Legislature, shall, except in regard to functions specified in the Constitution Act as exercisable in relation to Federated States commence from such date as shall be determined in this behalf by His Excellency the Governor-General.

7. I hereby further declare that the obligations assumed by me in the First Supplementary Instrument and in the Agreement executed by me on the second day of August, 1949, to make contributions to the Government of Pakistan for the maintenance of the forces of the State, shall cease with effect from the said date, and in lieu thereof, the proceeds of any taxes imposed and collected by the Federal Government in this State other than the Sales (Tax) shall be appropriated by the Government of Pakistan:

Provided that if the said proceeds, in any financial year ending the thirty-first day of March fall short of the sum of rupees 75 lakhs, the deficit from the said sum shall be made good out of the revenue of the State:

Provided further that without prejudice to any agreement between this State and the Government of Pakistan for allocation to this State of any portion of the proceeds of a sales-tax levied elsewhere than in this State, the proceeds of the sales-tax in the State shall be allocated between the Government of Pakistan and the State in the same manner as the proceeds of the sales-tax in a Governor's Province in Pakistan are allocated between the Government of Pakistan and the Provincial Government.

8. I hereby further declare that the express provisions of the Second Supplementary Instrument shall, as from the said date,

have effect notwithstanding anything inconsistent therewith contained in the Constitution Act on the date of the acceptance of the Second Supplementary Instrument by His Excellency the Governor-General, or in the Accession Instrument, or in the First Supplementary Instrument or in the Agreement executed by me on the second day of August, 1949, but in all respects, the said provisions of the Constitution Act, the Accession Instrument, the First Supplementary Instrument and the said Agreement shall be construed in such wise as to give full effect, in all relevant respects to the meaning and intention of the Second Supplementary Instrument.

9. Nothing in the Second Supplementary Instrument affects the continuance of my sovereignty in and over this State, or, in exercise of any powers, authority, rights, and jurisdiction now enjoyed by me as Ruler of the State or the validity of any law at present in force in this State, save as provided by the Second Supplementary Instrument.

10. I hereby declare that I execute the Second Supplementary Instrument on behalf of this State and that any reference in the Second Supplementary Instrument to me or to the Ruler of this State is to be construed as including a reference to my heirs and successors.

Given under my hand this twenty-ninth day of April, Nineteen Hundred and Fifty-One.

S. M. Abbasi
Ameer of Bahawalpur

I do hereby accept this Supplementary Instrument of Accession dated the thirtieth day of April, Nineteen Hundred and Fifty-One.

K. Nazimuddin
Governor-General of Pakistan

DOCUMENT SIX
AGREEMENT WITH HIS HIGHNESS THE AMIR OF
BAHAWALPUR REGARDING PRIVY PURSE, PRIVATE
PROPERTY AND RIGHTS AND PRIVILEGES

Whereas it has been decided that the constitution of Pakistan adopted by the Constituent Assembly of Pakistan shall be the constitution for the State of Bahawalpur as for the other parts of Pakistan and shall be enforced as such in accordance with the tenor of its provisions;

And whereas it is expedient that the rights, privileges and dignities, including the dynastic succession and the privy purse of His Highness the Amir shall be determined by agreement between him and the Government of Pakistan;

It is hereby agreed as follows:

Article I. His Highness the Amir of Bahawalpur shall be entitled to receive annually from the revenues of the State of Bahawalpur a sum not exceeding Rs. 2,950,000 (Rupees Twenty Nine lacs and Fifty Thousands Only) free of all taxes as detailed in the schedule annexed to this agreement.

(2) The said amount is intended to cover all the expenses of His Highness the Amir of Bahawalpur and his family including expenses on account of his personal staff, bodyguard tours, hospitality, maintenance of his residences, marriages and other ceremonies.

(3) The said amount shall be payable to the Amir of Bahawalpur in four equal instalments at the beginning of each quarter in advance.

(4) The payment of the said amount as herein provided is guaranteed by the Government of Pakistan.

Article II. His Highness the Amir shall be entitled to the full ownership, use and enjoyment of all the jewels, jewellery, ornaments, shares, securities and other private properties, movable as well as immovable, not being State properties belonging to him on the date of this agreement.

(2) His Highness the Amir shall furnish to the Government of Pakistan within three months of the date of this Agreement lists of all the movable and immovable property held by him as such private property.

(3) If any dispute arises as to whether any item of property is the private property of His Highness or State property, it shall be decided by the Governor-General of Pakistan whose decisions shall be final and binding on all concerned.

Article III. His Highness the Amir and the members of his family shall be entitled to all the personal privileges, dignities and titles enjoyed by them whether within or outside the territory of the State immediately before the date of this agreement.

Article IV. The Government of Pakistan guarantees the succession according to law and custom of the State of Bahawalpur to the Gaddi of the State and to the personal rights, privileges, dignities and titles of His Highness the Amir of Bahawalpur.

In confirmation whereof His Excellency the Governor-General of Pakistan and the Amir of Bahawalpur have respectively appended their signatures this 11th day of April, 1952.

Schedule

Privy Purse of His Highness the Amir of Bahawalpur.

Privy Purse	Rs. 2,000,000 per annum
Civil list reserve	200,000
Body guard	750,000

DOCUMENT SEVEN
BALUCHISTAN STATES UNION MERGER
AGREEMENT [9]

Agreement made this first day of January 1955 between the Governor-General of Pakistan and the Khan-e-Azam, the President of the Council of Rulers of the Baluchistan States Union (hereinafter referred to as the "Union") on behalf of the Council of Rulers.

Whereas the Rulers of Kalat, Mekran, Las Bela and Kharan entered into the Covenant for the formation of the Union on the 11th day of April, 1952.

And whereas the Khan-i-Azam executed on behalf of the Council of Rulers an instrument of accession on the 3rd November, 1952 which was accepted by the Governor-General on the 2nd December, 1952.

And whereas in the best interests of the Union as well as the Dominion of Pakistan, it is desirable to provide for the cession of the territories of the said Union to the Dominion of Pakistan and for the merger of the same in the proposed Unit of the said Dominion to be known as West Pakistan.

Now therefore it is agreed as follows:

Article I. His Highness the Khan-i-Azam hereby cedes to the Government of the Dominion of Pakistan his sovereignty and all his rights, authority and powers as President of the Council of Rulers of the Union, together with all his territories including the territories known as the leased areas, and, having been duly authorized to that end by the members of the Council of Rulers, that is to say the Rulers of Mekran, Las Bela and Kharan, their sovereignty and all their rights, authority and powers as such Rulers together will all their territories; and the authority jurisdiction and powers for the governance of the said Union and territories shall vest in the Government of the Dominion of Pakistan, hereinafter referred to as "the said day."

As from the said day the Government of the Dominion shall

exercise all powers, authority and jurisdiction for the governance of the said Union and territories in such manner and through such agency as it may think fit.

Article II. The members of the Council of Rulers shall be entitled to receive annually from the Government of Pakistan for their privy purse free of all taxes the amount given below:

His Highness the Khan-i-Azam of Kalat	Rs. 6,50,000 (Rupees, six lacs and fifty thousand only.)
The Nawab of Makran	Rs. 2,25,000 (Rupees, two lacs and twenty-five thousand only.)
The Jam Sahib of Las Bela	Rs. 2,00,000 (Rupees, two lacs only.)
The Nawab of Kharan	Rs. 70,000 (Rupees, seventy thousand only.)

The said amount is intended to cover all the expenses of the Rulers and their families including expenses on account of their personal staff, bodyguard, tours, hospitality, maintenance of their residences, marriages and all family ceremonies.

The said amount shall be payable to the Rulers in four equal instalments at the beginning of each quarter in advance.

The payment of the said amount as herein provided is guaranteed by the Government of Pakistan.

Article III. The Rulers shall be entitled to the full ownership, use and enjoyment of all the jewels, jewellery, ornaments, shares, securities and other private properties, movable as well as immovable, not being State properties, belonging to them on the date of this agreement.

If any dispute arises as to whether any item of property is the private property of the Ruler or State property, it shall be decided by the Governor-General of Pakistan whose decision shall be final and binding on all concerned.

Article IV. The Rulers, their wives and children shall be entitled to all the personal privileges, dignities and titles enjoyed by them whether within or outside the territory of the State immediately before the date of this agreement.

Article V. The Government of Pakistan guarantees the succession according to law and custom of the States concerned to the personal rights, privileges, dignities and titles specified in Articles II to IV, above.

Article VI. This agreement abrogates all the Instruments of Accession and agreements between the Governor-General of Pakistan and His Highness the Khan-i-Azam signed so far.

In confirmation whereof the Governor-General of Pakistan and His Highness the Khan-i-Azam have appended their signatures on this first day of January 1955.

This Agreement has been made by the President on our behalf and with our authority on behalf of our heirs and successors and shall be binding upon us, our heirs and successors.

Mir Ahmad Yar Khan, *Ruler of Kalat*
Bai Khan, *Ruler of Makran*
Habibullah Khan, *Ruler of Kharan*
Jam Mir Abdul Qadir, *Ruler of Las Bela*

Notes and

Bibliography

Notes

I. ISLANDS IN THE FLOOD

1. In Bahawalpur state, for example, the Resident preceded the ruler in certain processions of state and formal occasions.
2. A convocation resembling in function the present-day Privy Council of Britain.
3. Interview, Bahawalpur state, August, 1960.

II. PATRONS AND PATRIOTS

1. Quoted in R. C. Majumdar, H. C. Raychaudhuri and K. Datta, *An Advanced History of India*, p. 926.
2. Report of the Joint Committee on Indian Constitutional Reform (1918), in Sir M. Gwyer and A. Appadorai, *Speeches and Documents on the Indian Constitution, 1921–1947*, II, 708.
3. Quoted in V. P. Menon, *The Story of the Integration of the Indian States*, p. 23.
4. The central importance of this act in modern Indian history is now generally recognized. See Maulana Abul Kalam Azad, *India Wins Freedom*, pp. 187–89.
5. Sir Muhammad Iqbal, presidential address, All-India Muslim League convention, 1930.
6. Speculation concerning the origin of the idea, including possible British involvement, is summed up vitriolically in W. C. Smith, *Modern Islam in India*, pp. 254–55.
7. Bahawalpur's Act, quoted in *Pakistan Times*, January 9, 1948.
8. See Winston S. Churchill, *The Second World War*, IV, 209.
9. Choudhary Rahmat Ali, *Pakistan* (3rd ed.; Cambridge, Pakistan National Liberty Movement, 1947), pp. 117–18.
10. V. P. Menon, *The Transfer of Power in India*, p. 108.
11. See Penderel Moon, *Divide and Quit*, pp. 29–41, for a concise statement of the Sikh dilemma.
12. *Dawn*, September, 1944.
13. *Dawn*, August 20, 1944.
14. See the demands of the League's organizer in Baluchistan, Qazi Isa, *Baluchistan; Case and Demand*.

15. Reported in *Nawa-i-Waqt* and the subject of *Dawn's* editorial, February 19, 1945.

III. DESPERATION POLITICS

1. Quoted in V. P. Menon, *The Story of the Integration of the Indian States*, p. 59.
2. The text is reprinted in Gwyer and Appadorai, *Speeches and Documents on the Indian Constitution*, II, 767–69.
3. Quoted in V. P. Menon, *The Transfer of Power in India*, p. 493.
4. The party was banned during the war by the ruler of Kashmir who ruled more harshly than most of the princes. See the full party statement in *Dawn*, August 6, 1946.
5. Sir Sikander himself had once been chief minister of Bahawalpur.
6. Abdul Ghaffar Khan charged that the disturbances were the work not of the Muslim League but of the British Political Department. In fact, one Political Agent was tried for having lost control of his tribe but was acquitted. See *Dawn*, October 25, 1946. The full role of British officers in the states is not clear.
7. It is interesting to note the parallel with the earlier days of the Khilafat movement. See Choudhry Khaliquzzaman, *Pathway to Pakistan*, pp. 30–31.
8. The text is reprinted in *Dawn*, April 22, 1947.
9. V. P. Menon, *Integration of the Indian States*, p. 113.
10. Its chairman was the prime minister, Liaquat Ali Khan. Other members were Abdur Rab Nishtar, Sir Muhammad Zafrullah Khan, Kwaja Shahabuddin, Pir Allahi Bakhsh, and Ghazanfar Ali Khan.
11. See his offer as reported in *Dawn*, June 18, 1947.
12. Interview, Saidu Sharif, July 23, 1960.
13. Azim Husain, *Fazl-i-Husain*, p. 247.

IV. THE WAR FOR THE STATES

1. Quoted in Richard Symonds, *The Making of Pakistan*, p. 74.
2. Graphic descriptions of their plight may be found in Major General Fazal Muqeem Khan, *The Story of the Pakistan Army*, ch. 5, and in Penderel Moon, *Divide and Quit*, pp. 124–260.
3. Quoted in V. P. Menon, *The Integration of the Indian States*, p. 127.

4. Major-General Fazal Muqeem Khan, *The Story of the Pakistan Army*.

5. Estimates vary. This one is by V. P. Menon, *The Integration of the Indian States*, p. 396.

6. The discussion in this section relies upon Major-General Fazal Muqeem Khan, *The Story of the Pakistan Army*, pp. 100–46, and upon discussions with Lieutenant Colonel M. N. Hyder Alavi, chief, Historical Division, Pakistan army GHQ, who has written an unpublished history of the Kashmir war.

V. THE DOUBLE-EDGED SWORD

1. Liaquat Ali Khan, *Speech to the 1st Session of the Pakistan Muslim League*, p. 1.

2. Details of population, area, literacy, religion, language, and ruler's title may be found in the table on pp. 84–85.

3. Letter from M. A. Gurmani to Muhammad Zafrullah Khan, July 17, 1947, reprinted in M. A. Gurmani, "Princely States in the Polity of India," p. 55.

4. Testimony reported in *Dawn*, April 5, 1958.

5. The text is reprinted in *Dawn*, August 25, 1947.

6. *Ibid.*

7. Partial text of the letter is as follows: "[After formalities] With my best efforts His Highness has agreed conditionally about the accession of Bahawalpur with India provided Bikanir and Jaisalmir and Bahawalpur are put under him. . . . The religious sentiments of the Muslims of the State are at their climax, but the fury is temporary and will subside in the end as the intelligentsia of the State realize my stand. The army is pro-Pakistan. It is, therefore, necessary that you keep sufficient force on the State border to meet any eventuality. [signed] M. A. Gurmani"

8. Interview, July 29, 1961, M. A. Gurmani.

9. Penderel Moon, *Divide and Quit*, p. 157.

10. *Dawn*, July 18, 1946.

11. Letter to the author dated October 22, 1960.

12. Interview, July 29, 1960.

13. C. V. Aitchison, *Treaties, Engagements, and Sanads*, Vol. 9, p. 397, article 4.

14. *Dawn*, October 12, 1947.

15. Muhammad Murad Awarani, secretary, Baluch Jama'at, Karachi, in *Dawn*, November 14, 1947.

16. Mirza Rahmatullah Khan, the foreign secretary of Kharan, quoted in *Dawn*, December 14, 1947. His speech is more patriotic than historically correct.

17. See *Pakistan Times* (Lahore), January 14, 1948, for an account of the meeting.

18. His speech, carried in Pakistan *Times*, February 17, 1948.

19. Quoted in *Dawn*, February 27, 1948.

20. *Dawn*, February 28, 1948.

21. Quoted in *Dawn*, March 29, 1948. See also the *Pakistan Times* for an added report that India had offered the Khan three million pounds sterling to accede and that only after his cause was lost had they deserted him.

22. See "Early Reminiscences of a Soldier," Major-General Akbar Khan, Independence Day Supplement, *Dawn*, August 14, 1960. Brigadier Purves's report is in a letter from Lahri, dated 15 July 1948, to Mr. Fell.

23. Reprinted in *Pakistan Times*, November 4, 1947.

24. Government of India, Lok Sabha, *Debates*, Part I, V. 4, columns 4371–72.

25. The explanation of Soviet scholars concerning the rulers of the states and the "Pushtunistan" issue is that they allied with Pakistan to protect their feudal rights. See Y. V. Gankovskiy, "Ethnic Composition of the Population of West Pakistan," in A. M. D'yakov, ed., *Pakistan; History and Economy* (trans. USJPRS, 1961), pp. 10–11.

26. Interview, July 23, 1960.

VI. DILEMMAS OF REFORM

1. See the Muslim League resolution quoted in Mary L. Becker, "The All-India Muslim League, 1906–1947," p. 308, "*Fatwas* and manifestos should be issued on behalf of the Ulema in which the Muslims should be warned against joining the Congress and the disadvantages from a religious point of view of an association with the Congress."

2. For a fuller exposition of the roots of the federal controversy, see the author's paper to the Pakistan Political Science Association, "The Integration of West Pakistan," in *Proceedings of the Pakistan Political Science Association* (1962).

3. *Pakistan Times*, January 9, 1948.

4. Party press communiqué, reprinted in *Dawn*, February 12, 1948. There is no evidence that the mission penetrated into all the frontier or Baluchistan states. Even the government's geological survey teams were not welcomed in Kalat or Dir.

5. *Pakistan Times*, "Sind Newsletter," April 27, 1948.

6. The meeting on May 26 was between Lieutenant Colonel A. S. B. Shah, Joint Secretary of the Committee on States and Frontier Regions and Manzar-i-Alam, President of the States

League, and had been reported in *Pakistan Times*, May 27, 1948.
Pakistan Times, June 27, 1948.

7. Press note quoted in *The Times* (London), July 7, 1948. The act created a stir because of the unique precedent of a governor-general holding a cabinet portfolio. It was an attempt by Mr. Jinnah to play the same role as Lord Mountbatten played with the Indian states. In Pakistan, it was greeted with widespread editorial applause. See *Pakistan Times*, July 9, 1948.

8. Quoted in *Dawn*, November 10, 1948.

9. Government of Bahawalpur, *Extraordinary Gazette*, November 8, 1948.

10. Penderel Moon, *Divide and Quit*, p. 229.

11. Mohammad Aslam, representative of the Amb and Chitral state Muslim League, quoted in *Dawn*, November 4, 1948.

12. The cabinet was of one mind in wishing for the abolition of the states, according to Fazlur Rahman. Interview, June 26, 1960.

13. Reprinted in *Dawn*, February 20, 1949.

14. *Dawn*, April 5, 1949.

15. Quoted in *Dawn*, April 4, 1949.

16. The *Blitz* characterization of the Muslim League as quoted in A. A. Ravoof, *Meet Mr. Jinnah*, p. 206.

17. *Dawn*, April 5, 1949.

18. The full statement is reprinted in *Dawn*, June 2, 1949. Almost all officials did sign a loyalty oath to the League.

19. See Keith Callard, *Pakistan, A Political Study*, pp. 40–42, for a brief description of League structure.

20. As quoted in V. P. Menon, *The Story of the Integration of the Indian States*, p. 195.

21. Constituent Assembly of Pakistan (Legislature), *Debates*, March 5, 1949, p. 402.

22. The New York *Times*, May 2, 1949, p. 4.

VII. THE POLITICS OF PARITY

1. The full text is reprinted as Document 1 in the appendix.

2. The full text is reprinted as Document 2 in the appendix.

3. There is considerable controversy over the number of Hindu and Sikh casualties in Bahawalpur. Indian estimates were between 30,000 and 70,000 and K. M. Panikkar has written that 5,000 non-Muslims were killed on a single day. There are no official Pakistani estimates although Brigadier Naseer Ali Shah denies Panikkar's data in his *Sadiqnama*, p. 97. The most recent and convincing figures are given in Penderel Moon, *Divide and Quit*, pp. 177 and 293, and are much lower than previously believed.

4. *Dawn*, January 29, 1949.

5. *Pakistan Times*, November 10, 1948.

6. The full text is reprinted as Document 4 in the appendix.

7. Article 2(c) of Document 4, appendix.

8. Local self-government, medicine and public health, education, agriculture, veterinary affairs, cooperative societies, forests and gardens, and ancillary matters.

9. The Government of Bahawalpur Act, 1949, in *Extraordinary Gazette*, January 16, 1950, ch. 4, sec. 14.

10. Annex 1 of the Government of Bahawalpur Act, 1949.

11. As cited in *Dawn*, March 16, 1949.

12. *Dawn*, quoting Mahmud, May 30, 1949.

13. *Dawn*, January 16, 1951.

14. The full text of the agreement is in document 5, appendix.

15. The text appears in *Dawn*, March 2, 1952.

16. Ghulam Ali Talpur, quoted in *Dawn*, June 2, 1947.

17. This is the view of M. A. Gurmani, *Princely States*, p. 67.

18. *Ibid.*, p. 66.

19. Immigration to the states was considerably lighter than that to the provinces. The states had a bad reputation throughout India, and refugees were not welcomed. Moon quotes Gurmani as telling early refugees in Bahawalpur "that if they were seeking the promised land of Pakistan they had come to the wrong place and had better go on to Punjab or Sind." Penderel Moon, *Divide and Quit*, p. 110.

20. See Constituent Assembly of Pakistan (Legislature), *Debates*, March 5, 1949, pp. 402–3.

21. The Census of Pakistan does not enumerate Muslims by sect. The judgment that Sunnis are a clear majority comes from the deputy census commissioner.

22. The dynasty was allowed its own constituency.

23. Quoted in *Dawn*, September 17, 1951.

24. *Khairpur Legislative Assembly Reports*, March 1953, resolution no. 2 (no pagination).

25. See above, pp. 164–97, for an analysis of the role of the states in the federal controversy.

26. Press communique as quoted in *Dawn*, July 5, 1953.

27. *Dawn*, July 5, 1953.

VIII. CASE HISTORY IN THE DEMOCRATIC EXPERIMENT

1. The following narrative is based exclusively on an interview given the author by Hassan Mahmud on July 7, 1960.

2. Government of Bahawalpur press note reprinted in *Dawn*, February 23, 1949.

3. S. M. Akhtar, ed., *Village Life in Lahore District; Selected Political Aspects*, p. 17.

4. Quoted in *Dawn*, June 19, 1951.

5. See Majid Nizami, *The Press in Pakistan*, pp. 55–56, for the judgment that "in most cases, action under these public safety laws has been discriminatory, unwarranted and unduly harsh."

6. Quoted in *Pakistan Times*, February 6, 1952.

7. Quoted in *Dawn*, March 31, 1952.

8. Quoted in *Pakistan Times*, February 6, 1952.

9. Quoted in *Pakistan Times*, April 23, 1952.

10. This account is based solely on an interview with Hassan Mahmud, July 7, 1960.

11. See the cogent remarks of Mumtaz Daultana in *Pakistan Times*, April 30, 1952.

12. Quoted in *Dawn*, May 1, 1952.

13. See the transcript in *Gazette of Bahawalpur*, November 15, 1953.

14. *Ibid.*, August 18, 1954.

15. For a detailed study of legislative structure and procedure in Pakistan, see Munir Ahmad's capable study, *Legislatures in Pakistan, 1947–1958*, especially pp. 40–92. He devotes barely two pages to the princely states.

16. See *Bahawalpur Legislative Assembly Report*, January 26, 1953, pp. 32–43 and April 1, 1954, pp. 1–20 for major speeches.

17. Introduced in the January, 1953, session.

18. In 1954 it was made compulsory that all bills brought before the Majlis should be in English "for the precision and certitude required for statutory provisions." Government of Bahawalpur Act (Interim Constitution, Second Amendment), 1954, reprinted in *Bahawalpur Review*, I (February–March 1954), 25.

19. Hassan Mahmud, interview, July 7, 1960, in which he described the pattern of Pakistan's politics.

20. S. M. Akhtar, *Village Life*, pp. 16–17.

21. *Ibid.*, p. 14.

22. *Ibid.*, p. 29.

23. Government of Bahawalpur, *The Bahawalpur Scheme of Educational Reorganization*, p. 3.

24. Comparative data may be found in the Chief Minister's budget speech before the Bahawalpur Majlis, March 24, 1954, pp. pp. 34–61 of the Assembly *Report*.

25. *Ibid.*, p. 60.

26. See, in addition to *Village Life*, Zekiye Eglar, *A Punjabi Village in Pakistan*; John Honigman, "Field Research in West

Pakistan," in *Research Previews*, 1959; and Fredrik Barth, *Political Leadership Among Swat Pathans.*

IX. WATCH AND WARD ON THE FRONTIER

1. Major General Fazal Muqeem Khan, *The Story of the Pakistan Army.*

2. It is sometimes suggested that the outpouring of tribal forces would have been released inside Pakistan had not the Kashmir rebellion offered an alternative.

3. The report is in *Dawn*, April 2, 1948.

4. Quoted in *Dawn*, February 19, 1950.

5. He was later summarily recalled because of apparent government dissatisfaction with his conduct.

6. Quoted in *Dawn*, February 12, 1950.

7. Cited in *Dawn*, October 2, 1950.

8. Its members were Dr. Mahmud Husain, chairman; M. A. Khuhro, Malik Khuda Bakhsh, Nur Ahmed, and Bhabesh Chandra Nandy. See *Dawn*, October 14, 1950.

9. Constituent Assembly of Pakistan (Legislature), *Debates*, March 28, 1951, pp. 530–31.

10. *Ibid.*, November 17, 1951, pp. 23–46 for its text.

11. The system has three tenets: (1) Government works through the tribal chief; (2) tribes are responsible for law and order in their area; (3) the government pays for tribal levies to keep the peace.

12. Constituent Assembly of Pakistan (Legislature), *Debates*, November 17, 1951, p. 38.

13. *Dawn*, March 21, 1952.

14. It had been officially dissolved by the Working Committee of the parent party on March 7, 1952, a fact ignored in Quetta.

15. *Pakistan Times*, April 3, 1952.

16. Texts are in Constituent Assembly of Pakistan (Legislature), *Debates*, IX; Kalat, 1570–78, Makran, 1578–86, Las Bela, 1586–93, and Kharan, 1593–1601.

17. Constituent Assembly of Pakistan (Legislature), *Debates*, March 28, 1951, pp. 531–32.

18. *Ibid.*, November 17, 1951, p. 21.

19. For a detailed monograph on local Swat politics and organization see Fredrik Barth, *Political Leadership Among Swat Pathans.*

20. See, for example, Barth's story of the rifle-butting of mildly dissident landlords by the Wali's bodyguard, *Ibid.*, p. 132.

21. The pronouncements of the revolutionary government of General Muhammad Ayub Khan on legal reform implicitly accept

the Swat system as ideal with its emphasis on local, simple, and personal law.

22. *Khyber Mail*, February 14, 1954.

23. The author is indebted to Professor Fredrik Barth for much of the information on Dir state.

24. This discussion rests on information given the author by Professor Fredrik Barth, who has conducted brief researches in the state.

25. *Khyber Mail*, January 13, 1953.

26. *Dawn*, February 7, 1953.

27. The text is in Constituent Assembly of Pakistan (Legislature), XII, 84–92.

28. *Khyber Mail*, April 14, 1953.

29. Reprinted in *Dawn*, February 17, 1949.

X. THE CONSTITUTIONAL MORASS

1. The text may be found in Constituent Assembly of Pakistan, *Debates*, V, March 12, 1949, 100–1.

2. An evaluation of the numerous factors in Bengali-central politics may be found in Lawrence Ziring, "The Failure of Democracy in Pakistan; East Pakistan and the Central Government, 1947–1958."

3. See Keith Callard, *Pakistan, A Political Study*, pp. 89–98 for an analytical discussion of the Basic Principles Committee and its work. G. W. Choudhury, *Constitutional Development in Pakistan*, describes the proposals in considerable detail, see especially pp. 104–6, 109–16.

4. A. E. H. Jaffer in Constituent Assembly of Pakistan, *Debates*, October 10, 1953, pp. 110–11.

5. *Ibid.*

6. *Ibid.*, October 22, 1953, p. 298.

7. Reported in *Dawn*, March 14, 1954.

8. *Dawn*, June 11, 1954.

9. Quoted in *Dawn*, June 21, 1954.

10. Quoted in *Khyber Mail*, June 24, 1954.

11. Cited in *Dawn*, July 31, 1954.

12. *Dawn*, September 16, 1954.

13. Mohammad Ali, in Constituent Assembly of Pakistan, *Debates*, September 20, 1954, p. 454.

14. *Ibid.*, p. 468.

15. Public and Representative Offices (Disqualification) Act, 1949, which provided for the disqualifications of politicians for breaches of conduct or law and, it was charged, political discipline.

XI. STATE INTEGRATION AND THE CONSTITUTION

1. Quoted in *Dawn*, October 31, 1954. When these remarks, intended for foreign readers, were reprinted in Pakistan, there was a considerable reaction from "uninterested" readers.

2. Quoted in *Dawn*, November 3, 1954.

3. Mohammad Ali's national broadcast, as reported in *Dawn*, November 3, 1954.

4. Interview, Saidu Sharif, July 23, 1960.

5. Reprinted in *Dawn*, December 14, 1954.

6. Quoted in *Khyber Mail*, December 21, 1954.

7. There are rival claimants. See Mohammad Ahmad, *My Chief*, pp. 86–93 for the view that General Mohammad Ayub Khan originated the idea.

8. The text is reprinted as Document 6 in the appendix. It has never been publicly revealed and this copy must be considered unofficial even though its source is reliable.

9. The Khan of Kalat, as Khan-i-Azam of the Council of Rulers, was given an additional allowance for his tenure in that office. The consolidation agreement made it hereditary with his dynasty.

10. For a technical, first-hand discussion of the legal issues and problems involved, see Sir Ivor Jennings, *Constitutional Problems of Pakistan*.

11. The need for these agreements is questionable if the regime intended to promulgate a constitution. Under the federating instruments each ruler was bound to accept the constitution. More likely, the government bought princely support for One Unit as is clear from the Kalat agreement. None of the instruments has been made public.

12. Sardar Bahadur Khan, quoted in *Dawn*, March 6, 1955.

13. See the press communique, reprinted in *Dawn*, March 28, 1955.

14. Mian Iftikharuddin's characterization.

15. Governor-General's Order VIII, *Gazette of Pakistan*, April 15, 1955, reprinted in *Pakistan Law Digest*, p. 117.

16. Governor-General's Order IX, *Gazette of Pakistan*, April 20, 1955, reprinted in *Pakistan Law Digest*, p. 138.

17. H. S. Suhrawardy, Constituent Assembly of Pakistan, *Debates*, I (July 9, 1955), 27.

18. *Ibid.*, p. 28.

19. The speech is in Constituent Assembly of Pakistan, *Debates*, September 12, 1955, p. 674.

20. Constituent Assembly of Pakistan, *Debates*, November 9, 1955, pp. 1665–66.

21. The so-called secret manifesto of the Punjab Muslim League, portions of which were read into the record by Mr. Zahiruddin (East Bengal) on September 7, 1955. See Constituent Assembly of Pakistan, *Debates*, I, 558.

22. A long survey of this problem through the eyes of the Republican party may be found in M. Syed Hassan Mahmud, *A Nation is Born*. (Privately published but probably publicly financed.)

23. *The Constitution of the Islamic Republic of Pakistan*, 1958, p. 147.

XII. THE BLOODLESS REVOLUTION

1. For one example, see the letter from Agha Khan III to General Ayub reprinted in Colonel Mohammed Ahmad, *My Chief*, p. 85.

2. Richard Symonds detected this position as early as 1950, see *Far East Survey*. XIX, pp. 45–50.

3. Hasan Mahmud, *A Nation is Born*. It is unlikely that the busy minister actually wrote the text.

4. Keith Callard's estimate, *Pakistan*, p. 77.

5. Munir Ahmad, *Legislatures in Pakistan*, p. 37.

6. See Colonel Mohammed Ahmad, *My Chief*, p. 97.

7. Interview with I. I. Chundrigar, July 4, 1960. Note the parallel arguments in General Ayub's One Unit draft as reprinted in Colonel Mohammed Ahmad, *My Chief*, pp. 86–93.

8. Cited in Colonel Mohammed Ahmad, *My Chief*, p. 103.

9. The Secretary of Zikri Anjuman, quoted in *Dawn*, April 16, 1957.

10. "Baluchistan Newsletter," *Dawn*, April 16, 1957.

11. A comprehensive summary of activities may be found in Muhammad Sardar Khan Baluch, *History of the Baluch Race and Baluchistan*, p. ii.

12. General Mirza's speech reprinted in the New York *Times* October 8, 1958. The reference may, or may not have been directed at the Khan since there were also Leftist and pro-Indian targets of the administration.

13. The official government press note on the Kalat affair is reprinted in *Dawn*, October 7, 1958. Subsequent developments and the Khan's case were gathered in interviews.

14. A record of these warnings and Dir's response has not been made public but from the secretary of the States' Ministry, the late Ataullah Jan Khan, it was gathered that they were more con-

cerned with foreign and tribal affairs than with domestic reform, although it too was mentioned. Interview, July 9, 1960.

XIII. ON TREATING WITH PRINCES

1. The financial agreement of 1954 is in *Instruments of Accession and Schedules of Federating States, 1954*, pp. 21–23 and is reprinted as appendix Document 6.
2. See above, p. 187.
3. *Explanatory Memorandum on the Budget of the Government of Pakistan for 1956–57*, demand 73, p. 52.
4. *Instruments of Accession 1954*, pp. 21–22.
5. Quoted in *Dawn*, May 29, 1952.
6. Constituent Assembly of Pakistan, *Debates*, August 23, 1955, pp. 275–76.
7. Constituent Assembly of Pakistan (Legislature) *Debates*, March 28, 1951, p. 529.
8. There is a conspicuous absence of evidence showing an interchange of information on the states between India and Pakistan. Nonetheless the parallel experiences and the later policies of Pakistan would indicate a debt to India.
9. Brigadier Nazeer Ali Shah, *Sadiqnama*, p. 95.

APPENDIX

1. Dominion legislature finds use in other forms of this instrument.
2. All after "areas" excluded on other instruments.
3. Other instruments say only arms; firearms; ammunition.
4. Other instruments say explosives.
5. Other instruments say naturalization.
6. Others add Elections to the Dominion Legislature, subject to the provisions of the Act and of any Order made thereunder.
7. Khan Bahadur Nabi Bakhsh was Revenue Minister of Bahawalpur.
8. G.O.C. General Officer Commanding.
9. The merger agreements of the States have not been published officially by the Government of Pakistan. This is not an official text although there is no reason to doubt its authenticity.

Bibliography

GOVERNMENT PUBLICATIONS

AFGHANISTAN

Pakhtunistan; The Khyber Pass as the Focus of the New State of Pakhtunistan. London, Royal Afghan Embassy, n.d.

The Pakhtun Question. London, Royal Afghan Embassy, n.d.

Voice of Pushtoons. New Delhi, Publicity Department, Pushtoonistan, 1955.

BAHAWALPUR (all published at Baghdad-ul-Jadid)

Bahawalpur Review. 1953–54.

Bahawalpur Scheme of Educational Reorganization. n.d. (1954?)

Gazette of Bahawalpur. 1950–54.

Legislative Assembly of Bahawalpur, *Report*, April 1951; January–October 1953; March–April 1954. (Urdu.)

BRITISH INDIA

Administration Report of Bahawalpur State. Lahore, Government of the Punjab, 1926–27 through 1945–46.

Administration Report of the Baluchistan Agency. Calcutta, later New Delhi, Government of India, 1890 through 1939–40.

Administration Report of the Border of the North-West Frontier Province. Peshawar, Government of the North-West Frontier Province, 1924–25 through 1944–45.

Administration Report of the Khairpur State. Khairpur Mirs, Government of India, 1912–13 through 1944–45.

Baluchistan District Gazetteer, Kalat (Sarawan, Jhalawan, and Kachhi). Vol. VI, VIa, and VIb. Bombay, Bombay *Times* Press, 1907.

—— Makran and Kharan. Vol. VII and VIIa. Bombay, Bombay *Times* Press, 1907.

—— Las Bela. Vol. VIII. Allahabad, Pioneer Press, 1907.

North-West Frontier Province Gazetteer. Peshawar, Government of the North-West Frontier Province, 1913.

Punjab District Gazeteer, Bahawalpur State. Lahore, Government of the Punjab, 1913, 1935.

REPUBLIC OF INDIA (all published at New Delhi)
Lok Sabha, *Debates, Official Report.* 1956.
States' Reorganization Commission Report. 1955.
White Paper on the Indian States. 1950.

KHAIRPUR
Khairpur Legislative Assembly. *Official Report.* Khairpur Mirs, 1953. (Sindhi, Urdu, and English.)

PAKISTAN (all published at Karachi unless otherwise noted)
Census of Pakistan, 1951. Vol. II, Baluchistan; Vol. IV, North-West Frontier Province; Vol. V, Punjab and Bahawalpur; Vol. VI, Sind and Khairpur, 1952.
Constituent Assembly of Pakistan. *Debates, Official Report.* 1947–56.
—— *Final Report of the Basic Principles Committee (as adopted by the Constituent Assembly).* 1952.
—— *Instruments of Accession and Schedules of States Acceding to Pakistan.* 1949.
—— *Instruments of Accession and Schedules of Federating States* (Confidential). 1954.
Constituent Assembly of Pakistan (Legislature). *Debates, Official Report.* 1947–56.
Durand Line. N.d.
Economic Planning Board. *The First Five Year Plan, 1955–60.* 1955.
Explanatory Memorandum on the Budget of the Government of Pakistan 1956–57. 1956.
Financial Enquiry Regarding Allocation of Revenue between Central and Provincial Governments. 1952 (The Raisman Report).
Gazette of Pakistan. 1947–62.
Geological Survey of Pakistan. *Records.* Muree, 1948–55.
Liaquat Ali Khan. *Speech to the First Session of the Pakistan Muslim League.* 1949.
Ministry of Finance. *History of Services of Officers holding Gazetted Appointments in the Civil Services of Pakistan: Ministry of States and Frontier Regions, Ministry of Foreign Affairs and Commonwealth Relations, and Baluchistan Administration* (corrected up to January 7, 1952). 1955.
Ministry of Law. *The Constitution of the Islamic Republic of Pakistan.* 1956.
—— *Federal Court Reports.* 1947–56.
—— *Supreme Court Reports.* 1956–62.

—— *Unrepealed Constitutional Legislation* (as modified up to April 26, 1951). 1951.
National Assembly of Pakistan. *Debates, Official Report.* 1956–58.
Pakistan; The Struggle for Irrigation Water and Existence. Washington, D.C., Embassy of Pakistan, 1953.
Races of Afghanistan. 1956.

UNITED KINGDOM
Parliamentary Papers. (Command Paper) Cmd. 324. "Papers Regarding Hostilities with Afghanistan." London, 1919.
—— Cmd. 4843. "Views of the Indian States on the Government of India Act, 1935." London, 1935.
—— Cmd. 5064. "Correspondence Relating to the Government of India Act, 1935." London, 1936.

OTHER MATERIALS

Aga Khan III. *The Memoirs of the Aga Khan.* New York, Simon and Shuster, 1954.
Ahmad, Jamil-ud-din, ed. *Speeches and Writings of Mr. Jinnah.* 2 Vols., Lahore, M. Ashraf, 1947, 1952.
Ahmad, Colonel Mohammad. *My Chief.* Lahore, Longmans, 1960.
Ahmad, Munir. *Legislatures in Pakistan 1947–1958.* Lahore, University of the Panjab, 1960.
Ahmad, Z. A. *Excluded Areas under the New Constitution.* Allahabad, K. M. Ashraf, 1937.
Aitchison, C. U. *Collection of Treaties, Engagements and Sanads Relating to India and Neighboring Countries.* Calcutta, Government of India, 1931 (5th ed.).
Akhtar, S. M., ed. *Village Life in Lahore District; Selected Political Aspects.* Lahore, Social Science Research Centre, University of the Panjab, 1960.
All-India National Congress Committee. *The Indian National Congress Resolutions, 1934–36.* Allahabad, 1936.
Aslam, A. H. *The Deputy Commissioner.* Lahore, University of the Panjab, 1957.
Attlee, C. R. *As It Happened.* London, W. Heinemann, 1954.
Azad, Maulana Abul Kalam. *India Wins Freedom.* New York, Longmans, Green and Co., 1960.
Bahawalpur State Department of Irrigation. "Abbasia Canal Project, Bahawalpur State," *Pakistan Geographical Review,* VI (1951) 26–32.
Baluch, Muhammad Sardar Khan. *History of the Baluch Race and Baluchistan.* Quetta, privately printed, 1958.

Barth, Fredrik. *Political Leadership Among the Swat Pathans.* London, Athlone Press, 1959.

Becker, Mary L. "The All-India Muslim League 1906–47." Ph.d. dissertation, Radcliffe College, 1957.

Birdwood, Christopher Bromhead. *Two Nations and Kashmir.* London, Robert Hale, 1956.

Bolitho, Hector. *Jinnah.* London, J. Murray, 1954.

Bruce, R. I. *The Forward Policy and Its Results.* London, Longmans, Green and Co., 1900.

Callard, Keith B. *Pakistan, A Political Study.* New York. Macmillan, 1957.

—— *Political Forces in Pakistan, 1947–1959.* New York, Institute of Pacific Relations, 1959.

Campbell-Johnson, Alan. *Mission With Mountbatten.* London, Robert Hale, 1951.

Caroe, Sir Olaf. *The Pathans.* New York, St. Martin's Press, 1958.

Casey, R. G. *An Australian in India.* London, Hollis and Carter, 1947.

Chamber of Princes Directorate. *The British Crown and the Indian States. London,* P. S. King, 1929.

—— *The Handbook of the Chamber of Princes.* Simla, Narendra Mandal, 1942.

—— *Proceedings of the Meetings of the Chamber of Princes.* Simla, Narendra Mandal, 1916–46.

Choudhury, G. W. *Constitutional Development in Pakistan.* Lahore, Longmans, 1959.

Churchill, Winston S. *The Hinge of Fate,* Vol. IV of *The Second World War.* Boston, Houghton Mifflin, 1950.

Chudgar, P. L. *Indian Princes Under British Protection.* London, Williams and Norgate, 1929.

Cobb, E. H. "The Frontier States of Dir, Swat and Chitral," *Journal of the Royal Central Asian Society,* XXXVIII (1951), 170–76.

Coupland, R. *The Constitutional Problem in India.* London, Oxford University Press, 1944.

—— *The Cripps Mission.* London, Oxford University Press, 1942.

Cumming, John, ed. *Political India, 1832–1932.* London, Oxford University Press, 1932.

Dames. M. L. *The Baloch Race.* London, Royal Asiatic Society, 1904.

Das Gupta, J. B. *Indo-Pakistan Relations (1947–1955).* Amsterdam, Djambatan, 1958.

Davis, Kingsley. *The Population of India and Pakistan.* Princeton, Princeton University Press, 1951.

Durand, Algernon. *The Making of a Frontier*. London, Thomas Nelson, 1900.

D'yakov, A. M. ed. *Pakistan; History and Economy*. Moscow, USSR Academy of Sciences, Institute of Oriental Studies, 1959 (trans. U.S.J.P.R.S. 1961).

Eglar, Zekiye. *A Punjabi Village in Pakistan*. New York, Columbia University Press, 1960.

Emanuel, A. E. L. "The Baluchis of Upper Sind," *Anthropological Society of Bombay Journal* (1911) 76–84.

Emanuel, W. V. "Some Impressions of Swat and Afghanistan," *Journal of the Royal Central Asian Society*, XXVI (1939), 195–213.

Feldman, H. *A Constitution for Pakistan*. Karachi, Oxford University Press, 1956.

Fitze, Kenneth. *Twilight of the Maharajas*. London, J. Murray, 1956.

Franck, Dorthea. "Pakhtunistan," *Middle East Journal*, VI (1952), 49–68.

Fraser-Tytler, Sir Kerr. *Afghanistan, A Study of Political Developments in Central Asia*. London, Oxford University Press, 1958.

Gopal, Ram. *Indian Muslims, A Political History (1858–1947)*. New York, Asia Publishing House, 1959.

Griffin, L. H. *The Rajas of the Punjab*. London, Trübner and Co., 1873.

Gurmani, Mushtaq A. "Princely States in the Polity of India," mimeographed, n.d. (1958?).

Gwyer, Sir Morris and Appadorai, A. *Speeches and Documents on the Indian Constitution, 1921–1947*. 2 Vols., London, Oxford University Press, 1957.

Harrison, Selig S. *India: The Most Dangerous Decades*. Princeton, Princeton University Press, 1960.

Hasan, K. Sarwar. *Pakistan and the United Nations*. New York, Manhattan Publishing Co., 1960.

Holdich, Sir Thomas. *The Gates of India*. London, Macmillan, 1910.

Hollister, John N. *The Shia of India*. London, Luzacs, 1953.

Honigman, John J. "Field Research in West Pakistan," *Research Previews*, 6 (1959), 20–24.

Husain, Azim. *Fazl-i-Husain*. Bombay, Orient Longmans, 1946.

Inayatulla. "The Administration of Amb State," M.A. thesis, University of the Panjab, 1956.

Isa, Qazi M. *Baluchistan; Case and Demand*. Karachi, Daily Gazette Press, 1944.

Ismail, Sir Mirza. *My Public Life*. London, G. Allen and Unwin, 1954.

Jennings, Sir Ivor. _Constitutional Problems in Pakistan._ London, Cambridge University Press, 1957.

Khaliquzzaman, Choudhry. _Pathway to Pakistan._ Lahore, Longmans, 1961.

Korbel, Josef. _Danger in Kashmir._ Princeton, Princeton University Press, 1954.

Khan, Major-General Fazal Muqeem. _The Story of the Pakistan Army._ Karachi, Oxford University Press, forthcoming.

Lee-Warner, Sir William. _The Native States of India._ London, Macmillan, 1910.

Leech, Major Robert. "Brief History of Kalat, Brought Down to the Disposition and Death of Mehrab Khan Braho-ee," _Journal of the Asiatic Society of Bengal,_ XII (1843), 473–512.

Lumby, E. W. R. _The Transfer of Power in India._ London, G. Allen & Unwin, 1954.

Luni, Abdul Aziz. "Jirga System in Quetta Division." M.A. thesis, University of the Panjab, 1959.

Mahmud, M. Syed Hassan. _A Nation is Born._ Lahore, privately printed, 1958.

Majumdar, R. C., Raychaudhuri H. C. and Datta, K. _An Advanced History of India._ 2nd ed. London, Macmillan, 1956.

Mian, N. I. _A Preliminary Economic Survey of the Tribal Areas Adjoining West Pakistan._ Lahore, Punjab Board of Economic Inquiry, 1956.

Menon, V. P. _The Story of the Integration of the Indian States._ New York, Macmillan, 1956.

—— _The Transfer of Power in India._ Princeton, Princeton University Press, 1957.

Moon, Penderel. _Divide and Quit._ Berkeley, University of California Press, 1962.

Mosley, Leonard. _The Last Days of the British Raj._ New York, Harcourt, Brace and Co., 1962.

Mountbatten, Lord Louis. _Time Only to Look Forward._ London, N. Kaye, 1949.

Muhammad Iqbal, Sir. _Presidential Address, Allahabad session, 1930._ Delhi, Muslim League Printing Press, 1945.

Munshi, Mohan Lal. "A Brief Account of the Origin of the Da'ud Putras and of the Power and Birth of Bahawal Khan, Their Chief, on the Banks of the Ghara and Indus," _Journal of the Asiatic Society of Bengal,_ VII (1838), 27–33.

Nasr-ul Mulk, Captain Shahzada (The Mehtar of Chitral). "The Ismailis or Mulais of the Hindu Kush," _Journal of the Royal Central Asian Society,_ XXII (1935), 641–45.

Newman, K. J. _Essays on the Constitution of Pakistan._ Dacca, Pakistan Cooperative Book Society, 1956.

Nizami, Majid. *The Press in Pakistan.* Lahore, University of the Panjab, 1958.

Noman, Mohammad. *Muslim India.* Allahabad, Kitabistan, 1942.

Pakistan Law Digest. Karachi, Pakistan Legal Decisions Press, 1948–58.

Panikkar, K. M. *The Indian Princes in Council.* London, Oxford University Press, 1936.

—— *Interstatal Law.* Madras, University of Madras, 1934.

Parsons, Sir Arthur. *The Administration of Customary Law through the Frontier Crimes Regulations in Baluchistan.* Simla, Government of India Press, 1938.

Pithawalla, M. B. *A Geographical Analysis of Khairpur State.* Karachi, Haroon Press, 1935.

—— *The Problem of Baluchistan.* Karachi, Government of Pakistan Press, 1952.

Qasimi, Abdul Ghafoor. *History of Swat.* Peshawar, privately published, 1939.

Qureshi, I. H. "Islamic Elements in the Political Thought of Pakistan." Mimeographed, 1960.

Rajput, A. B. *The Muslim League, Yesterday and Today.* Lahore, M. Ashraf, 1948.

Ravoof, A. A. *Meet Mr. Jinnah.* Lahore, M. Ashraf, 1955.

Roberts, P. E. and Spear, T. G. P. *History of British India under the Company and the Crown.* London, Oxford University Press, 1952.

Robertson, G. S. *The Kafirs of the Hindu Kush.* London, Lawrence, 1896.

—— *Chitral; The Story of a Minor Siege.* London, Methuen, 1898.

Robertson, W. R. *An Official Account of the Chitral Expedition 1895.* Calcutta, Government of India, 1898.

Roman, M. A. "The Brahuis of Quetta-Kalat Regions," *Journal of the Pakistan Historical Society,* VII (1959), 252–74.

Rudra, A. B. *The Viceroys and Governors-General of India.* London, Oxford University Press, 1940.

Sack, John. *Report from Practically Nowhere.* New York, Harper, 1959.

Saiyid, M. H. *Mohammad Ali Jinnah, A Political Study,* Lahore, M. Ashraf, 1945.

Sayeed, Khalid B. *Pakistan; The Formative Phase.* Karachi, Pakistan Publishing House, 1960.

Shah, Brigadier Nazeer Ali. *Sadiqnama.* Lahore, Maktaba Jadeed, 1959.

Shahab, Qudratullah. *Pathans.* Karachi, Pakistan Publications, n.d.

Siddiqi, A. H. "Population and Settlements Along the Baluchistan Coast," *Oriental Geographer,* II (1958), 131–39.

Smith, Wilfred C. "Hyderabad: Muslim Tragedy," *Middle East Journal*, IV (1950), 27–51.

—— *Islam in Modern History*. Princeton, Princeton University Press, 1957.

—— *Modern Islam in India*. London, Gollancz, 1946.

Spain, James W. "Pakistan's Northwest Frontier Province," *Middle East Journal*, VIII (1954), 27–41.

—— "Pathans of the Tribal Areas," *Pakistan: Society and Culture*, Stanley Maron, ed., New Haven, Human Relations Area Files Press, 1957, 135–53.

Spate, O. H. K. *India and Pakistan: A General and Regional Geography*, London, Methuen, 1954.

Symonds, Richard. *The Making of Pakistan*. London, Faber and Faber, 1950.

—— "State-Making in Pakistan," *Far Eastern Survey*, XIX (1950), 45–50.

Tate, G. P. *The Frontiers of Baluchistan*. London, Witherby and Co., 1909.

—— *Kalat; A Memoir of the Country and Family of the Ahmadzai Khans of Kalat*. Calcutta, Government of India, 1896.

Tuker, F. I. S. *While Memory Serves*. London, Cassell, 1950.

Ware, Colonel Webb. "The Nushki Railway and Some of the Problems on Which it Bears," *Journal of the Royal Central Asian Society*, I (1914), 44–50.

Wilcox, Wayne A. "The Integration of West Pakistan," *Proceedings of the Pakistan Political Science Association*, (1962).

Williams, L. R. "The Indus Canals Water Problem," *Asian Review*, 51 (1953), 137–54.

Ziring, Lawrence. "The Failure of Democracy in Pakistan; East Pakistan and the Central Government, 1947–1958." Ph.d. thesis, Columbia University, 1962.

Index

Princes: functions and power before partition, 12-14; position after 1919 reorganization, 15, 16, 17; three classes of, 32

Privy purses: of rulers of Baluchistan States, 150; allowances at time of integration into West Pakistan, 187; importance in Pakistan's negotiations with princes, 214, 217; agreement between Amir of Bahawalpur and central government concerning, text, 238-40

Provinces of British India, 8-11, 25

Provinces of Pakistan, 109, 184

Public and Representative Officers (Disqualification) Act (PRODA), 134

Pukhtunistan dispute, 213; *see also* Afghanistan

Punjab, before partition, 34, 41-42; partition between India and Pakistan, 46; plan for union of Punjab states, 71-72; *see also* West Punjab

Punjabi (people), 70

Punjab League, 127

Qadir, Manzur, 209

Qizilbash, Mumtaz Hasan, 120, 176-77, 200, 220

Qayyum Khan, Abdul, 43, 130, 161, 205

Qazi, Isa, 77, 144

Qazi, Musa, 144, 149

Quetta, 75, 144

"Quit India" campaign, 30

Qureshi, I. H., 132

Rahman, Fazlur, 219

Rahmat, Ali, Choudhary, 31

Rashid, Sardar Abdur, 176

Rasulkhanji, Mahabatkhan, 56

Razakhars (para-military force in Hyderabad), 64, 65

Razwi, Kasim, 64

Reform Committee on Baluchistan, 146, 148

Refugees: partition and population transfers, 53-55; Pakistan problems concerning, 68; Settlement program in Khairpur, 120-21; role in Bahawalpur politics, 125-26, 134, 136

Regency, Council of (Khaipur), 119, 120, 121

Religion, importance of, in Indian politics, 9, 26

Representative government, 124

Republican Party, 196, 199, 200, 201

Resident of princely states, in British India, 12

Rural education, in Bahawalpur, 138

Sahib, Dr. Khan, 180, 189, 200, 205

Sahib, Ghulam Haider Khan, 133

Salam, Chaudhuri Abdus, 194, 195

Sandile, Jan Mohammad, 122

Sardars (chiefs), 78, 147, 150, 204

Shah, A. S. B., 71, 80, 98

Shahi Jirga (Kalat Royal Assembly), 78, 145-46

Shari'ah, enforcement of, 135

Shi'a Muslims, in Khairpur, 120

Short, Major, 72

Sikhs, 33, 41, 42

Simon Commission, 24-25

Sind: question of Khairpur's merger with, 119; proposed grouping in Mohammad Ali Formula and, 172; consolidation of West Pakistan and, 183, 186; court ruling on dissolution of Constituent Assembly, 183, 187; representatives to Constitutional Convention, 190

Smuggling, federal intervention in